DOWN TO EARTH WITH A BUMP

The Diary of a First-time Dad

Andrew Watson

Book Guild Publishing
Sussex, England

First published in Great Britain in 2011 by
The Book Guild Ltd
Pavilion View
19 New Road
Brighton, BN1 1UF

Typesetting in Garamond by
Keyboard Services, Luton, Bedfordshire

Printed in Great Britain by
CPI Antony Rowe

A catalogue record for this book is available from
The British Library

ISBN 978 1 84624 573 2

For Zoë and Polly who, between them, pretty much wrote this book themselves

Two reasons why you should read this book

The reference books can't tell you everything

That didn't stop us getting one, though, and if you're about to have a baby, you should do the same. Between your big, worthy reference book and the internet, you'll get all the dry facts you could ever want. And I should know, because I wrote one of them.

The problem is that, informative and reassuring as they often are, in trying to cover everything with authority and objectivity, those reference books just don't have the space to tell you what it's really like to *experience* those facts. And that's where the properly interesting bits lie: in the noises, the smells, the exhaustion, the terror and the incomparable delight of becoming a parent.

They might tell you that 'snoring in pregnancy is normal', but they won't warn against husbands wearing earplugs in case they never actually hear their partners wailing from the bathroom when her waters have broken. And they'll probably recommend you 'keep up to date with your child's immunisations', but are unlikely to mention your competitive determination *not* to be the parent forced to pin your baby down while the needle-wielding nurse stalks ever closer.

So reassure yourself by keeping a reference book to hand, certainly, but if you're after the far more colourful reality behind the dry facts then you want a diary or memoir, something personal, dripping with hard-won experience. Like this one, for instance.

The path to parenthood is a shared one

Of course, there are thousands of parenting books out there, and almost without exception they're aimed at women *or* at men. The books for women are generally cosy and comforting and wrapped in pastel-coloured, smiley-faced covers, while the books for men seem to be based on the assumption that we all face fatherhood reluctantly and need a desperate gag in every paragraph to stop us losing interest and turning on the telly.

But to split and package parenthood according to gender seems to miss the point, because while having a baby may highlight the differences between men and women, above all it emphasises the similarities. Breasts and wombs aside, the modern path to parenthood is a shared one, an evolution that – in the face of the same challenges, the same hopes and the same fears – unites a man and a woman far more than it divides. After all, a baby doesn't stop to check if you're in pants or knickers before it yacks all over you.

So if you and your partner are about to start down that same path and are wondering what to expect, if you want to learn how another couple have coped with a similar journey, if you're hoping to prepare yourself for the enormity of the experience, from the conflicting emotions and the effect on your relationship to the joys and the terrors of parenting together, then you want a story that isn't split down the middle. A story about how a man and a woman faced the most challenging months of their lives, and came out the other side, smiling and together. Like this one, for instance.

Andrew Watson,
London, 2011
www.awwa.co.uk

PART ONE

Early Days

5.45 a.m. Somewhere on the south coast of Spain.

'Andrew! *Andrew*! Wake up!'

Reluctantly, I raise my head from the pillow and, through squinting eyes, see Zoë collapsing onto the bed beside me, a terrified smile across her pale face.

'Look!' she says in a shaking voice, thrusting towards me a small, slightly smelly white stick. 'I'm pregnant.'

Sleep-starved and hungover, my response is not the most sensitive. I give my wife a weak hug, then roll over and go back to sleep.

I wake again a few fitful hours later to see Zoë examining her body before the mirror, turning from one profile to the other and running a hand over her enviably flat belly.

'Zoë?'

She turns, matches my nervous grin, and skips back to bed.

'I knew it!' she says, cuddling up alongside me. 'I thought something was different.'

'How?'

'My period was late, for a start.'

'But you told me your periods have always been irregular.'

'I know. But there are these spots on my back as well.' She points towards her bare shoulders where last week's small invasion of acne now seems to be colonizing in all directions.

'You told me that was stress with all the builders in the house.'

'Come on!' she laughs. 'You must have suspected *something*! What about this?' She thrusts her breasts towards me, the left one recently swollen far larger than the right – an embarrassing development if the plan is to spend the week's holiday in a bikini. 'You can't tell me that looks normal.'

'I never said it did. But you're a woman – who am I to say what's normal?'

She'd pointed out the bizarre lack of full-frontal symmetry a few days before, but despite her immense appetite for anxiety, hadn't seemed worried. And so I'd shrugged it off, not thinking twice. After all, she's the GP, not me, and I long ago accepted that there are things about women that will remain forever beyond my understanding.

But now I realise that Zoë has been suspicious for days, enough to sneak a couple of pregnancy tests into our suitcase. The first, she tells me, succumbed to her nervousness early on; result: negative. And she reached for the second only when her patience could no longer hold out, at – when else? – a quarter to six in the morning.

'If you suspected you were pregnant,' I ask her, 'why didn't you tell me?'

'I didn't want to jinx it,' she says.

'But you're a professional medic – you're not meant to be superstitious! Did you really think that, just by sharing your suspicions, those spots were going to disappear, that boob would shrink back into place and your fertilized egg would spit my sperm back out?'

'Of course not,' she says, raising herself onto one arm so she can look me in the eye. 'But when you're in the theatre, even if you know your lines before you go on stage each night, you still get nervous, don't you?'

'Sure.'

'Right. And knowing all the facts won't stop me worrying either.'

I nod and squeeze her tighter. It's meant to be reassuring, to disguise the chasm of bewilderment opening before me.

Zoë spends much of her working week dealing with pregnant women and screaming babies – they're a staple of the job. Over the last five years, every baby-related problem imaginable has walked through her door, and she's dealt with them all. In fact,

I've always reckoned that, if it weren't for an initial requirement of sperm, she could easily do this whole thing herself. But now, as we lie together tingling with the realization of what's to come, it dawns on me; I have an epiphany similar to the one that struck me, aged 15, at three in the morning after a friend's party in the loft of a barn in Fife: there's a whole world of difference between talking about something and actually experiencing it.

Thursday, 15th June – About four and a half weeks pregnant?

We're going to be parents. A fantastic and altogether terrifying thought – not totally unexpected, but just a little sooner than anticipated. Yet despite that churning mix of delight and fear that Zoë's sudden announcement has produced, our holiday might actually turn out to be more relaxing. Not only because the words 'Let's have an early night' will now actually suggest a bit of rest, but because – at last – the pressure's off.

Ever since my eventual, cautious nod of agreement that we should start trying for a baby, Zoë has been impatient to be pregnant – so much so that, when her period returned after just one month of trying, she took to casting upon her stubbornly flat stomach a look of hatred as the words 'I'm barren' echoed around the building site that passes for our home, usually delivered in a melodramatic wail and accompanied by the protrusion of a lower lip. When Zoë decides she wants to get something done, she wants it done NOW, to the exclusion of all else.

The situation didn't improve when Sally and Martin flew out to join us on Tuesday, delayed because of a 12-week pregnancy scan. In they walked with enormous grins clutching a black-and-white photo of a blob that's apparently their baby. And of course we're delighted for them, all the more so because they had to undergo ICSI treatment – a bit like IVF, but instead of putting a sperm and egg in a test tube and shaking it up, they actually have to inject the sperm into the egg. Success rates are similar, but ICSI costs even more – meaning that their relatively early positive result is nothing but fantastic news.

Unfortunately, though, the very fact that the treatment was necessary for them at all gave Zoë an unstoppable fear that she'd be unable to conceive naturally herself. Add to that her professional awareness of all the possible problems, and it's easy to see how the presentation of Sally's scan photo only further stirred her fears. Well concealed beneath her greater joy at their good news was a quietly smouldering jealousy.

Now, though, she's able to dive willingly into the mass of baby chat without worry – that it's Sally's stomach pulling focus and not her own is the small price to pay for our secret. And since the guys are out on the golf course all day, I've little opportunity to blurt out our news to them. Instead, I find myself just wandering silently around in a little world of my own. I'd expect to be panicking at how our lives are about to change; instead, all I feel is a strange sense of manly pride that I could make it happen so quickly, and the contentment that comes from knowing that Zoë and I are about to share in something amazing.

Friday, 16th June

'It didn't take us long, did it?' I'm trying to disguise the growing sense of unease beneath a tone of swaggering pride, but yesterday's self-satisfaction has definitely dissipated overnight.

Zoë looks up from her book and smiles. 'Feeling pretty virile, huh?'

I shrug to suggest a magnanimous acceptance of my immense powers of fertility. 'So what was all your worrying for? You made out it was going to take us much longer.'

'It might have,' she says, her eyes back on her chick lit. 'For healthy couples, there's a 20% chance of conception every month.'

I can't work out if that seems high or low. Is it high enough to justify all those years of condom-related awkwardness and fumbling, those endless books and movies where women fall pregnant after one quick knee-trembler against a wall? Or low enough to excuse Zoë's disapproval whenever she caught me in a boiling hot bath or found my mobile phone in my front trouser pocket?

'The problem is,' she continues, 'you can't know if you're going to have problems until you've been trying for a while. And, as a doctor, you don't send patients for tests until they've been trying for at least twelve months.'

Put like that, I can understand why some might think it wise to get on with it. But then another thought strikes me. 'So how many people trying for a baby actually *do* turn out to have problems?'

Suddenly, Zoë is vague. Her face slides further behind her book. 'I think it's about 10%. But,' she hurries on, 'it depends how late you leave it. And we're not getting any younger...'

I've only just turned 29; Zoë's a few months younger. That doesn't seem old. Thankfully, we're both healthy and – despite the regular horror stories in the press about falling fertility rates – the statistics seem to be on our side. In fact, given that stress can hinder ovulation, I'd have said the biggest threat to Zoë getting pregnant was her frustration at not being pregnant.

Now, under duress, she admits that 25% of couples trying for a baby conceive within the first month. Yet somehow I'd gained the impression that it was all going to take longer, that I'd have more time to get used to the idea. And now I'm getting the distinct feeling that Zoë was only too happy to allow that misconception.

It's not that I'm unhappy that she's pregnant – far from it. I'm absolutely delighted, albeit a little shell-shocked. And I'm grateful for how relatively easy it's been, especially when the likes of Martin and Sally have gone through so much just to get to the same position. But I can't shake off a mild feeling of discomfort.

It's like I've just left a shop thinking I've haggled a great deal but seen the shopkeeper's sneaky grin as I leave – thrilled though I may be with what I've got, I can't help feeling someone else knows more than me.

7

Saturday, 17th June – Almost five weeks pregnant?

Sitting at the dinner table, I look at our friends and realize that, of them all, I'm the one who least deserves to be enjoying this week abroad. While they all have successful professional careers and are already several rungs high on those ladders leading to partnership or management, I'm struggling just to pay my way. That's the cost of the flexibility that acting demands in order to run off to auditions at sometimes only an hour's notice, or to disappear to a small regional theatre for a couple of months. So for the last few years I've earned not very much writing articles for magazines and papers, doing the occasional voice-over and running role-play training sessions for doctors.

As for what that flexibility has achieved, my acting credits after five years are sadly typical of the industry: a number of theatre runs and radio jobs, several brief scenes of TV, and one recent CBBC series, all of which have paid nothing like enough to put me on an equal footing with these others round the table.

Yet despite my embarrassingly low income and the ongoing costs of renovating our new house, I still secretly daydream about somehow buying back our family home in Argyll. And now we have the very real cost of a baby.

Zoë, it seems, has no such worries. She's spent another day floating around the apartment with a beaming grin that, were it not for everyone focusing on Sally, would surely have tipped them off. Perhaps she can allow herself to smile because – in typical style – she's got our future all planned. Maybe I'm worrying about nothing, and a simple inquiry into her meticulous life schedule would reveal how she plans to balance the books, and so set my mind at rest. But just to ask is to suggest doubt that a baby is 'a good thing', and I'm really not doubtful.

Am I?

Sunday, 18th June

Back home. We're lying peacefully side by side, recovering from our first efforts at intimacy since we learnt that she's pregnant, and instead of blissful sighs or soulful whispers of gratitude and wonder, Zoë's first words are, 'I'm glad we've got that over with.'

Squinting from the pillow alongside, I manage to look offended.

'I know there's nothing to worry about,' she continues. 'I know having sex won't induce a miscarriage or anything. But it's still worrying, don't you think?'

Admittedly, it did feel slightly uncomfortable, almost inappropriate, as though I was intruding. For the first few seconds.

'So it's good to know it's possible,' she says. 'It's reassuring now that we've done it this first time.'

Already, it's no longer just the two of us. It's not that I'm intruding on our baby, but that even in our most private moments – or perhaps *especially* in our most private moments – our baby is intruding on us. The dynamic is already changing.

Monday, 19th June

'I'm worried about my sperm,' I tell Zoë when she finally returns from work.

Dumping her bag on our tarpaulin-covered floor amongst the dust and the tools, she visibly musters her tolerance. She has, after all, just spent ten hours dealing with demanding patients and should, by rights, be entitled to the evening off.

But it's been bothering me all day. After all, just as a hair sample can provide evidence of a drug ingested months before, our bodies can record a particular condition long after circumstances have changed. From a cut that takes weeks to heal to the pits of illness on a fingernail not yet grown out, our physical selves testify to our past as well as our present. Surely, then, my sperm at any given time must be – at least to some extent – indicative of my state of health at the time they were created?

'I was wondering,' I continue, ignoring her heavy sigh and impatiently cocked head, 'which exact attempt was it that proved successful at getting you pregnant?'

'Yeah, I was wondering that myself. But I'm not entirely sure. It might have been that weekend down in Itchnor.'

I struggle to remember. Does that mean the lazy morning, hungover and half-asleep? Or the sneaky, late-night effort when the creaking bed forced us onto the floor? Were the resulting sperm sent weaving on their way, still heavily under the influence, or did they slip furtively out on the spermatic equivalent of tiptoes?

'Why?' asks Zoë.

'Because surely the condition I was in will have an effect on the sperm that develops – all being well – into our baby?'

'I'm pregnant, aren't I?' says Zoë, displaying her typically practical approach to such questions. 'So of course there's nothing wrong with your sperm.'

'Yes, you're pregnant. But all that means is that one particular sperm made it. It doesn't tell me what state that sperm was in.'

'It tells you that it was in good enough condition to outdo the tens of millions of other sperm up for the same job.'

'But sometimes if I've had a few drinks, I've been able to do things I'd never have managed when I was sober, like sprinting hundreds of yards for a bus, or meeting your parents for the first time. So how do I know I've not impregnated you with an alcohol-fuelled sperm that, only minutes after breaking into your egg, isn't just going to collapse on the sofa and order a kebab? The sort of sperm that, had I not had a few drinks on the night we conceived, would have been naturally selected to die young prying burnt toast out of the toaster with a knife?'

'It doesn't matter! Once the sperm merges with the egg, it's the DNA that takes over and grows into our baby – it doesn't matter if the delivery boy's drunk, as long as the package gets there safely.'

'But that's assuming all sperm contain the same DNA, that each is as good as the next. And that can't be true, or else every child of the same partner would be identical.'

'Look, you don't need to worry. It takes over two months for sperm to develop, and another two weeks for them to wriggle their way along the ducts of the epididymis until they're ready for action. If they're representative at all, it's of a very general state of health; you'd have to be hitting the bottle for months to make any difference.'

'So sperm sent out when totally sober are no different to sperm sent out when blind drunk?'

'... Exactly.'

But I recognize the tone of her voice, the slight hesitation. 'You don't really know, do you?'

'Not really,' she admits.

And there we have it. From this I learn two things. If we ever decide to start trying for a second child, I should actually *go* to the gym rather than just talk about going to the gym. And the clue to Zoë's knowledge is in the title: *General* Practitioner. Despite the many pregnancies and babies she's dealt with over her career, much of what lies ahead will be new for her too. That realization is a little disconcerting – and strangely exciting.

Wednesday, 21st June

South-east London. I spend the day pretending to be ill in a variety of ways so a group of GPs can practise their diagnostic and communication skills and, ultimately, improve the doctor-patient relationship.

By lunchtime, I'm struck by what should have been obvious before: as much as GPs are scientifically trained, what they do from day to day isn't science.

While clinicians in the lab can perhaps follow logical and linear rules as they work towards exposing and identifying an illness, when it comes to dealing with the person presenting that illness in the first place, a GP's task is of a quite different nature. To expose the real issue, they must often first navigate endless variables and vagaries.

From prejudices, fears, beliefs and expectations, to language barriers or just a bad mood after a sleepless night, these variables can influence not just the patient's presentation, but also the doctor's interpretation. As a result, such complex human factors play an enormous role in how doctors come to treat their patients.

There's never been any doubt that, between the two of us, Zoë's the scientist while I, perhaps through default more than ability, aspire to the creative. And so I wonder if I haven't allowed myself to step back, to view this pregnancy as a medical condition and therefore her domain, in full expectation that she'll handle it all in a logical and linear manner.

But not only is pregnancy far more than a medical issue, this time Zoë's both the doctor and the patient. And while I might have thought that such a dual role should make communication between the two all the clearer, I suspect I'm wrong. I suspect that relating her own hormone-fuelled feelings with her knowledge of the dry facts is all the harder. So where do I stand – and what's my role – within this doctor-patient relationship?

Thursday, 22nd June

I'm standing in the newly tiled shell of our converted loft measuring how much space we'll have to install a shower when my phone rings.

'Right,' says Zoë, without any preamble. 'Here it is. There's somewhere between 40 and 120 million sperm in the average ejaculate, shot out at 10 miles an hour, although as much as 25% of those could already be dead. Only 30% of your sperm will be of normal shape and form, but at least 25% will be swimming with rapid forward movement. Less than 50 make it all the way to the ovum, taking anything from 45 minutes to 12 hours. Your one successful sperm has swum what would be the equivalent of you or me swimming over 5,000 metres. In other words, whether hungover, lazy or just easily distracted, you don't need to worry. Your single successful sperm is nothing less than an Olympian.'

That's one advantage of Zoë being a control freak. If she doesn't know the answer, she has to find it out.

Saturday, 24th June

A gastropub in Shepherd's Bush, and a belated twenty-fifth birthday lunch for wee brother Rob. We fight our way through the packed building to join him and his mates at their table, all of them so blurry-eyed from their Friday night that they never stop to question why Zoë's drinking only water. They themselves go straight onto the Bloody Marys in a bid to perk themselves up in preparation for what they're planning to be a long day ahead.

I catch Zoë's eye and we exchange a glance of bubbling excitement. We're comfortably cocooned in our shared secret, a million miles from the chat around us: talk of holidays to Ibiza and New York, and of the alcohol-fuelled antics of last night, when they said goodbye to a friend going to work in Cape Town for a few years. They joke and laugh as they plan their afternoon's itinerary of pub gardens and, unconnected to the conversation, I begin to look around.

At the next table are three men. They're jostling toddlers on their knees as they sip from wineglasses. I watch them, their discarded *Times* supplements spread out beneath sleep-starved faces. One of them nips to the bar for another bottle of white. Another has baby dribble running down the shoulder of his pink shirt; as it drips onto his jeans, he wipes it off without a second thought, sipping at his wine as he expresses his relief that the rising cost of private schooling has not yet outstripped the rising value of his west London home. I turn away; I'm eavesdropping on another country and, as they usually do in other countries, he's speaking another language.

Two mothers are standing by the impromptu pram park at the door, sipping Chardonnay and jiggling babies on hips. They look like they're comparing notes, chatting through each baby's development in probably the same way they previously discussed their PR accounts and client lists. Their make-up is immaculate, their clothes not more than a few months old clinging to model-thin figures in outright denial and no doubt regained within weeks – if not days – of giving birth. They both look every inch the mother and yet every inch the 30-something professional, and equally confident in either role.

I look across the table at my wife, the Chelsea GP, with every expectation that in a matter of mere months she will effortlessly blend in with those Yummy Mummies by the door. I imagine her taking to parenthood instinctively; where I will hear only an incomprehensible wail, she'll know exactly what our baby is saying, using the same uncanny female intuition that warns her when all that's left in our fridge is half a can of beans and some off milk.

Only then does it become clear to me. It really does take me this long to realize: I don't belong at either table. I'll never again talk about moving to Australia for a few years, or choose on a whim to spend a boozy afternoon in the sunshine or a late night with my mates. Yet nor am I a battle-hardened veteran immune to the drumming of toy cars on my chest, capable of calmly discussing childcare while wrestling with belligerent kids or flicking babywipes from packets like a masterful matador.

I now know where I am: on a hilltop border, looking back with nostalgia into the land behind me, but aware that I've already chosen to continue into a whole new country, a country about which I know nothing.

We drive home in silence. Zoë slumps in front of the telly, stroking her stomach, and I creep upstairs to sit in a corner, quietly panicking. What the hell have I agreed to? Zoë already has a medical career and shelves full of books telling her what

14

she can expect, but who's going to tell me? I want to be involved at every step, but haven't a clue what that means. I want to support my wife, but have no idea how. I want to be prepared for my new role, but don't know what that will be.

One of the consequences of an expensive education was being forced to learn Latin for eight years, at the end of which I still couldn't even ask the cost of a slave girl. So how am I going to learn the language of fatherhood in less than nine months?

Sunday, 25th June – About six weeks?

It's surely more than just that Jewish cliché, her determination to worry about whatever she can and find cause for guilt in her every action.

As long as it's piping hot, there's apparently no health risk in eating soft cheese while pregnant. So we go out for lunch and Zoë orders her starter, loves it, and then munches slowly, miserable with guilt, through the rest of the meal. Such remorse from putting our unborn child through a risk she knows is really no risk at all!

It's the same with sex. Though, admittedly, perhaps not quite so piping hot.

Monday, 26th June

It's easy to understand why, having married into a family with a surname like Watson, Zoë has decided to continue using her maiden name at work. Elementary, you might say. As a result, her married name remains available to be dragged out on those occasions when she'd rather people don't know she's a doctor, like when she's boarding a flight in dread of a medical emergency, or listening to people she's just met socially complaining about their irritable bowels. Or, like today, when she's pretending to be two different people and using her professional name to book herself in under her married name for an early pregnancy scan.

Being a ruthlessly organized medic and knowing all too well everything that can possibly go wrong, she's sneaked herself onto a hospital list with the aim of reassuring us that our baby, who until now has been nothing more than a longed-for line on a pee-stained stick, is alive and well. By this time tomorrow, we should have seen our baby for the first time.

Tuesday, 27th June – Official: 5 weeks and 4 days pregnant

I arrive a few minutes behind Zoë at Chelsea and Westminster Hospital's Early Pregnancy Assessment Unit to find that she's already filled in the forms, so we wait together in silence, surrounded by anxious couples.

'These scans often can't pick up a baby's heartbeat until week six,' she whispers, as much for her own benefit as mine, 'so if we can't see it beating, that doesn't necessarily mean something's wrong.'

Her name is called (another reason for using her married name – so she won't be recognized by former colleagues) and in we go. The doctor sits her on a reclining seat, gently pulls her legs apart, places a paper sheet over the top for modesty's sake, and then pushes a humiliatingly-sized and very well-oiled probe up and out of sight.

And there on the screen appears something like a grey fried egg on a string, pulsing steadily as it floats in a sea of black. Our baby, no more than 2.5mm in length, with a heart the size of a matchstick head already clearly able to outrace mine. They date it at five weeks and four days, with no abnormalities detected, and we leave the room with a photo in our hands and beaming smiles on our faces.

I don't realize – don't stop to think – that the EPAU is predominantly for people with problems: bleeding or abdominal pain, fears of a miscarriage or an ectopic pregnancy. I just think it's for people like us wanting simple reassurance, and that people like us would be bursting with wonder and delight. So perhaps giving the waiting women a goofish grin and the thumbs up isn't the most sensitive exit.

Wednesday, 28th June – 5 weeks, 5 days

Dinner with Zoë's parents in Putney. By chance, her grandparents and both brothers are there as well.

Fortunately I'm still treated as a guest, so my slice of roast beef is already safely on my plate when Zoë stands and tells them she has an announcement. The smile on her face makes words redundant, and her mum immediately drops the rest of the roast on the floor and bursts into tears. All eyes turn to the still totally flat stomach hovering, exposed, above the tray of roast potatoes, and there are kisses and handshakes all round.

The hints that Zoë has endured over the last months from all ages of her family should have reassured me that they'd take the news well, but I'm still instinctively awkward as the announcement is made. It's a novel sensation for a father to *congratulate* me for sleeping with his daughter.

Thursday, 29th June – 5 weeks, 6 days

Mum arrives off the train, come to claim her two ballot seats at Wimbledon, and Rob joins us all for dinner. We tell them the news as they're sipping drinks and nibbling crisps amongst the boxes and building dust.

There's a brief moment of shocked silence, then congratulations that, however heartfelt, can only seem subdued in comparison to the high drama of Zoë's family.

Mum doesn't mention it, but I can appreciate that the moment must be bittersweet, happy but achingly sad as well. Dad lasted just long enough to celebrate my engagement to Zoë. A few months more, and he would have seen us married. A few more still, and he would have met his first grandchild. So close, and yet so far.

Zoë's already emailing me every day with links to websites that show what the baby must look like. This week its inner ears should be forming. So I guess it was around this point when something went wrong with Mum's development, leaving her deaf from birth. The same genetic defect has struck a few of her generation, all of them female, and there's a chance – perhaps particularly if we have a girl – that our baby could be born deaf as well. And yet we couldn't have better examples before us of how that needn't be a disability.

Friday, 30th June – 6 weeks pregnant, 34 weeks to go

Zoë is one of those people who always need something to worry about.

'I didn't pressure you into this, did I?'

I look across the bed to where she's mid-way through another pregnancy guide. 'Why?'

'I just wonder sometimes if I did, because I was so keen to have a baby.'

And she was. There was definitely a sense of urgency. She'd always made it clear she was working to a timetable: to be married and pregnant by the age of 30. And as a doctor, because she's now married and will be 29 in a few months, it was predictable that the threat of infertility – be that hers, mine or a combination of us both – should have been the worry onto which she latched her immense appetite for anxiety. And as is the case with most of her fears, she can't rest – or let others rest – until they're proved groundless. And so, only a matter of weeks before we agreed to start a family, we'd had one of those conversations in

which my every effort to stall was met with an even more
determined response.

'I don't think there's really any great rush,' I'd say. 'My dad
was well into his thirties when Nathan was born; I'm still in my
late twenties.'

'But your mum was almost ten years younger, while I'm the
same age as you.'

'But don't you want to enjoy being just the two of us for a
while? We've barely been married 12 months.'

'Andrew, we've been together six years. And we both agreed
before we got married that we wanted children.'

'Sure, but so soon? I've just been through the worst years of
my life: months watching my dad die and then the sale of our
family home. I need time to adjust.'

'This will help; it's something positive to take your mind off
it all.'

'Shouldn't we just be aiming for a few years of plain sailing?
Give me time to focus on a career, to regain some stability and
build up a little financial security?'

'Since when has the work you do ever provided the sort of
security you're talking about?'

And with that last, usually delivered in an exasperated shout,
she had me. Realizing I would *never* be ready was, I suppose, the
point at which I realized I was ready. And so, with a part of me
still wishing I could rewind the clock about ten years and prepare
myself better, I agreed.

Without a doubt, Zoë piled on the pressure – pressure that
was all the more effective in coming from the one person I least
wanted to disappoint. So now, as I look across our bed to where
she's lying with our baby slowly growing in her belly and she's
asking me if she pushed me into parenthood, I wonder what I
can say.

'No,' I lie, and then immediately change my mind. 'Yes. I
mean, yes, you did push me into it. But, honestly, I'm grateful
for it, otherwise having a family would have been another of

those things I'd have liked to do but never got round to, like hang-gliding or learning German.'

'It's not a weekend hobby, you know. You can't just give it up if you get bored.'

'Of course you can,' I say, turning out the light. 'If things aren't working out, they come and take the kid off you.'

Saturday, 1st July – 6 weeks, 1 day

I lose the toss, so it's Rob who joins Mum for a scorching day at Wimbledon and comes back buzzing at the idea of taking his future nephew to tennis tournaments and football games. When I ask if he'd be willing to take a niece to ballet class instead, he fudges the answer and turns on the sports channel.

Sunday, 2nd July – 6 weeks, 2 days

Zoë's a great doctor. I know that from the steady stream of gifts she brings home from patients, and from all the time and worry she expends on them far beyond what's expected. When it comes to matters of health, she knows it all, or at least knows someone who does.

She's so capable that it's only dawning on me now how much of this experience I might never know and never share. For the first three days of our holiday in Spain, whether through women's intuition or a professional hunch, Zoë knew what was going on, and I did not. While she was experiencing a mix of panic and excitement, I was working on my tan, oblivious. While, for weeks before that, she was sneaking pregnancy tests out of work and riding the roller coaster of hopes and fears as she sought confirmation, I was unaware.

That's not how I want this to be. I want to be involved. Short of offering to give birth or breastfeed myself, I want this to be an equal, shared experience. Yet so capable is she that I worry I'm going to have to try all the harder to get involved, to carve out a role.

Monday, 3rd July – 6 weeks, 3 days

A bad day for Zoë. She returns home exhausted, having spent all last night worrying.

Just to spite that first negative pregnancy test in Spain, she allowed herself more than a few glasses of wine. But now she knows she was actually pregnant at the time. So did she drink too much?

Will our baby be deaf?

Will our baby be healthy given that – without the prenatal screening that allows the option of termination, 1 in 50 would be born with some serious physical or mental handicap?

Will she even carry our baby through to term, when one in five first pregnancies miscarry, most commonly within the first 12 weeks?

That last one seems to be her main concern. Although the risk of miscarriage drops considerably once you've seen a heartbeat and continues to fall with every passing day, that scan was almost a week ago. And since not every miscarriage is automatically flushed out of the system, it's possible for women to go on thinking they're pregnant, with no bleeding or other signs to suggest otherwise.

Our baby may already be dead, and we wouldn't even know it. This seems one of those cases where a little more ignorance of all these worst possibilities would be bliss.

Friday, 7th July – 7 weeks pregnant, 33 weeks to go

Dan and Becky call, wondering if they can pop round to see the new house. Remembering Zoë's pregnancy books littered on every dusty surface, we gather them up and throw them in a box with only seconds to spare.

Now that the loft's largely finished, the builders are starting next week on the rear extension. For an estimated three months, we'll be without a kitchen. So much for a healthy pregnancy diet.

Sunday, 9th July – 7 weeks, 2 days

Zoë's manuals say that, in trying to get her pregnant, we were doing it wrong – news to me, because doing it at all, I've always thought, is only doing it right. But apparently for the best chance of conception it wasn't enough to just go at it whenever we could. Nor was her abstaining from alcohol or her post-coital leaning of legs on the wall any guarantee of success, as she willed her own internal big bang and shouted, 'Swim, my pretties, swim!' in the direction of her groin.

The real secret, the books now tell us, is to give the man every second day off, thereby allowing whatever he has to contribute to the mix time to regroup in between. It makes sense, I suppose – even God took a break from creation on the seventh day. I just wish I'd known so I could have exploited the situation to the full: 'But Zoë, I can't get up off the sofa to cook dinner; my sperm are sleeping.'

'Every second day,' the books say, without any concern for the realities of life, where the concomitant pressures of time, sleep, stress, nights out and must-see TV all conspire to get in the way.

Thursday, 13th July – 7 weeks, 6 days

I'm still waiting for the profundity of this looming experience to make itself known. Shouldn't I feel different now I'm a confirmed expectant father? But it's just too surreal to consider seriously; nothing has really changed.

Zoë feels a little light-headed at times, and is tired and sick in turn. She's given up eating meat which, while sharing a home with a confirmed carnivore, isn't easy. And her breasts are swelling nicely. That, at least, is one aspect of pregnancy that's easy to get used to.

Friday, 14th July – 8 weeks pregnant, 32 weeks to go

Zoë returns home victorious. Barely pregnant, already she's negotiated a vastly improved maternity package.

When I worked in an office, I saw people taking cigarette breaks every half hour and it made me want to take up smoking so that I could be paid to leave my desk for a chat by the back door. If for no other incentive, I think if I were a woman I'd want to get pregnant for the same reason: the paid leave, flexitime and legislated security.

Month Three

Saturday, 15th July – 8 weeks, 1 day

A sudden thought induces instant panic.

'Zoë, were you expecting a present from me now that you're pregnant?'

'Why?'

'Isn't that what you're meant to do, buy flowers or something?'

'For some people, I suppose. But I'm far too superstitious for that – the same reason I don't want a baby shower. Imagine getting all your friends round with presents for a baby, and then something going wrong...'

For once, I find myself siding with her superstition, and not just because it saves me finding her a present. And yet I'm still not wholly comfortable. A few years back, I asked Zoë if there was anything particular she wanted for her birthday.

'I can't think of anything right now,' was her answer. 'Why don't you wait until I see something I really want rather than waste your money?'

Admiring her practicality, the day of her birthday arrived without any further suggestions from her and I handed over a card with an IOU for one present. Before I know it, Zoë's sitting on her sofa in quiet tears. 'Is this it?' she wails. 'You've not got me *anything*?'

Sunday, 16th July – 8 weeks, 2 days

Zoë wakes with a discharge that, when held up to the light, could just be the lightest of pink colours. This prompts a day throughout which she morphs within minutes from Dr Jekyll to Mrs Hyde and back again, the roles overlapping only so far as to allow the doctor's knowledge to inform the mother's worst nightmare.

'It's not like I'm actually bleeding, and it's not unusual to bleed in the first few weeks anyway, and there's no pain so I'm not really worried ... But I could just get a scan to be on the safe side ... Although if a patient came to me in the same way, I'd just reassure them that there's nothing wrong ... Then again, if it turns out I've wrongly ignored something serious, I'd never forgive myself ... But I don't want to take advantage of my position and start over-investigating every little thing just because I can...'

Finally, we agree to listen to the doctor, and create a benchmark for the future: 'If I was one of my patients, what would I tell myself?'

Apparently (as it turns out later when I catch Zoë poring over the computer) she'd tell herself to ignore her doctor's best efforts at reassurance and instead sneak off to look it up on the internet.

Tuesday, 18th July – 8 weeks, 4 days

To Will and Cath's for dinner. Zoë waits until they're both in the kitchen getting coffee before sliding her wedge of Brie onto my plate and switching her full glass of wine for my empty one.

Saturday, 22nd July – 9 weeks, 1 day

Now that we've a home of sorts to house them, we finally retrieve our wedding presents from Zoë's parents' loft. It's been so long since we got them that it's like receiving them all over again. And it makes me realize – our wedding itself should have warned me to think ahead and be better prepared.

Zoë and I have been married for 14 months. When I proposed, we were both 27, and had been going out for five years and living together for three. Knowing I wanted no one else and that she was getting impatient, I brushed aside concerns about self-inflicted responsibility and got down on one knee. (Specifically,

I leant against a wall to calm my nerves and bobbed downwards slightly, more a gesture than a carefree romantic declaration as the beach around us was liberally splattered with cow shit.)

It was Christmas Day and, less than half a mile up the muddy track leading to Ardburdan, my dad was sitting at his desk, slowly dying.

Though marriage remained a terrifying prospect, I had come to realize that it was as inevitable for us as it was desirable, and I saw little point in putting it off any longer, particularly as I wanted Dad to share in at least the start of our happiness. Besides, I figured, surely by popping the question I'd be stalling the chat of more serious adulthood? We'd be able to sit back, I thought, content that we'd each committed to the other, and take the rest of our lives at a gentler pace.

How wrong I was.

That one small question released an avalanche that swept me up and deposited me in my Sunday best before an altar. Those few words, 'Will you marry me?' led to months of planning on a scale not seen since the Normandy landings, soon after which Zoë spotted the perfect house and – almost immediately after that, it now seems – we started trying for a baby.

Young girls are supposed to daydream about their wedding day, but Zoë must have gone one further. While her classmates were sketching ponies on the backs of jotters and writing about what they did in their summer holiday, I reckon she was drawing up graphs of optimum fertility and flicking through Mothercare catalogues. When I finally succumbed to her timetable, she began to put her long-awaited campaign into effect with characteristic precision.

After years on the pill, she wanted the reassurance of her ability to conceive, reassurance that would come from giving her body a chance to regain something close to a natural monthly rhythm. As a result, while still working to erode my resistance and already taking her daily folic acid supplements, she had given up the pill and begun to look around for an alternative method of contraception.

With a medic's knowledge of the options, she opted for a diaphragm, a device as impulsively romantic as a cold, wet shower curtain. So up until a few months ago, Zoë was counting on the diaphragm to stop her getting pregnant. I, meanwhile, fancied myself as one step ahead: not only was I counting on the diaphragm to stop her getting pregnant, I was also hoping that the subsequent return of her natural cycle would reassure her and so stall the inevitable next step. And, I thought, even if she's determined to breed, it would still take us months to get her pregnant, right?

Now that I know better, now that I'm waking up to Zoë's determined timetable, I'm beginning to feel like I've stepped into a Bond film, one of those scenes when the full extent of the arch-villain's cunning plan for world domination is at last revealed.

Sunday, 23rd July – 9 weeks, 2 days

Zoë and I visit an old university friend in north London. Her baby's over two months old and, in all that time, we've spoken to her no more than twice. It's like she's slipped off the edge of the world. To a place where it's fashionable to look utterly bedraggled.

The baby looks just like any other, and I wonder if I'm going to be as blinkered into thinking my own as uniquely beautiful as this mother clearly imagines hers to be.

'She's adorable,' I say, having first ransacked my memory to confirm that this bundle of blankets and raw flesh is actually a girl rather than a boy.

And then there's that awkward pause, when I know I'm expected to comment further but have no idea what to say. It's a baby. It does what babies do – whatever that may be. The thought that Zoë and I are due to have one of our own in a few months is such an abstract thought that I still can't summon up much interest when I'm faced with one. Consequently, without any friends or other family with babies, I know nothing about them. I know I'm going

27

to have to learn, but it's too distant and alien a concept to prompt me to delve into the books the way Zoë's doing.

Tuesday, 25th July – 9 weeks, 4 days

I'm not a reluctant dad. I'm really not. I always knew that some day I'd want children. It's just that, unlike Zoë, I've never really thought about it that much and have certainly never taken the time to add any detail to the occasional daydream. I suppose when I've considered it, it's always been an indistinct possibility in a far-off future – I've imagined myself playing outside with maybe two or three children, rolling around with them on the Ardburdan lawn, laughing with them at some shared joke, and trying to support them as they face their futures as individuals, just as my parents supported me.

The problem is, if I'd ever bothered to look around inside that same daydream world, I'd have seen myself living comfortably and with a reasonable income, either in Ardburdan itself or nearby, confident of my place in the world around me.

Worryingly, as a largely out-of-work writer and actor whose family has been forced to sell Ardburdan, it seems that fatherhood is the only part of that dream that's an imminent reality. In the face of such deficiencies, I feel I'm playing catch-up with my life. And the clock is ticking.

Friday, 28th July – 10 weeks pregnant, 30 weeks to go

I swing daily, almost hourly, between a state of bouncing excitement and outright terror.

The reasons for excitement are obvious – horribly ecclesiastical though it sounds, my relationship with Zoë has been made flesh, cemented in a whole new generation that should last long after we're gone. According to Zoë's favourite website, our baby's face is now forming, the eyes gaining colour; it has a mouth and a tongue, the beginnings of hands and feet. All being well, this little growth, not much more than two centimetres in length, should become a tangible, walking, talking human, that most awe-inspiring, exasperating, capable, irrational and wondrous of creations. This child will be undeniable evidence of our love, something to share in and wonder at.

Unfortunately the reasons for terror are pretty obvious, too. Those who claim that women who resent the loss of their bodies to a parasitic bump are in some way unsuitable for motherhood are lacking imagination. Physically, I'm nothing to do with what lies ahead – it's not me who's going to swell up as something grows inside me, feeding off me until it's ready to force its way out. And yet I still feel trapped beneath the same ticking inevitability, so fearful of all I've yet to learn that I'm grateful for my ignorance.

That it's Zoë who has to endure so much of what lies ahead only emphasizes those areas in which I should be contributing: financially and emotionally. As such, it's just not fair to admit to feeling terrified.

Saturday, 29th July – 10 weeks, 1 day

Zoë and I spend the morning trying to work out our accounts. And as it becomes more and more clear how much we depend on Zoë's income, I can't shake off the feeling that, with the imminent arrival of fatherhood, I should at last be putting my private school and university education to use and getting myself a proper job. Nor can I shake off the feeling that it would only be irresponsible and egotistical to even try to shake off that feeling.

'I don't want to give up being a doctor,' says Zoë, when I voice my concern. 'So I'll go back to work afterwards.'

And with that commitment to support the instability of my career with the solidity of hers, my selfishness wins through. As long as we can pay the bills, the status quo will remain.

Tuesday, 1st August – 10 weeks, 4 days

Our Polish kitchen fitter comes round to measure up the space and check we've ordered the right bits. Unwilling to share any responsibility, Zoë opts to sit the whole thing out in front of *EastEnders*, employing the already typical excuse echoing round the house, 'But I'm pregnant!'

Thursday, 3rd August – 10 weeks, 6 days

Although Zoë's only just 11 weeks, we've the 12-week nuchal scan tomorrow, which can apparently be done any time between 11 and 14 weeks.

As well as simply letting us know that our baby's still going strong, by measuring the level of fluid at the back of the neck they can work out the probability of Down's Syndrome.

'Maybe we should talk about what we'll do if the test shows a high risk,' says Zoë, wolfing down her bangers and mash as though determined to make up for the last few weeks when she's not been eating meat.

'What are the options?'

'If the probability is high, there are a couple of procedures where they go in and take a sample of amniotic fluid or placenta. But both those procedures have risks of their own and can induce miscarriage.'

'And even if the scan reports a high risk of Down's, it's still not definitive, right?'

'Right. It's only an expression of probability.'

'And in that circumstance, we'd have to have further procedures anyway?'

'Yes.'

'So why not wait until that point before we worry about it?'

'Because then we can start to plan. Isn't it worth working out what we'd do now, rather than being swayed by emotion later on?'

'But shouldn't emotion play a role anyway?'

Eventually, we agree to wait and see, to save that conversation for when it's necessary. Not only do we then avoid lingering on the grim possibilities, but we don't have to reveal to ourselves the type of people we might really be, the sort that flush away a life if it doesn't match our expectations or requirements.

Friday, 4th August – 11 weeks pregnant, 29 weeks to go – the nuchal test

It takes me an hour and a half to drive less than eight miles back from a 15-minute dentist's appointment in Kingston. As a result, where I'd hoped to be calmly curious, balanced and prepared for my first real involvement in the pregnancy since those foundational few minutes 12 weeks ago, I'm fuming.

We park in the car park of the shop where we bought our kitchen and walk down the road, hand in hand, to the hospital, figuring that since we're paying them so many thousands, they won't mind lending a parking space for an hour or so.

We pass a slow-moving procession of black cars following a hearse. Inside, a bundle of flowers spells 'Nan'. One out, one in.

The fetal ward is full of families. I shrink into my seat wondering if I'll ever get used to the sound of screaming kids while Zoë fills in the paperwork, taking a string of dates from her Blackberry and scrawling copious marginalia as though the doctors aren't asking the right questions.

Not long after the appointed time, a smiling ultrasound operator appears and leads us into a room. Zoë lies down, I sit beside her holding her hand, and the gel is squelched liberally on her lower belly. Then, eyes on a screen that's tilted to give us no more than an angled view, the operator starts looking … and looking … and looking.

Just before my hand is crushed entirely, she finds something vaguely baby-shaped but, needing to get a clearer picture, keeps moving the scanner, so much so that I can't see any independent movement amidst the blur of grey. And all the time she's mumbling, 'It's very small … very small … and lying at an awkward angle … very small.'

Zoë, naturally assuming the very worst scenario her years of medical experience can imagine, is convinced the baby's dead. It's small, she's thinking, because it's stopped growing and, with the scanner constantly moving, we can't latch onto that heartbeat that was so amazingly clear when it was all of two and a half millimetres in length. Then, just as I'm beginning to believe the scenario the pain in my clutched hand is describing, the operator freezes and the image of our baby settles on the centre of the screen. And it jumps like a guilty thing, as though suddenly aware that it's the focus of attention. It twitches in surprise, two arms, two legs and a bulbous head, with all the grace and rhythm of its father on the dance floor.

'It is OK, isn't it?' asks Zoë, assured doctor become pleading young hopeful.

'Fine,' says the woman at last, 'absolutely fine. But you're not as far as we'd thought. We'll have to arrange another scan for a week's time to run the tests.'

At last, she gets a fix on our baby that she can measure, and the due date is confirmed: 23rd February.

Ticking the box that reads 'Normal Development', she ushers us out. Then, after a few long minutes searching the bookings for a free space, she asks us to sit in the corridor. For 15 minutes we stare at the printed artwork and I'm relieved when Zoë quietly agrees that it's all been something of an anti-climax. Nothing seems to have changed; with the scan being so indistinct, we don't even have a photo to show family and friends.

Finally, the ultrasound operator returns. 'The next available appointment is in three weeks.'

I'm already nodding my acceptance when I hear Zoë, her voice rising. 'But won't that be leaving it a bit late to run the tests for Down's?'

The operator looks down at our notes in her hand, an obvious prop as she's not really reading them. 'No, that should be fine.' 'Are you sure?' asks Zoë, once more the hard-nosed medic. 'Because that'll put us on the 14-week mark.'

With a smile and what I suppose is meant to be a reassuring shake of the head, the operator can only repeat herself. 'Three weeks will be fine. If you can hand this in at the desk on your way out...'

And we're shepherded back down the corridor, Zoë forced to accept what anyone else would have taken without question.

Saturday, 5th August – 11 weeks, 1 day

'Zoë is with child.' As a way of delivering the news, it seems suitably portentous.

While I understand the desire to make it seem like we're in this together, I can't go with Zoë's preferred line, ' *We're* pregnant', because, as I'm sure is going to become increasingly clear, *we* are not pregnant. *She* is. We're pregnant in the same way that we're sick when she's eaten something I've cooked and is retching into the toilet: I may have contributed to her condition, I may even hold her hair back out of her face, but my experience of the process just can't compare to hers.

With mixed feelings, especially as some friends have been trying for a baby for far longer, we make a few calls. It's difficult to avoid the inevitable question, 'And what was so-and-so's reaction?', as a few of them probe to work out where they stand in the pecking order of information-sharing.

Maternity package negotiations aside, Zoë's made no mention of the pregnancy at work. But it's already having an impact; whenever she's late home, I know she'll have been seeing at least a couple of new mothers. And they always have to ask for their babies to be handed back.

33

Sunday, 6th August – 11 weeks, 2 days

That period before we told anyone, in which we shared the secret of our own expanding future, was the most equal part of the pregnancy. Bloated tits aside, there were no physical changes to be seen in either of us; things seemed balanced, just a delicate, inescapably intimate, fecund and physical fact that drew us closer.

But now, while I remain as I ever was, she's becoming something else. Those two words of revelation act like a dam bursting. Because now that we're telling everyone, she's starting down a path I can't follow and there's no going back. Suddenly, it's *her* event, and sometimes even that's not enough – while some of Zoë's friends have cried at the news, others have been brave enough to share her joy but then allow conversation to creep back to the everyday. At which Zoë, in her excitement, has to fight the urge to shout out, 'Hang on! I'm still pregnant here! Let's keep talking about that.'

Meanwhile my own friends – none of whom has yet been in a similar position – have offered dutiful congratulations, asked a few typical questions ('Was it planned?') and then moved rapidly on to more familiar ground. Strangely, it was much the same when Dad died. Those who hadn't lost their own fathers offered dutiful condolences, made a few polite inquiries, and then hurried back to the everyday. And no doubt I'd have reacted the same had the situation been reversed.

If I thought too much about it, perhaps I'd feel a sense of isolation, especially as I'm struggling to comprehend what lies ahead. But right now it feels so much something that Zoë and I are facing together that I feel a confidence, as though we're capable of anything. And after an enjoyable evening with her folks, plenty of chat and a bottle of champagne (a cup of tea for Zoë), this whole thing is starting to become a little more exciting, a little more real. And suddenly February seems very close...

MONTH THREE

Tuesday, 8th August – 11 weeks, 4 days

With the ground floor given over to wheelbarrow traffic as the builders dig out our new kitchen foundations, it's no surprise to find clouds of dust sneaking stealthily up the stairs. The air is so thick with it, it's as though I'm permanently wearing a tubful of hair gel. Not daring to ask Zoë what damage it could be doing to the baby, I look it up on the internet.

And there it is, in big letters: 'Lead is poisonous.' Passing freely from mother to unborn child, high blood lead levels can affect the developing brain and cause developmental problems. 'Large amounts of lead can be found in paint, dust, soil, building products, wall and ceiling cavities and carpets.' Which pretty much describes our home environment these days.

Wednesday, 9th August – 11 weeks, 5 days

'32DD!' comes the ecstatic shout down the phone. 'I know I always wanted bigger boobs, but this is ridiculous!'

Zoë has gone for a special maternity bra fitting and our shared delight at the official recognition of her enormity is stalled only by the news of the ensuing cost. And still the irony isn't lost on me: just as an aspect of this pregnancy arises in which I could offer devoted and hands-on involvement, she won't let me near them. It's surely a critical biological design fault; isn't this around the time that, having successfully impregnated one female, a male might be tempted to move on, to seek out others with whom to mingle his genes? If that's the case, it's at this stage that biology should grant pregnant women a few extra, alluring qualities that encourage their mates to stick around, not balloon the breasts until they're too tender to touch. What's the point in that? It's like telling me I've got a free upgrade on my mobile phone but can't make any calls.

The morning sickness comes and goes at all times of day, and

Zoë complains of being permanently exhausted. But while others would view being nauseous and knackered as negatives, she contrarily draws comfort from her discomfort, seeing all the typical causes of complaint as reassuring confirmation that our baby's alive and well.

'What about you?' she asks. 'How are you feeling?'

And the truth is that, beyond laying my head on her still totally flat stomach or listening to her quiet moans about how she's feeling, this pregnancy has affected my day-to-day life not at all. It's at night that I notice the changes.

Because she's having to pee at least once in the small hours of every morning, I find myself waking and needing to do the same. It's happened so frequently now that my bladder seems to think it's some sort of competition and, rising to the challenge, is now waking me regardless of Zoë's movements.

Thursday, 10th August – 11 weeks, 6 days

'I think we must be on a stork migration path.'

Zoë and I are working in the front garden; she's helping by sitting on what will become a cupboard door while I plane it down to size.

'What?'

I stop and gesture at the street. 'Everyone around here is pregnant! It's like a swollen belly's part of the local uniform. And for every expectant mother, there are at least two pushchairs already full.'

'So that means this is a popular area to raise kids. What's wrong with that?'

'Nothing, I guess. I just didn't realise when we bought this house that we were buying into that same lifestyle.'

'What lifestyle?'

'Look around. It's safer dodging cars on the roads than the stampede of prams on the pavements. If you don't move fast enough, you get run down by some bulldozing mum on the way to the park, her pram nipping at your ankles like a ratty dog. Either that, or they roam in pairs, blocking the way.'

'At least we've *got* a park nearby.'

'Which itself is like an obstacle course of weaving scooters and dropped ice creams.'

'So stay in the garden. We're lucky to have that too.'

'The only time I'm ever in that mudbath is to return balls lost over the fence! That's what I mean: we've moved to a breeding suburb, where coffee shops overflow with pregnant women avoiding caffeine, and the streets are lined with people carriers and 4x4s parked between every skip – everyone's renovating, extending kitchens and converting lofts. I've never heard so many high-pitched shrieks in one neighbourhood, or seen so many taut tummies ready to pop. Any minute now, the earth's going to tilt on its axis.'

'They're not renovating; they're *nesting*.'

'Exactly! And I thought we were just refurbishing. But we've bought into the whole package. We are now officially suburban cliché.'

'If this is the life we want, what does it matter?'

'It doesn't. It's just weird. Because I don't feel old enough, respectable enough, mature enough or secure enough to be part of that lifestyle. And somehow I've skipped that stage where I buy a sports car with my disposable income.'

Friday, 11th August – 12 weeks pregnant, 28 weeks to go

My brother Nathan calls to say he's finally received the plaque for Dad's grave. After his death, we were all so busy trying to find a way to keep Ardburdan and then, with every avenue exhausted, so busy preparing for a sale, that we never got round to having the plaque made up or fitted.

As Nathan and I talk, we both arrive at the same question:

where is Dad? Or, rather, where is the focus for him to be? Am I going to allow myself to believe that a small patch of grass in an Argyllshire graveyard is the place to focus my thoughts, or am I going to go along with the old cliché that Dad is 'in each and every one of us', living on wherever Nathan, Rob, Mum and myself may be?

Sitting in our new loft, high above the clatter of builders below, I suddenly have a vision of walking along Ardburdan beach. Instead of tiled rooftops and straggled gardens beneath an endless criss-cross of planes and helicopters, I see green fields and vast, empty skies, hear the crunch of pebbles underfoot, and smell the sea wind and the cow-streaked fields. And I have something like a panic attack, a sudden shortness of breath at the enormity of the loss, and the knowledge that I will never be able to share it with my child as my father shared it with me.

Month Four

Tuesday, 15th August – 12 weeks, 4 days

Lacking a kitchen, we put up a shaky old card table in the middle room of the first floor – in what should become the nursery – and splash out on a microwave with built-in grill and oven, and a mains-operated freezer box. Then we order a takeaway.

Yet, increasingly conscious that today's fast food is tomorrow's baby food, Zoë does try to eat healthily. And while I scoff curry and she munches on a lettuce leaf, our baby has now reached the stage where it's also able to swallow.

Unfortunately, not having access to its mother's meticulously arranged 'local takeaway menu folder', its options are limited, so our child is currently knocking back amniotic fluid and then – wait for it – peeing it out again. So already, months before I've even thought about how to feed or clean a baby, it's learning how to eat and make a mess, though at least for the moment it has the decency to be self-contained.

Friday, 18th August – 13 weeks pregnant, 27 weeks to go

I meet Zoë at her surgery and she drives me to her friend's Belgravia flat, inherited recently from a wealthy aunt. We're 15 minutes early for dinner so Zoë pulls up across the street.

'Check this out,' Zoë says with a grin, pulling up her shirt and smearing some sort of lubricant gel over her belly. Before I can ask what she's doing, her hand darts behind the driver's seat and reappears holding a smooth, cylindrical plastic appliance about the size of a handheld electric whisk. Or a vibrator.

Though delighted that Zoë seems to have thrown off her conservative shackles, I'm still wondering exactly what happened at work today to have accelerated our sex life down this novel route when she places the vibrator against her skin and, suddenly, I can clearly hear the beat of our baby's heart.

'It's a fetal Doppler,' she says. 'I've nicked it from work. It's like sonar on a stick.'

Suddenly, the baby is there with us, not just on a sepia screen in the sterilized world of the hospital, but right there, inside my wife, along for the ride as we head out for dinner. And I'm still beaming when there's a tap at the window. A policeman has strolled over from the nearby Turkish embassy and is peering in to where Zoë's wiping off the gel. His expression is bemused, as if to say, 'You see all sorts in this job.'

Wednesday 23rd August – 13 weeks, 5 days

Our second '12-week' scan, double-booked to squeeze us in before it's too late. We arrive far too early but, both armed with a book, we're looking forward to an enforced period of rest.

To escape the extortionate hospital parking rates, I feed a meter just outside the gates. But when we finally make it to reception via the slowest lifts ever engineered and I see the long line of wallowing bumps awaiting their turn, I start worrying about how long we're to be left lingering. For five minutes I dither in the corridor; should I run back out to top up the meter and risk missing the scan, or just accept the possibility of a parking ticket for another glimpse into the dark depths of Zoë's belly?

As it turns out, I needn't worry. Perhaps word has got round that she's a GP, because only minutes after our appointed time we're greeted by the top consultant in the unit who leads us to his office and, within seconds, is showing us our baby, sleeping soundly, on a sepia screen.

Zoë begins chuckling almost insanely with excitement as, with one quick, expert prod from the scanner, our baby starts swatting and kicking. The doctor zooms round to give us views from every angle of two arms, a normal-sized skull, the stomach, bladder and two legs. Then he turns on the 3D scan.

Only the confidence that he has inspired from the start cushions the sense of shock. For there on the screen is our child: a perfect little body, an immense umbilical cord (not the hereditary gift from me I'd thought at first) and – where only moments before we'd seen a head – something that looks like an exploding pumpkin.

'Nothing to worry about,' he says, noticing our reaction. 'That's just the placenta blocking your view.' Disconcertingly aligned, it's making our baby look like a mini Medusa with a low fringe. 'I'll try and get a better angle,' he says.

But no matter how much the doctor presses into Zoë's belly and we will our baby to move, it refuses to show its face, remaining obstinately hidden, like the sun beyond the curve of a hill. As the child of an actor, it should give us at least a smiling headshot but, when the machine spits out a string of photos, none of them is very distinct. And yet we know what we're looking at: that smudge, which to everyone else who nods with polite enthusiasm must look like a butterfly about to land on its nose, is actually a thumb seeking out a mouth. And those blurred blobs to the left are its feet as it tries to loop the loop.

There's a moment, when the 3D scanner is showing the baby straight on with two clearly identifiable legs and such a flagrantly large length of something in between, that I have to ask. Although I can't make out exactly what I'm seeing, there's clearly *something* there, something that perhaps he can interpret.

But despite the fact that this 12-week scan is nearer 14 weeks, it's still too early. And that's fine with me. Because when it seems for a moment as though he might be able to tell us, I feel something like panic – more because it seems like we're getting too many presents at once than because I'm worried one way or the other.

Fortunately, Zoë and I are in agreement that we're happy to wait and see. Friends of hers in a similar position are not: he wants to know, she doesn't. And so, in a style of decision-making that I well recognize, they don't know.

Thursday, 24th August – 13 weeks, 6 days

Zoë comes home and goes straight to bed, exhausted. One of the secretaries caught her sleeping on the examination table in the lunch break.

Despite the healthier meals, her belly is now protruding to the point that one or two items of clothing are getting tight around the waist. If she had the energy, she might actually consider putting her gym membership to use.

She's still terrified of anything but the gentlest of sex in case it prompts bleeding afterwards and, in a move that will trigger concerns for China's economy, has stopped drinking tea altogether.

I take her a cup of hot juice instead. 'How are you feeling?'

'Irritable,' she says. 'But the books say I'm allowed to be. Tell you what, though: I'm having to shave my legs more often. I think it must be a boy.'

'Is that something to do with male hormones, then?'

'No. I think it's something to do with Leo passing into Virgo.'

Friday, 25th August – 14 weeks pregnant, 26 weeks to go

The fetal Doppler is now Zoë's closest friend – spot the relieved grins and telltale smears of gel on her stomach. I persuade her to leave it behind and, with the entire back of our house propped up by a malnourished floor jack and a few scaffolding bars, we hurry to Heathrow for our flight to Scotland.

Saturday, 26th August – 14 weeks, 1 day

Paul's thirtieth birthday celebrations in Elie. We're staying in one of the old houses right on the beach, with views across the Firth of Forth towards Lothian and beyond. I used to come here with my brothers and grandparents in their motor caravan. More recently,

I spent a memorable part of my stag weekend fighting off friends as they tried to strip me and throw me into the North Sea.

I had decided to wear for that night a pair of Dad's old school socks, more a gesture than a serious tribute, a light-hearted means of having him along with us for the evening. Naturally after a few drinks they'd gained sufficient significance as a memento that, when I discovered my attackers had mislaid them in the dark somewhere between the pub and the house, I broke down in tears.

The next morning, while everyone else was still sleeping, I made a cup of coffee and walked out onto the beach. Gulls were wheeling over the waves, children were chasing kites across the sand already warm beneath my bare feet and, in a fishing boat pulled high above the line of seaweed, an old man was crouching over a net. And there, in the middle of the bay, lay a pair of hugely over-rated socks, happily high and dry having escaped the tide. In full awareness of my sentimentality, we sat together, Dad's socks and I, and enjoyed the vastness of the sea, the fresh breeze and the open skies.

As I sit here again now with Zoë, I want to ask her once more why we've found ourselves living in London, so far from the world I expected to be able to call home. But it's a conversation we've had often enough before, and while she's the main source of income, it seems only fair that her work dictate our location. So instead we sit, my arm over her shoulder and her hand on her belly, enjoying the moment in silence.

Sunday, 27th August – 14 weeks, 2 days

With little else to worry about and having got up to pee three times during the night, Zoë decides to settle on the possibility of a urinary tract infection.

'Surely it's more likely that, as other bits grow, your bladder has to shrink?' I suggest. 'Isn't that what all the books say?'

'Yeah, the growing uterus presses on the bladder and you need to pee. But a growing uterus can also interfere with the drainage of urine from the bladder. And that's when you get an infection. And pregnancy can mask some of the other symptoms.'

'Leading to what?'

'At worst, the infection can spread all the way up to the kidney. And a kidney infection can cause early birth or reduced weight in the baby. So I'm not taking any chances.'

At Edinburgh airport, Zoë arranges a prescription for antibiotics, then diverts us via the hospital on our way back through London where she drops off a urine sample for testing.

Monday, 28th August – 14 weeks, 3 days

For Zoë's birthday, I buy her a treatment in a local spa. And because it's like any other local store keen to exploit the abundance of ripe women with money to spend, I'm able to pay extra for a 'mother-to-be' massage. I don't know why the grocer doesn't get in on the act and start selling 'pregnancy potatoes' for twice the price.

Tuesday, 29th August – 14 weeks, 4 days

The results of Zoë's urinary tract infection test come back negative. Determined not to be reassured, she's almost triumphant having found continuing cause for concern. 'This only proves I didn't have an infection when I took the test, and that was two days ago. Anything could have happened since then!'

Friday, 1st September – 15 weeks pregnant, 25 weeks to go

However much I may like to consider myself worldly and wise, it doesn't take much for Zoë to demonstrate how much more of life she's exposed to, and how much wider a spectrum. So much so that she shares a statistic from her hospital days with weary acceptance.

If a pregnant woman's blood is rhesus negative but the baby is rhesus positive, it can cause problems in any future pregnancies; the two blood groups unavoidably mix, causing the mother to develop antibodies that can then attack any subsequent pregnancies with similar rhesus incompatibility. Thanks to frequent blood tests and injections given immediately after birth to those faced with such a problem, the implications aren't huge.

But a baby's blood will only be rhesus positive if the father's blood is also rhesus positive. A simple test, then, would be to test the father's blood just as they test the mother's, to see if incompatibility will be an issue.

But in the hospital where Zoë worked before she became a GP, there's a 20% non-paternity rate. In other words, one in five of the 'fathers' aren't the real fathers at all.

Monday, 4th September – 15 weeks, 3 days

Zoë discovers a study suggesting a link between repeated ultrasounds of pregnant mice and diminished brain development in their fetuses. Until I'm one of those Hollywood actors able to afford an ultrasound scanner to peer into my wife's innards on a daily basis, there's not much to worry about.

But even though the handheld Doppler is so much weaker than a proper ultrasound, she's decided to play safe and stop using it. Which is perhaps a good thing, because it can be reassuring to listen to our baby until it moves quite normally to a point that the Doppler can't pick it up, and then suddenly Zoë becomes a whirling panic of prods and jiggles.

Friday, 8th September – 16 weeks pregnant, 24 weeks to go

After dinner, Zoë unbuttons the top of her trousers, as much a result of her second lemon pancake as her impatience to be showing. Sixteen weeks of frantic growth inside her, and yet the biggest change to our lives is the frequency of night-time bathroom breaks. Cards still line the shelves, but the handshakes and backslaps have died down, and still Zoë barely looks pregnant. If she lies on her side, there's a little belly to cup as I fall asleep, and her breasts remain frustratingly tender. But on the whole it's frightening how much things remain the same – frightening because I know it must be the calm before the storm.

Month Five

Tuesday, 12th September – 16 weeks, 4 days

8 a.m. A steady trickle of suited men pass our window en route to the childminder a few doors down, their faces fraught with the pressure of handing over their kids in time to make it to the station and on to work.

And only now does it really dawn on me what I've let myself in for. Distracted by the overarching concerns – the cost and the responsibility – I'd never fully appreciated that, while Zoë's intended return to work might answer any financial worries, it leaves me staying at home and caring for the kid. I've sleepwalked into the role of househusband, twenty-first-century man, content to change nappies and wipe bums while my wife provides.

If I thought that meant I could spend my days lunching with friends or strolling round the park, basking in the wonder of my child's daily development, I would be facing the future with overwhelming impatience. No career could appeal as much. But in a society where gender supposedly never discriminates, all the prams around here are still pushed by women. Overwhelmingly it's the men who, far from meeting for lunch, are still trudging to the trains. I'm to be a man in what remains, undeniably, a woman's world, and that makes me more than a little apprehensive. It's little consolation to think that, if the stereotypes hold true, I should at least be the best pram driver in the park.

Saturday, 16th September – 17 weeks, 1 day

An article in the paper today warns pregnant women against eating too much fish while pregnant. The same article warns against not eating fish while pregnant.

I ask Zoë if she's managing to abstain from her frequent McDonalds lunches. She smiles disarmingly. 'All things in moderation,' she replies.

The ultimate message of the article is that 'you are what your mother ate'. In which case we face the challenge of raising a ketchup-smeared quarter-pound cheeseburger with fries. Given the conflicting advice trumpeted from all corners, 'all things in moderation' seems an admirably common-sensical approach. But when it comes to fast food, Zoë can be moderate even in her moderation.

Monday, 18th September – 17 weeks, 3 days

'What's wrong?'

Zoë's just got out of the shower, her face grey. She ties the towel tightly around herself and, close to tears, reaches out for my hand, guiding it towards her right breast. 'Feel this.'

Not daring to think, I rub a few fingers the way she's showing me on the outer side of her breast. And I can feel it, a small area of thicker tissue beneath the surface, no bigger than a 10p piece.

'It could just be normal pregnancy changes,' she says. 'But I think I need a scan.'

'How long will that take?'

'They've got to see me within two weeks.'

Two weeks is a long time to be worrying. I see it stretching out before us, 14 days of unchecked terror. 'Is there nothing more you can do?'

'I'll call the hospital. Maybe they can squeeze me in sooner.'

As soon as she gets to work, she books an appointment. By admitting that she's a local GP, they find a slot for her first thing tomorrow.

Fortunately, it's a busy day; she has no time to sit and think. We go through the evening without mentioning it. I do all I can to fill the silences with talk of other things, and she plays along.

Tuesday, 19th September – 17 weeks, 4 days

She tells me not to come with her. 'I'll go straight to work from the hospital.'

Within the hour, she calls. 'It's fine,' she says.

'Tell me what happened.'

'They gave me an ultrasound, told me to put my finger on where I can feel it then scanned it, but there's nothing there. I feel so stupid, like I've been panicking for nothing. I barely slept last night.'

'What did they say?'

'They just said it's normal to feel changes in pregnancy. But they were really nice. I said I was sorry to have wasted their time, but they said that's what they're there for. And I know as a doctor myself that they'd rather be telling me it's nothing to worry about than that it's something more sinister.'

Because Zoë's a doctor, we benefit and we suffer. She can exploit the system to gain the sort of reassurance for which others would have to wait weeks, but she can also latch onto the smallest symptom and see in it every fatal possibility.

Saturday, 23rd September – 18 weeks, 1 day, just under 22 weeks to go

We're driving north for another thirtieth birthday party outside Edinburgh, and escaping London once again highlights the difference between the life I'd expected to lead in Scotland, and the life I now face, into which we're about to bring a child.

In London our son or daughter will grow up thinking it's normal to travel for a whole hour to meet for coffee, that the suffocating heat of the city centre in mid-summer is bearable, and that it's worth venturing abroad beyond the M25 now and again because, once you get there, cabs and drinks really are so cheap.

Half-Scottish, half-English, its northern half will be inescapably stifled by the daily onslaught of London life, with only intermittent visits to a Scottish granny and the nostalgic gibbering of its father to awaken any sense of its roots lying deep in the damp soil of Argyll.

Passing through the desolate hills of Cumbria, my brooding only solidifies. When Zoë tells me that, assuming our baby hasn't inherited my mum's deafness, he or she should now be able to hear, I succumb to the temptation and put on the *Braveheart* soundtrack.

Minutes later, Zoë shrieks from the passenger seat.

'That was it! I think that was it! I just felt the baby move.'

It's sentimental; it's stupid; it's coincidence. But it's also heartening to think that, at the sound of the pipes and drums, my baby has been inspired to perform its own little Highland fling.

Sunday, 24th September – 18 weeks, 2 days

As Zoë's tentative bump is admired by a long line of northern relatives and friends, it becomes clear: as long as she doesn't smoke, drink excessively or start playing contact sports, she can bask in the spotlight and, as she grows bigger, exhibit to one and all the success of her continuing pregnancy.

Meanwhile, what can we men do? I begin to understand why some choose to grow in tandem, sympathetically matching their partner's belly pound for pound, just to feel involved. There seems to be no other way in which to gauge the success of our ongoing contribution to the process. That's my excuse anyway.

Wednesday, 27th September – 18 weeks, 5 days

Back home. Rebecca comes round for mid-afternoon tea and is dispensing advice on the myriad of baby equipment available before she's even through the door. Having worked as a nanny in the US, she's tested most of the market, so quickly opens our eyes to the many opportunities we now face to waste our money.

Listening to her, I begin to wonder how I'll ever forgive my parents for not having had a 'wetwipe warmer' – a plug-in box that acts like a mini oven for your baby's wetwipes, the idea being that the little darling will then escape the unforgivable shock of having a cold bum. The fact that you can apparently then only use half the pack because the rest has dried into a crusty brick is a small price to pay for avoiding the lifelong burden of 'cold crack trauma' (as my psychiatrist calls it).

When Rebecca's chat progresses from the perils of warming milk to the plethora of pushchairs available, I latch proudly onto the one label I recognize. I'd thought that the 'Bugaboo', merely by virtue of my knowing its name, was the most popular make. It's certainly the favoured option around these streets.

'Don't go for that, though,' says Rebecca. 'It'll only last you a few months and it's so expensive. What you want is a Maclaren.' She shakes her head wearily at my sudden interest. 'No, it's nothing to do with Formula One.'

To be honest, I don't listen to why the Maclaren is the one for us – I'm thinking back to the enormous spokes of the cast-off travelling tank I was pushed around in as a baby and marvelling at how I developed into an even vaguely balanced adult without all the expensive extras available to children today.

'So do any of them come with alloys and in-stroller music systems?' I butt in, thinking I'm hilarious.

'Probably,' she answers, not even recognizing my question as a joke. 'I've heard talk about electric covers and speedometers, so I wouldn't be surprised.' She turns to Zoë with an exaggerated roll of her eyes. 'Honestly, guys get so competitive about their prams.'

'What?'

'Yeah. I've known dads who take their prams out at the weekend for a wash and a polish.'

'You are kidding!'

'Not at all. You're going to be out and about with it a lot, so there's a lot of pressure to look good with the right pram.'

What strange world have we slipped into?

Thursday, 28th September – 18 weeks, 6 days

The cheerful wee Australian plumber has just installed our showerhead at a height that's fine for him but would only just splash my belly. I'm asking him to adjust it when my agent calls with news of an audition, the first in about six weeks.

It's for *River City*, Scotland's answer to *EastEnders* – a regular role that offers experience, profile and a good income. They film it just west of Glasgow; ironically, if there's one acting job that would have been just about commutable from the wilds of Argyll, it's this.

When Zoë comes home she matches my excitement with a polite smile, torn between sympathy for my hopes, and terror for the immense disruption it would bring.

Friday, 29th September – 19 weeks pregnant, 21 weeks to go

Realizing that I'm to be responsible for another, my thoughts turn inevitably to myself, as though seeking a firm base, a foundation on which to build another generation. And it's with great delight that I realize I can now judge myself according to a whole new set of criteria, by which my less exciting characteristics can be reassessed as credits. In fatherhood, plodding constancy is surely just paternal stability; timidity is but a degree of respect for others, while a tendency to sit on the fence is a wise appreciation of conflicting views. Perhaps I'm ready for this after all...

Saturday, 30th September – 19 weeks, 1 day

Our first meal in our newly fitted kitchen.

'I spoke to Lorna today,' says Zoë. 'She and Alex are getting a Bugaboo.'

'That doesn't surprise me.'

'Maybe we shouldn't rule it out. There must be–'

'I don't want to spend all that money just so we can keep up with everyone else.'

Zoë sighs. 'But there's a good reason why people buy Bugaboos, and it's not just to keep up with their neighbours.'

'You heard what Rebecca said.'

'Yes, but I've also heard what Dan and Becky have said. They think theirs is great.'

'I don't want one.'

'Why have you got such a thing against them?'

'Because I don't want to get into the habit of reaching beyond our grasp for something that's just not necessary. And I don't like the idea that someone's making money out of our fear and ignorance, or exploiting our instinctive desire to want only the best for our baby. There are men and women in marketing departments all around the world whose enormous salaries depend on the fact that parents have a hard time saying 'no' when it comes to their children.'

'I'm just saying let's not rule it out. We probably wouldn't be able to fit a Bugaboo into the car anyway.'

Later, back in front of the telly, I wonder why I'm getting so uptight. Is it because, in a world that revolves around money, I know that having some to spend on your child does, if only at a shallow level, equate to being able to provide for that child? And if you provide for your child, you are a good parent. And yet, just like our baby, it looks like I'm going to be reliant on Zoë.

Wednesday, 4th October – 19 weeks, 5 days

'I've changed my mind,' says Zoë. 'I don't want to find out.'

I look across the bed. She's lying on her back, her belly tucked beneath a gently rising duvet, and I sigh. Of all the conversations prompted by the pregnancy, this has to be the most revisited: how keen are we to peer at our baby's genitals?

Months ago, when Zoë first asked if I'd want to know our baby's sex, I shrugged and nodded. After all, if you can, why wouldn't you? Short of peeking at their diary in a few years' time, I hope I'll always want to know all there is to know about my son or daughter.

'What's the usual thing to do?' I ask.

'Most people find out.' She turns carefully onto her side to face me. 'But I don't want to know.'

'So what's changed your mind? Your mum?' Despite her obvious excitement at the prospect of becoming a grandmother and her willingness, almost impatience, to be as involved as possible, Zoë's mum has been one of the vocal many warning against 'spoiling the mystery'.

But Zoë shakes her head. 'It's since the baby started moving. I was impatient before for any sign of life. But now that I'm getting regular kicks, I don't need that same reassurance.'

Looking at her expression, I sense that her typically intuitive approach, which at times leaves her as whimsical as the wind, has resolved this time into a firm decision. 'So what about you?' she asks.

'I'm still not sure. It would make it easier to choose a name, I suppose. And then we could get on with all the clothes shopping, and painting of the nursery, and all the other boring things that we'll have to organize.' But I know as I'm saying it that I'm in no hurry to embroil our child in the mundane, to map out its life before we've even set eyes on it. Nor do I really think that knowing its sex is going to guarantee a ceasefire to the late-night feuding as we fire names across the pillow.

'It is traditional to wait,' parrots Zoë.

'Maybe, but you could also say it's traditional to deliver babies without painkillers. Or to live without central heating.'

'It would spoil the surprise.'

'No, it would *relocate* the surprise. But it would still be a surprise, whatever day we find out.' I think for a bit. 'Wouldn't it be good to know what we're having so we can picture it a bit better and ... just start identifying with it?' It would certainly give me time to swat up on football strips or limber up in preparation for being wound around little fingers.

'Perhaps,' concedes Zoë. 'But you don't need to know its gender to begin forming a relationship. And anyway, they don't always get it right, you know. About one in 15 get it wrong.'

I smile and wonder how our kid would ever live down such a mistake.

'And would you rather find out from our baby itself or from some sullen, overworked ultrasound operator?' Instinctively, her hand disappears beneath the covers to caress her bump. 'They can write it down and put it in an envelope, you know. Then we've got the answer if we change our mind later.'

I shake my head; such a cruel exercise in self-restraint seems tantamount to telling us anyway.

We lie in silence.

'OK,' I say at last. 'What about this? Right now, neither of us feels any preference for a boy or a girl. But what happens if we develop a favourite between now and the birth, and then we're disappointed?'

'I suppose that's possible,' admits Zoë. 'But then by finding out, you lose the ability to daydream about both. If I found out one way or the other, I think I'd feel a bit disloyal to the child we're not going to have.'

'That's ridiculous!'

'It's not! There are whole psychiatry papers written about it; it's a type of mourning.'

'So if you find out on the day itself, you're just too busy to grieve, is that it?'

'I guess so,' shrugs Zoë.

'But I don't want to spend the next few months latching onto those unofficial "signs". Like if you carry the baby high rather than forward, we're having a boy, or if we pass four magpies in the park rather than three...'

There's another short silence as we weigh up the pros and cons. This scan could tell me if I'm to spend the years ahead shielding my eyes from a constant pink glare, or struggling to differentiate one dinosaur from another. It's exciting, and I wonder what need there is for restraint.

'It's a bit like knowing there's a present under the tree with our name on it,' says Zoë. 'Do we want to peek months before Christmas and see what we're going to get, or are we happy to wait, savouring the anticipation, until the day itself?'

It's a good analogy. Everything's going so well; why lose the fun that comes from guessing if we've still got to wait several months until we can play with our present anyway?

'And there's another reason for not finding out, Andrew. Deafness has so far only affected females in your family. If we're told we're having a girl, I'm going to worry for the next five months whether or not she's deaf as well.'

I hadn't thought of that.

So at last we come to a tentative decision; we're not going to find out. The next problem is how to explain that to Zoë's mum without admitting she might be right.

Friday, 6th October – 20 weeks pregnant, 20 weeks to go

The audition. Waking at six with nerves, I'm in town 40 minutes early and forced to loiter around Leicester Square, convinced that everyone who's not obviously a tourist is there to steal the role from me.

Barely ten minutes after I've walked into the casting room, I'm walking out, and already replaying my every comment while second-guessing their every requirement. Did I read the script right? Is my accent strong enough? Do I look too old? Did I come across as the sort of person they'd want to be working with every day for months on end?

Walking back to the tube, I check in with my agent.

'How did it go?' she asks.

'Fine. I think. Now I guess we just wait until they come back to us...'

'Absolutely. Oh, they emailed this morning with the character's shoot dates; it's to start around the end of February.'

In other words, within days of our baby being born, I might have to leave London for Glasgow. Yet I hesitate only a fraction of a second. 'Great,' I say, hiding the mounting worry. 'Keep me posted.'

I haven't told my agent that Zoë's pregnant yet. With auditions so few and far between, I don't want to give her any reason to think my availability is going to be in any way reduced in the future. I'm guessing not many leading men have built their careers around childcare.

Month Six

Tuesday, 10th October – 20 weeks, 4 days

The books say that, in order to bond with the bump, I can try reading a book – it doesn't matter what type as long as the baby can hear my voice. Which would be fine if there wasn't a requirement for Zoë to be around at the same time and if I liked bodice-ripping historical romances.

'Why don't you sing something to it, then?' says Zoë, gesturing at my guitar sitting largely untouched in the corner of the room. She leans back on the sofa and exposes her belly, and I start strumming a few old favourites.

I stop pretty soon, feeling stupid. I don't ever sit and sing to Zoë, so it's all the stranger to be serenading a stretch of skin. And I still can't shake off the pressure to work while I've got the chance, to trawl for article commissions, to chase up voice-overs. Jon's sent the details of an American publisher looking for authors for a series of original fiction aimed at adults learning English as a foreign language, and I've an idea for a thriller I want to pitch – if I can ever find the time.

The thought makes me ditch the guitar and propels me upstairs, accompanied by a niggling guilt: is this where it starts, being so tied up worrying about the future that I neglect the here and now?

Friday, 13th October – 21 weeks pregnant, 19 weeks to go

We're well past the halfway point, so I try again to read up about our baby, as though immersing myself in the details will bring it all home, but it's a bit like watching a David Attenborough documentary: I gape in amazement at the pictures, hear a few brain-boggling facts, and then, shaking my head in wonder, get up and get on with life, rapidly dismissing such trivia as nothing to do with my day-to-day reality.

If our baby is a girl, the books tell me, then the two million eggs now in her ovaries will have halved in number by the time she's born. Beneath its white coat, a polar bear's skin is actually black. Already, over four months before it's born, our baby is preparing its first bowel movement. Toads are more susceptible to attack from the right-hand side. Interesting, perhaps, but still distant enough from my everyday life as to be comfortably forgotten.

Saturday, 14th October – 21 weeks, 1 day

'You know,' I say to Zoë as I hand her a cup of tea and we sit down to another night in front of the telly, 'this baby won't change us at all.'

'What do you mean?'

'Look at us! We're just about the dullest people I know. In the prime of life, and we spend every evening on the sofa. We've both got slippers beside the bed and a favourite mug; we never go out, and the few times we do, you want to drive so you can get back to bed even quicker. This baby's only going to give us the perfect excuse to stick to our cosy routine.'

'Maybe,' nods Zoë. 'But we don't go out now because we don't *want* to. Are you still going to feel so happy about it when you don't have the choice?'

'What difference will it make?'

'Because it's nice to know we *could* go out if we wanted to.'

In the end, we agree to hope that we'll fail to recognize such a loss of choice as a restriction if we're holding in our arms the best possible reason for staying in.

Monday, 16th October – 21 weeks, 3 days

I wake briefly at three in the morning when Zoë gets up for the loo, then slip into a nightmare.

I'm back at Ardburdan. The building is covered in damp patches of moss, gutters are streaming onto cracked and blistering render, windows are rotting, foliage grows out of the walls. The whole place is suffering from terminal neglect.

Somehow I find myself inside, walking in dismay from one dilapidated room to the next. Passing the cloakroom, I notice, through the half-open door, that someone is sitting on a sofa that was never there before, staring out of the window. Thinking it must be the new owner, I walk hesitantly in.

And it's Dad. He's sitting there smoking, looking as haggard and ill as he ever did, his leathered neck, burnt from the treatment, hanging in wrinkled folds. He glances up and I don't know from his confused glance if he's recognized me.

'I don't know what I'm doing here,' he says. 'Do you?'

I shake my head, and my heart's aching with the realization that, although he's come back, I can't stay with him; I'm only visiting, I have responsibilities elsewhere.

'I don't understand,' he says, his voice weak. 'I don't know what's happened.' He turns and looks properly towards me. 'They've all left me, you see,' he says.

I wake then, and stare at the curtains without moving, for fear of waking Zoë. And even though I don't believe in ghosts, I think of him walking back up the hill from the graveyard to tell us he's come home, to sit at his desk and pick up his life as before, only to find those he's loved gone and the house dislocated, full of strangers. And I wonder if I can imagine anything more sad.

Tuesday, 17th October – 21 weeks, 4 days

In a few days we've got the anomaly scan. Still hungry for anything that will help to bring it home to me that in just a few months we'll be three, I'm wavering over our decision to remain ignorant of our baby's sex.

Zoë doesn't need anything else – the constant kicks are notice enough. They stop her mid-sentence, or start her giggling inexplicably in a manner that must be hugely disconcerting for her patients. I watch her sitting quietly, happily stroking her ever-growing belly as her body changes almost daily in what must, for her, be the perfect scenario: all the attention and promise, all the anticipation and maternal contentment, with none of the noise, pain or mess. And for one who experiences solitude as punishment, she has the constant comfort of a captive companion.

I, meanwhile, feel a little uninvolved. I run around the house, juggling plumbers and decorators, tilers and carpenters, slowly turning our house into a home. But apart from the ultrasound photo on my bookshelf and the beautiful bulge on my wife, our baby is not yet something I feel I've really engaged with.

Even my sperm have done more for this baby than I have – naturally, I don't want to belittle my contribution in sending them on their way, but while I was rolling off to turn on the telly, they were already fighting and dying, struggling valiantly through the most hostile of environments, overcoming Goliath-like odds with a single-minded dedication as they gave all they had to fulfil their destinies. By contrast, I've not even painted the nursery.

Wednesday, 18th October – 21 weeks, 5 days

'Quick! Feel this!'

Zoë grabs my hand and places it on her belly. I'm only inches away from our baby, but I can't feel anything.

'There! Did you feel that?'

Again, I have to shake my head.

We wait.

Soon Zoë screeches as though two sumo-wrestling contortionists are battling it out for supremacy of her innards. 'You must have felt that!'

Disappointed, I give up, almost offended that, at my mere touch, our baby seems to shrink for cover beneath its mother's lower intestine.

Zoë tries generously to give our baby's apparent unwillingness to engage with its father a positive spin. 'It's because you're a calming influence,' she says.

Maybe calm is what I should be grateful for, as Zoë's body nurtures our child noiselessly and messlessly in a perfectly self-contained little package. Perhaps in a few months' time I'll be dreaming of these quieter, pre-storm days. But right now I could do with a more tangible sign of what's to come, something to latch onto and identify with. And mightn't the knowledge of our baby's sex be just that?

There was that point during our 12-week scan when I panicked, suddenly realizing I might find out for sure. I wanted time just to savour the stage at which we'd found ourselves. Now, though, after several weeks of little change, I think I'm ready to learn more, to experience at least a degree of the same connection that Zoë so obviously feels.

This isn't a clichéd wail of insecurity as I complain that the baby's coming between us (although of course it is, literally, as Zoë's belly now keeps us several inches further apart). It's simply that I'm impatient for any opportunity to get to know it better.

Not long ago I thought I was content just to know that there's a present under the Christmas tree with my name on it. Why should I have to know what that present is, I wondered, in order to enjoy the anticipation? What good does it do to know what you're getting if you can't play with it anyway? Now, though, I'm thinking that if those presents were tantalizing you every day for nine months and if your wife was giggling constantly as though she knew that little bit more than you, surely you could be forgiven for taking a little peek?

Thursday, 19th October – 21 weeks, 6 days – the anomaly scan

I never thought I'd be so keen to get a glimpse of someone's genitals, but my instruction to the doctor as Zoë and I walk into the examination room is dutiful, if a little half-hearted: 'If you see anything, don't tell us.'

Zoë's still firmly against finding out our baby's sex, but I squirm on my seat as, for the most excruciatingly frustrating few seconds of my life, I force myself to turn away from the screen.

The sonographer checks all the bits, then, with a smug smirk at my obvious turmoil, reports simply, 'Everything's fine down there.'

Then on she goes, her voice so quiet and her language so laden with medical jargon as she speaks to Zoë as a fellow doctor that I don't catch or understand half of it. And then, after only a matter of minutes, I could swear I've just heard the woman refer to our baby as a 'he'.

I turn to Zoë to see if the mistake has registered but she's chatting on, oblivious, so I study the sonographer's face. Is that a look of guilty realization? Or has she simply used the masculine pronoun as default? Or have I just heard wrong?

Suddenly, I feel cheated. I've shown such strength, such resolve in looking away, only to find out anyway through a slip of the tongue. And the quandary now facing me slowly dawns: do I tell Zoë, despite her not wanting to know? Can I really keep it from her anyway?

I think of Dan and Becky. They'd planned to keep their baby's sex a secret, until he let it slip in conversation with a work colleague. Within minutes, his whole office knew. If he couldn't even keep it from water-cooler gossip, how will I ever keep it from pillow talk?

What should I do? Ask for confirmation while I have the chance? Or just ignore it, but risk it gnawing away at me for another four months as I prepare – perhaps wrongly – to have a son? A son! A mini-me, someone to take to the park for a kick around, another body to help vote in an evening of sport rather than *Strictly Come Dancing*...

'And here you can see the vagina...' says the sonographer, that single word breaking through my plotting.

Vagina? Hang on...

This time there's no doubt what she's said because, only moments later, Zoë repeats the word as well, pointing casually at the screen as they mention EDDs and LMPs, CRLs and BPDs. So I *have* misheard – the sonographer couldn't make it clearer: we're going to have a daughter! A baby girl! After growing up with two brothers, at last I'll see life through the eyes of a girl as she grows into a woman, someone I can spoil with presents and protect from the wandering eyes and hands of smelly, sports-obsessed boys...

And then, the minute I start to question Zoë's calm acceptance of the sonographer's lack of discretion, my amazement at such gross professional misconduct is pervaded by a touch of common sense. The penny finally drops as Zoë turns to me to translate, and I realize the vagina in question is hers.

'The placenta's encroaching on the cervix,' she says. 'It's called placenta praevia – happens in about 0.5% of pregnancies.'

'What does that mean?' I ask, turning to the doctor. 'Is it serious?' With all the ferment over our baby's sex, I realize I've forgotten the main point of the scan: to ensure that our baby and Zoë are both doing well.

'It's nothing to worry about at this stage,' the doctor answers. 'As the uterus continues to grow, it often resolves itself.'

Zoë seems reassuringly unperturbed. 'It just means we'll have to come back for another scan in a few months.'

At which point I'll have to go through it all again...

Friday, 20th October – 22 weeks pregnant, 18 weeks to go

Friends have gone to a wedding and left Archie, their ten-month-old boy, with us for the night. He's so calm and cheerful that I begin to feel calm and cheerful myself at the prospect of having a baby of our own.

'I think a boy would be fun, don't you?' asks Zoë as we're falling asleep.

I grunt noncommittally, determined not to admit that I've been thinking the same in case any expression of preference backfires.

Saturday, 21st October – 22 weeks, 1 day

Archie's parents return to pick him up, and suddenly the house seems a bit empty, something I take as a reassuring sign of our own readiness.

That evening, we visit Zoë's cousins. They have an 18-month-old girl, so loving and smiley that we're soon undecided once more.

Tuesday, 24th October – 22 weeks, 4 days

I guess it's to be expected that we're in front of the telly when I feel our baby move for the first time. Apparently. We're sprawled across the sofa, my hand on Zoë's belly, and there's the smallest ripple beneath my palm that could easily have been a muscle tensing.

And much as I will myself to match the wonder in Zoë's eyes, I still find it impossible to equate this twitching belly to the impending seismic shift we face in just a few months, when we're to be responsible for an utterly helpless, fragile little blob. It's enough to catch the breath, perhaps why my mind is cheerfully refusing to make the connection.

Tentatively, I share the thought.

'I do know what you mean,' agrees Zoë. 'We've ordered up so many new things for this house, from lights and bedheads to mirrors and radiators, that it almost feels like a baby will be just another item on that list.'

And she's right. As long as one of us is in to sign for it on the day, surely we'll be able to take it through to the kitchen, hold it up to the light to see if it matches the colour scheme and, if the worst comes to the worst, send it back for a refund?

Friday, 27th October – 23 weeks pregnant, 17 weeks to go

We've still not got any back doors on the kitchen, and the house is freezing. I'd turn on the heating if the plumbers had got it working.

As I walk to the shops, I still feel so out of place amongst the tarmac and the concrete. Here in the city, we work so hard to ensure we're unhindered by nature's variety that only its most heavy-handed attributes still intrude on our comfort, leaving us sweltering in the summer or shivering in the winter. And even those, with the click of a switch, we do our best to avoid.

Living in the country, you're exposed to the seasons in a way you totally miss in the city, and are aware of a cycle of life of which we're merely a part, however much we may try to rise above it. I enjoyed growing up in the country so much it's hard not to want the same for my child, and I find myself wondering how far I should gauge my success as a parent by my ability or otherwise to give them what meant so much to me.

Does it really matter that my child will grow up a city-dweller, better used to feeling concrete underfoot than unsullied soil? Does it matter that, here in London, our child will be lucky to find one frozen puddle that hasn't already been cracked underfoot? Or that the closest they'll get to seeing a shooting star will be a 747 on its descent into Heathrow's Terminal 5 – assuming they can make it out through the glare of thousands of street-lights?

Doubtless, growing up in one of the largest cities in the world will offer my child endless benefits and opportunities that I never had. But I worry that they'll also miss something we're all at risk of overlooking. Or is this just me already trying to impose my own values on my child? Or making excuses for broken central heating?

Sunday, 29th October – 23 weeks, 2 days

A lazy, bed-bound morning as any question of a decreasing libido is resolutely answered. Midway through our efforts, Zoë's left breast begins to leak, prompting a brief but fascinated interlude as we discover that both are now offering up small drops of creamy liquid.

'Colostrum,' declares Zoë, in wonder and triumph. 'Full of carbohydrates and protein. Loads of antibodies.'

'A bit like a protein shake, then?' I say. 'Just the thing for a mid-marathon athlete.' I lean closer, with more bravado than intent, so it's a relief when Zoë pushes me away with a shriek. 'Don't waste it!' Quite apart from stealing from my unborn child, it's slightly uncomfortable to have it confirmed that these enormous breasts are gearing up to be nothing more than feeding stations.

Wednesday, 1st November – 23 weeks, 5 days

'Not long now!'

Every time I hear those words, usually offered up with an anticipatory grin of *Schadenfreude* from those with kids already, the practicalities of having a baby force their way a little further through the warm, fuzzy cloud of abstract sentiment. And my main concerns about those practicalities revolve principally – and somewhat egotistically – around my future identity.

As a hugely valued doctor, Zoë will be the one going out each day to earn our daily bread while I, as the lower earner, will be left caring for the baby. Although I'll continue to act and write as much as possible, my principal role will be that of 'house-husband'.

It's interesting that my word processor seems totally comfortable with the word even if I'm not. In a world where one's occupation contributes so much to one's identity, it's just not a position I'd ever planned for or aspired to. As the teacher went round the class asking us what we wanted to do with our lives, I don't remember anyone saying they fancied a shot at househusbandry. The best recommendation the school's careers advisory programme could manage for me was a life of hairdressing – there was certainly no thumb-worn folder on the bookshelves listing the requirements of a stay-at-home dad.

They say that raising children is one of the most challenging yet rewarding jobs around. And I can certainly believe it's one of the most important: after all, in the decades to come, the world is going to need all the well-balanced, intelligent and sensitive individuals it can get. Today's parents could be responsible for the making or breaking of this little planet.

But while I can rationalize the role's worth all I want, there remain, inescapably, the residual expectations instilled by generations of men who went out to work while the women stayed at home and raised the children. And those fragments of past norms are still sufficiently substantial to prick the conscience and rouse me to something like shame when I imagine the response of others to our role reversal.

Zoë herself seems immune to those same stereotypes, remaining as supportive as ever, but will her family think that I'm letting her down, that I'm forcing her to trudge back to work because I've failed to assume my manly duties? Will our friends quietly consider me that little bit less responsible for failing to provide? I'm sure it wouldn't surprise them to learn that these days she even snores more than me.

More importantly, what will our child think of me? Will he or she get confused and claim to have two mums? Or face ridicule

in the playground as boasts are exchanged over what Daddy does?
Can I be a good mother to my child while still providing a
fatherly, masculine role model?

Month Seven

Saturday, 4th November – 24 weeks, 1 day, just under 16 weeks to go

'Apparently,' says Zoë, flourishing a paperback, '*this* is the book we need.'

'What is it?'

'Jackie says it's brilliant – she's been using it with Henry. It tells you exactly what to do every minute of the day.'

'Isn't that what a wife's for?'

Zoë answers by slapping the book down hard in my lap.

'*The Contented Little Baby Book*,' I read.

'It's a bestseller,' says Zoë. 'I think we should give it a go.'

'Why?' I ask, flicking through the pages. 'What's so good about it?'

'Because it gives you a 24-hour timetable.'

'Is that good?'

'It is if you've never raised a kid before and haven't got a clue what you're meant to do. If you follow the routine, you know exactly what you should be doing at any given time. And you know your baby's getting enough food and drink and sleep.'

'But doesn't that assume that all babies are identical? The one thing I specifically remember Dad telling me he'd learnt from being a parent is that no two kids are the same.'

'Andrew, this has worked for thousands of babies! Jackie was having a nightmare with Henry until she tried this book, and within the week he was sleeping through the night – that's good enough for me. She says Gina Ford's a miracle-worker. Although,' Zoë pauses, momentarily doubtful, 'she also said she's like Marmite – you either love her or you hate her.'

'Why?'

'Because the routines are so prescriptive. Some people get offended by the strictness, as though it undermines their own judgement.'

'It's a book! Surely if people don't want help or don't like what they read, they can just stop reading it?'

'You'd think so.'

'So you'd rather be told what to do?'

'Definitely. If the alternative is to trust to some untested, maternal instinct, yes!'

'So, just to clarify – because you've never been a mother before, you'd rather someone told you what to do?'

'Yes.'

'You've never been a wife before, have you?'

'I think I can see where this is going...'

Monday, 6th November – 24 weeks, 3 days

Suddenly, Zoë's stomach has become public property. People we barely know – and a few we don't – imagine they're free to stroke it or pat it as though it's a sweet-looking dog they're passing in the street.

If it's the novelty of her physical growth that's drawing them, I suppose I should just be grateful they're not trying to cop a feel of her breasts as well. Although give it a few more months and, with regular feeding, I suppose they'll be more or less public property as well. They certainly won't be private.

Thursday, 9th November – 24 weeks, 6 days

Dad would have been 64 today. I can't help wondering what he'd think of me preparing to sit at home with a baby while my wife goes out to work. As a forester, his hands were hard, his days physical. He worked the same open, Argyllshire lands that his father had worked, and his father and his father before him, returning each day more often than not covered in sawdust and soil, his body exhausted. By contrast, I sit in a mid-terraced London suburb preparing to coo nursery rhymes and spoonfeed mush.

I may still have a chance to make more of myself: I've been offered a contract from that American publisher so now have a thriller to write, and Zoë's mum has generously offered to take the baby for one day a week. And with Zoë working the equivalent of a four-day week, there should still be time – assuming Spielberg ever manages to track down my number – for a bit of acting work as well.

So when someone asks me, 'What do you do for a living?' how will I reply? I could adopt the butchest stance possible and say that I'm a househusband, daring further inquiry. Or, worse, I could pluck out that defiant title of 'homemaker' and talk incessantly about nothing but my child.

But I'm hoping that, if all goes to plan, there'll be a third option, and I'll be able to gloat as I mention both my worlds: the workdays when I'm acting or writing and so contributing financially, and the rest of the week when I walk with my child through the park.

Tuesday, 14th November – 25 weeks, 4 days, just over 14 weeks to go

One of the women from up the street catches us going into the house and points an arthritic finger at Zoë. 'You should think yourself lucky,' she says. 'I used to be a slim little thing like you before I started having children; never got my shape back. You're going to be all right, though, I can tell. You haven't put on any weight at all.'

At least that's one thing that Zoë hasn't yet started to worry about. And it looks like that woman might be right: apart from her newly inflated breasts and a tautly stretched belly that regularly kicks and writhes, Zoë looks the same as ever. Which is reassuring, however base it makes me feel to admit it. If our marriage lasts 50 years – and here's hoping – I'd like to think that she was looking like the girl I fell in love with for a bit more than two of them.

Wednesday, 15th November – 25 weeks, 5 days

'Check this out,' says Zoë, digging around in her bag for a magazine. 'I found this article today, thought it was interesting.' We're stopped at lights en route to Ikea in search of a new sofa for our front room. I glance across. She's found her marked page and I can see the title: 'Boy or Girl?'

'A bit late, isn't it?'

'Yeah, but listen.'

As much as the streetlights and passing headlights allow, she begins to read. Within a few paragraphs, Zoë's message is clear: whatever happens, it'll be my fault.

If we have a riotous boy who turns our home into a chaotic whirlwind of noise and mess, it's my fault. If we have a delicate little daughter who manipulates the world around her with all the charm and cynicism of a politician, it'll be my fault. As the provider of the all-important, determining chromosome, be it X or Y, it seems that I am to be held forever accountable for the sex – and therefore the resulting characteristics – of our child.

'And this is the interesting bit,' she continues. 'Apparently, if you want to try and influence whether it's the male Y sperm or the female X sperm that wins the race, it's all about exploiting their differing characteristics.'

Zoë finishes the article as we arrive at Ikea and soon the unwitting aptness of the article becomes frighteningly clear as I

73

realize that the attributes exhibited by the male and female sperm when chasing an egg are near-identical to those shown by myself and Zoë when hunting for a comfortable sofa.

I like to know what we're after, go directly to it as quickly as possible, then leave at top speed before I succumb to a life-sapping despair. Zoë, meanwhile, likes to look around, to wield her tape measure and wander for hours as she talks through the options. Her stamina is Olympian.

To produce a girl, the article suggests, we should be sent off on our quest in full knowledge that not only is Ikea out of stock having just menstruated their last sofa, but that they aren't expecting another delivery for several days. Within minutes, I as the male sperm would be found collapsed and gasping for air somewhere between the cookware and textiles departments, overwhelmed by a sense of futility and without hope of ever reaching my goal. Zoë, on the other hand, would browse for hours, comparing different models of loo brush or obscure kitchen utensil, happily hovering until they restock. At which point, a pastel-coloured, thoroughly female sofa would be born.

If, however, the sofas are already in stock when Zoë and I are sent in together, I would be victorious. While Zoë's journey is slowed by the distraction of plastic flowers and wicker baskets, I would be responsible for the arrival of a black leather, thoroughly male Scandinavian. And only once he's home would it become clear he's got a screw loose.

As we wheel our enormous sofa-shaped bundle of plastic and cardboard to the checkout, I share with Zoë the beauty of my analogy.

'I suppose that's about right,' she allows. 'Sex straight after menstruation sends the faster male sperm on a fool's errand, while the female sperm will linger for longer and still be around when it matters.'

'Right.'

'But if you want a boy, there's another trick – and I don't just mean calling ahead to check there's a sofa in stock.'

'Well?'

'Male sperm prefer alkaline conditions, the sort typically found higher in the vagina and heightened when a woman has an orgasm.'

I think it through. 'So if the guy's well hung and a good lover, he'll have a boy.'

'Exactly,' Zoë grins. 'No pressure...'

Monday, 20th November – 26 weeks, 3 days, 13 and a half weeks to go

At the sight of my agent's number flashing on my mobile, my stomach coils in excitement, the hope rising before a glimpse of the life I could be living. Impatiently, I endure the small talk, waiting for the purpose of the call.

'Anyway,' she says, finally coming to the point. 'I heard back from *River City* this morning.'

'Yes?'

'I'm afraid they've decided to go for someone younger. They really enjoyed meeting you and said they'll definitely try to get you in again for something else, but you just weren't quite what they had in mind for this part.'

There's nothing to say. I can't add the line 'But they really liked me' to my CV for the benefit of future auditions. Nor can I guarantee – even if they do ever ask me to go back in – that I won't be inescapably buried by then beneath nappies and playdough.

Tuesday, 21st November – 26 weeks, 4 days

I'm working my way round Sainsbury's, marvelling at how much money we spend on nuts and chocolate in the name of peace on earth and goodwill to all men, when, in the midst of the fruit and veg, a piercing screech suggests I'm nearing a pram. But when I turn round I see only a mother and her no-more-than-five-year-old daughter. And it's the mother who screamed.

For the next few minutes I fight against a desire to intervene as the girl is wrenched from aisle to aisle, tugged along by a rope that's jerked to emphasize her mother's every second word. 'Shut UP! If YOU don't SHUT your MOUTH, girl, I'm gonna' SLAP you SO hard!'

As far as I can see, the girl's only crime is to be as sluggish as my shopping trolley. It's late evening, she's wet from the rain and grumbling in a subdued voice at being violently dragged faster than her little legs can manage.

'Right, that's IT!' shouts her mother. 'I'm leaving you here NOW. You're gonna be on your OWN. Goodbye!' she shrieks, disappearing behind a wall of discounted cheese. Cue frightened howls as the girl's relatively calm complaints double in decibel level, rising to such glass-cracking intensity that I throw an anxious glance towards the wine section.

I finally shake them off somewhere around the frozen foods, leaving the girl to be raised under a cloud of resentment, fully expecting her to pass on her experience of parenting to her own children in just a few years' time, deepening each generation's faults like Larkin's coastal shelf.

Wednesday, 22nd November – 26 weeks, 5 days

After yesterday's example of how *not* to do it, it's serendipitous that the products of another of Zoë's recent Amazonian spending sprees should drop onto our doormat today. Until our antenatal classes start, it seems we're to get the bulk of our expertise from books and magazines.

Succumbing to every conflicting recommendation, Zoë has already spent a fortune on books, and forages voraciously through the growing pile beside our bed. Having not yet felt sufficiently panicked to start reading, I've little idea what to expect when I pick one out of the pile of newcomers.

It's like my old biology textbook. In microscopic close-ups like those used to illustrate bedbugs, our child has developed from a minute pod smeared against a desolate, rock-strewn valley to something like a baby rat, and now looks spookily similar to those bog bodies found buried in peat banks. Weighing in at just under 2lbs, it's a wrinkly little thing that, any time now, will open its eyes and begin to blink.

But books and magazines – even with the benefit of a resident doctor – will only enlighten so far. When it comes to the continual testing reality of parenthood, I'm guessing that easy answers can't be cut from pages.

What I saw yesterday in the supermarket just instinctively seems wrong. And for that, I've my parents to thank. Because, aside from trial and error, I'm guessing that the greatest contributor to how we raise our child will be our own experiences as children: depending on how we've been raised ourselves, a certain action or approach might just feel right. Or wrong.

Recognition of that fact brings with it another terrifying realization: in raising our child, we'll be teaching them how to act with their own children as well. Directly or indirectly, we're to be at least partly responsible for the raising of at least two generations. They should mention that in family planning classes.

Thursday, 23rd November – 26 weeks, 6 days

Around 5.30 a.m. I'm woken by a kick in the back. I look round to complain to Zoë – a notorious night-time twitcher and flailer – only to find her dozing peacefully, her big belly turned towards me. As she sleeps on, oblivious, the bump and I chat briefly in Morse code through the thin layer of skin, and suddenly it's easier to understand that this is a separate entity about to burst upon us, not just a growing extension of Zoë.

Friday, 24th November – 27 weeks pregnant, 13 weeks to go

Although Zoë's frustratingly superstitious when it comes to arranging for life beyond the birth, I'm desperate enough for all the help we can get, and arrange a meeting with our financial advisor.

As a father of two, when Danny arrives he appears more sympathetic than excited. He tells us the good news: the government are going to reward our sex life with a cheque for £250, and another £250 if we can keep our kid alive to the age of seven. And, along with the daunting chat about redrafting wills, life insurance, mortgage cover, income protection, inheritance tax, Child Benefit and everything else, he comes bearing a gift – a cot, something his youngest has now outgrown.

Intending only to see how it looks in place before dismantling and storing it, instead I'm begged by Zoë to leave it standing in the corner of what will be the baby's room, and she giggles with excitement every time she walks past the door.

Saturday, 25th November – 27 weeks, 1 day

My mum sends down her baby book from the 1970s. From the number of clippings still tucked into the pages, it seems the written word was as important a part of a parent's education then as it is now. As I add it to the bookshelf wondering if I'll ever find the time to read it, I catch a glimpse of a phrase: 'Example is more forceful than precept.' Since one of Dad's favourite tongue-in-cheek quotes was 'Do as I say, not as I do', I'm guessing this is a book he never got round to reading either.

Sunday, 26th November – 27 weeks, 2 days

Zoë's really feeling the baby now – her belly is causing her some back pain and the pile of clothes discarded for being too tight grows daily. In all, she's holding up well, although she tells me she intends to complain from here on right up until the birth. She's also – and with good reason – intent on complaining about the building work. We now face our twentieth week of an eight-week project, yet still I spend the day papering and painting, sanding and varnishing, and picking up so much stray hair that Zoë's clearly skipped the paragraph about pregnant women shedding less. But by the end of the day, with our new sofa and a wedding present rug in place, the front room looks pretty cosy. Ready for little feet.

Wednesday, 29th November – 27 weeks, 5 days

Zoë's dad comes round with an article claiming that the cost of raising a child to the age of 21 is close to £200,000. Whether it's a warning or a request for a refund, he doesn't say, but it makes me grateful that our baby's arriving *after* Christmas, so we'll escape for a few more months the need to fork out for expensive toys that will only be eaten or forgotten by New Year.

I browse through one of Zoë's parenting magazines and, having braced myself for the worst, am actually pleasantly surprised at the average price of each accessory. Then I realize it's suggesting we get one item from each category. I begin considering the viability of hammering together a baby chair, playpen and car seat out of the debris left by the builders.

Month Eight

Sunday, 3rd December – 28 weeks, 2 days pregnant, just under 12 weeks to go

Zoë tells me I should now be able to hear our baby's heartbeat. I lean down in expectation of a tender moment, and get an immediate and almighty kick in the face. When my reproachful prod is answered only by a second flailing attempt to make contact (lacking the space for a good backswing, presumably), I'm caught between relief at such encouraging vigour, and a resolve to ground our child for three months the moment it shows its face.

Monday, 4th December – 28 weeks, 3 days

8 p.m. Our first NCT class. It's only a few streets away, but we're still late. We walk in apologetically, both of us fiddling with our hands: I'm peeling off dried paint and she's rubbing where her wedding ring should be. Amidst fears that she'll never be able to get it back on, she was finally forced to take it off this morning.

I've heard about these classes – Dan says he was made to lie on the floor and pretend to be a woman giving birth – so I'm sceptical before we even walk through the door. After all, I've always thought myself pretty expert at 'breathing'. And will the simple fact that we're all having children at the same time really be enough to draw us amicably together so often and for so long?

The suspicious silence is interrupted as we go round the room introducing ourselves with names and due dates and then, within minutes, the men are separated from the women and sent through into the next room to compile on a whiteboard a list of 'our greatest fears about pregnancy and birth'.

'Changing nappies', 'health concerns', 'financial implications', 'terrorism/state of the world', and, spelt out in capitals and underlined, '*LACK OF SLEEP*'. As an afterthought and to bulk it out, one person suggests we add 'the environment'.

I can't believe it. Have none of these people seen *Jack and Sarah*? A father-to-be played by Richard E. Grant falls down the stairs while rushing to get his labouring wife to the hospital. Losing consciousness, he wakes a little later to find that his wife has died in childbirth.

'There were complications,' the doctors tell him.

Can it really be that no one in our class has considered such a scenario? Complications swirl through life all the time – why should they choose to swerve clear of the six of us?

Regrouping, we're told that, since the fundamentals of feeding and nappy changing can be learnt, loss of sleep is the single biggest concern for first-time parents. I keep quiet, thinking that if no one else is worried about losing their wife or baby, it would hardly help to mention it now.

'Above all,' our teacher says, 'don't worry about these things. A lot of what you've got to do will very soon feel instinctive and, because it's done out of love, it all becomes so much easier to bear.' My worry is whether or not that instinctive love which should bear all things doesn't need a good eight hours itself.

By ten o'clock, Zoë and I are walking home through the dark.

'That made me really uncomfortable,' says Zoë.

I'm surprised. 'Why?'

'Because I wasn't sure if I should mention that I'm a GP or not.'

In two whole hours, we hadn't spoken about our professions at all, a change from the routine that I'd found liberating. And why should we? City banker or street sweeper, their babies all come out screaming and squishy.

'I didn't want to look a prat by answering all her questions,' says Zoë. 'But they're bound to find out that I'm a doctor at some point, so I don't want them to think I don't know the answers either. And if I tell them I'm a GP, they'll wonder why we're bothering with these classes.'

'So why *are* we bothering with these classes?'

'Because I want to be a normal mum, and get to know others who are going through it all at the same time. And there's more to having a baby than medical stuff – I want to be able to recognize when things go *right*.'

So it's simplistic to say that she's trapped between gratitude for the reassurance her profession can bring and envy of others' ignorance. Every problem so far has, of course, arisen because she doesn't know *more*.

As ever, it's fear of the unknown.

Friday, 8th December – 29 weeks pregnant, 11 weeks to go

John and Christine come round for tea with Archie, now one year old. As I raise him towards my head with the friendly intention of blowing a welcoming raspberry on his belly, the baby casually hooks one delicate finger into my right nostril and, giggling with glee, wrenches it round until my nose bleeds.

That glint in his eye I'd naively taken for a joyful greeting was obviously nothing more than a calculating assessment of how best to spray my blood over our new rug. With no option but an immediate withdrawal in the face of such an attack (cunningly camouflaged beneath a veneer of 'vivaciousness'), I quickly place him well out of range on the floor. Without so much as acknowledging my slowly draining life force, he turns with all the detachment of a psychopath to insist on total domination of his Lego box. Twenty minutes later he leaves, presumably to mark another notch on his cot post.

In the face of such unprovoked hostility (not to mention the frequent ass-kicking from my own child as I'm repeatedly woken by hefty blows to my backside from Zoë's belly), I decide to broach the emotive issue of discipline.

'Are we going to smack our kid if it's naughty?' I ask Zoë.

To my surprise, she isn't immediately horrified. 'Not sure,' she says. 'Isn't it illegal?'

'Not yet. But some people reckon it should be, that children should be given the same legal protection against physical force as adults. Apparently smacking your kid is against the European Convention on Human Rights.'

Zoë thinks. 'But you can't always reason with a child, can you?'

And that, I think, is the crux of the argument. Because my current view, reinforced by the hard but fair hand of my own dad, is that a smack – when employed conscientiously as a tool rather than an expression of anger – is the clearest means of communicating with a child for their ultimate benefit. It's the most basic, immediate and primal establisher of limitations. So to state that smacking can never be right is to claim that a child can be made to understand those same boundaries when communicated in another form, and to understand them as clearly and as immediately. In which case presumably those same children can also be made to understand when they overstep certain other boundaries, such as launching a pre-emptive nosebleed on their host before a room full of witnesses?

In which case, I shall instruct my lawyer to pursue the matter in the European courts, where I'll sue for considerable compensation for trauma and mental anguish. And the cost of a new rug.

Sunday, 10th December – 29 weeks, 2 days

More than ten whole weeks before we're scheduled to play host to round-the-clock screaming, our house is already home to a regular cacophony. There's the sighing through the night as Zoë wallows and rolls with all the agility of a square wheel. Then, when she can sleep, there's the dry-mouthed snoring, followed, when she wakes, with the thirsty slurping of water. There's the unfortunate downside to our conscientious increase in fruit and veg, and there are the regular chuckles erupting at all hours of the day as either the baby makes its presence felt with particular vigour, or Zoë's again amusing herself in the mirror, walking into her reflection and giggling when she sees that the bump has got there first.

Monday, 11th December – 29 weeks, 3 days

Rousing myself to the vertical, I stumble into the bathroom, brush my teeth and then, my thawing brain still on autopilot, climb straight back into bed. For a brief moment, as my body conspires to fool me into believing it's night time again, a wave of relief washes over the bone-deep, paint-flecked exhaustion I've been dragging round the house for weeks. I'm counting down the days until Christmas not with lumps of chocolate torn from an advent calendar but with buckets of paint.

Then, through blurred eyes, I see Zoë up and about, charging ahead with her day's preparations as though she's already been up for hours, as alert and efficient as ever and all the time carrying a tightly clad, vampiric bump. Shame throws me from the bed once more to pull on my brilliant white, quick-drying, easy-wipe t-shirt and trousers, and arm myself for battle.

Twelve hours of solid painting later, we're back for another NCT class and a game in which each couple takes it in turns to answer the teacher's questions with one of three options: 'Go Back To Sleep – Everything's Normal', 'Phone The Labour Ward For Advice', or 'Hurry To Hospital'.

'You're in your last few weeks,' says the teacher to one couple, 'and you can't feel your baby moving. What do you do?'

The woman's answer is immediate and confident. 'I reckon that's pretty normal,' she says. 'At that stage in the pregnancy, there can't be much room to move around. I'd go back to sleep.'

'No!' interrupts Zoë, unable to contain herself. 'If you feel less than ten movements in twelve hours, you've got to go for a CTG.'

The urgency of her voice makes everyone turn in surprise,

while the woman looks at Zoë with the same frozen smile of feigned admiration you'd offer the class swat.

Realizing the game's up, Zoë comes clean. 'I'm actually a GP,' she admits to the room with an embarrassed laugh. 'And we'd recommend that you definitely go for a check-up. It's probably nothing to worry about, but if you've not felt ten movements or more in twelve hours, you should see your doctor or midwife as soon as possible.'

From that point on I feel slightly sorry for the teacher, who sits patiently as Zoë threatens to steal the show, fielding questions from every corner. And it reminds me once more how proud I am of her and her ability to offer such practical help and reassurance, especially when compared to the impact I make on people's lives with my work – it's not often I get to offer such dramatic reassurance with a few pointers on voice projection or apostrophe usage.

Thursday 14th December 2006 – 29 weeks, 6 days

The coldest night of the year so far, due to drop to minus five degrees, and our new boiler has already broken down, leaving us without hot water or heating. After so many months of building work, it still feels like one of those camping trips with Dad: it's cold and basic, and you know that whatever you're looking for is around somewhere but you're not sure where, and all the time you're wondering if you'll step on something you shouldn't.

We can but hope that this ever-present blanket of dust will be that little bit thinner and there'll be fewer nails littering the floor by the time our baby puts in an appearance.

Friday, 15th December – 30 weeks pregnant, 10 weeks to go

When Zoë lies down, her nose blocks up. The result is a snore that sounds like the *Titanic* scraping across an iceberg, and regular sighs and grunts as she shuffles about trying to get comfortable.

And since I can feel our baby's kicks and squirms even though her belly is cushioned by an extra pillow, I can only imagine what it must be like for her.

Yet still she storms on with her days, barely pausing for breath between patients seeking miracle cures in time for Christmas, and the house, where a London-wide search for soft furnishings has now given way to a hunt for light fittings.

'Ninety-three per cent of first babies are born at full term or later,' she says. And though I'm reassured by such a high figure, she's brooding on the early 7%, and pushing me to finish the house while she orders up a cot mattress and baby carrier. So for every heartbeat housed by Zoë, I slide a brush over fresh plaster. For every hair now poking through the baby's scalp, I'm hammering a nail into floorboards. Unable to contribute directly to the development of our child, I can only turn my attention to the environment into which it will arrive.

By the time I travel into Soho for an early evening audition (a car advert), I'm so tired that the outside of my left eye has started twitching. When I step in front of the camera I could swear I see the cameraman winking in reply.

Yet instead of rushing home to bed, I drag myself across town to see friends, determined to do it while I can. Zoë declines to meet me, opting instead, I imagine, for a lazy night in on the sofa. So it's a surprise on my return to find the house truly 'pottered', with tabletops cleared, presents wrapped and cards written. Which leaves me wondering: will I even notice if she kicks into that high-efficiency, pre-labour nesting mode?

Tuesday, 19th December – 30 weeks, 4 days

Pulling on my clothes, I hear a shriek from the bathroom, followed by fluent curses.

'Look at this!' spits Zoë, storming into the room and marching over to her dressing table, one finger pointing towards her face.

'What? What's wrong?' Knowing it's pointless, I still pretend not to see the cold sore sprouting above her top lip that she's rapidly burying beneath an avalanche of cream.

'Perfect!' she hisses, full of venom. 'Just in time for Christmas.'

Taking my life into my own hands by making the point while I have the chance, I say, 'It's not surprising, you know. It wouldn't hurt you to slow down a bit; you've been running in all directions for weeks.' And she has, with her usual energetic sense of purpose that overlooks the constant draw on her batteries from within.

'That's not exactly a sympathetic response,' she says.

'Well, at least you got to it early,' I try again, pointing at her face. 'That'll help.'

She brushes off this attempt at reassurance with all the vigour of her annoyance.

As our paths cross a few minutes later in the bathroom, she grumbles about the likely response of friends and family. 'Mum'll say I've been overdoing things.'

'Well, she wouldn't be entirely wrong,' I say, a thought that's met with a barely sustained silence.

'What really worries me,' she admits in the kitchen as she makes a sandwich for her lunch, 'is that it means I might not be caring for the baby as I should.'

Sitting at the table as I try to crawl into my first coffee of the day, I think again of all the running around as we hurry to finish the house by Christmas, not to mention the usual obligatory festive evenings out. We're both feeling drained, and yet the one word I've always been forbidden from saying to her is 'relax'. It's a tried and tested and by far the most effective means of winding her up.

My response takes a compromising middle course, somewhere between the immediate and unconditional support I should muster, and out-and-out smugness.

'There's not a lot I can say,' I tell her, 'without getting close to saying "I told you so".' Which is, of course, no better than just saying 'I told you so'.

She turns and freezes, staring down at me. 'That's not very

reassuring,' she says, and I can see it in her eyes: she's spotted a chance to transfer her infuriation onto something that will feed her frustration by answering back.

'At least you got to it early,' I try once more. 'It's only noticeable now because you've put cream on it.'

'Huh!' She snorts with derision, fuelled by her irritation and refusing to be consoled. 'The studies show that creams only reduce duration by half a day. It'll get worse before it gets better.' Then, exaggerating the offer of a cheek to be kissed rather than an infectious lip, she gathers her bags and walks out the door.

The house settles back into silence as I wearily contemplate the day's painting that lies ahead. And then suddenly the family of phones around the building leaps noisily to life. It's Zoë, wailing at the realization that she's left her lunch behind.

And a very tasty lunch it is.

Thursday 21st December – 30 weeks, 6 days

With the tactical application of make-up and the benefit of these darker days, no one at the antenatal class seems to notice Zoë's cold sore. The men are told to stand back against the wall with knees bent at right angles, and to hold that position for three minutes while the women watch us in relative silence.

Unable to guess the point of the exercise and stiff from another day's frantic painting, I'm struggling, but naturally try to make out I'm not.

Then, with only a few minutes to recover, we're asked to do it again. This time, interspersed with a few gentle words of encouragement, the teacher lets the chat run free and soon one of the women mentions the words 'Gina' and 'Ford', a combination that triggers the usual mix of admiration and vitriol.

'You know she hasn't got any kids of her own?'

'The timetables make it look easy. It's like join-the-dots parenting...'

'What if your baby's screaming for something to eat? Are you just meant to ignore your own child?'

'I'll try anything if it gets them sleeping through the night...'

'Are you just meant to leave your own kid to cry?'

'I'm just going to use the bits that work...'

'But how do you know which bits are important without doing the whole routine?'

'You know what I think? I think it's just so parents can feel like they're in control, so they can dictate how the day goes instead of the baby...'

'What's wrong with that? If you're not happy, your baby's not going to be happy...'

Within what seems like less than a minute, the teacher interrupts. 'That's three minutes!' she says, looking round at the men. 'Easy, wasn't it?'

Point well made, I think.

It's gone ten o'clock as we walk home. 'I'm absolutely knackered,' sighs Zoë. 'Maybe it's time to start taking things easier.'

Still scratching the dried paint off my hands, I agree – as softly as possible. So used to propelling herself through her days with awesome drive, it's surely only a matter of time before she'll be forced to allow for a slippage of standards. And maybe then I'll be able to leave the occasional dirty bowl in the kitchen sink.

Friday, 22nd December – 31 weeks pregnant, 9 weeks to go

Dustsheets are tucked away and paintbrushes banished to the back of the shed only minutes before my mum and granny arrive off the train, and their reaction on seeing first Zoë's bump and then the changes to the house are priceless and suitably profuse, even in comparison to Zoë's family's typical exuberance.

The garden still looks like a 1914 festive football pitch but at last, give or take a dab here and a touch there, we have a house to be proud of. I just hope, in rushing to finish it completely, we're not exhausted before the baby even arrives.

Sunday, 24th December – 31 weeks, 2 days

This is my first Christmas in a city, ever. And so, understandably, it feels nothing like Christmas. So many of those actions that the years have cemented as indispensable to the festive ritual, from the cutting of a tree to the nursing of an overfilled belly before a log fire, have no place here in London.

And the remaining customs only highlight the change, in our surroundings as well as in us. Already we're feeling the slide towards a more adult role, where – as first-time hosts – giving takes over from receiving.

Instead of being able to assume it'll all be done for us, we make beds, steer overladen trolleys round the supermarket, fight for freezer space, stuff stockings and tuck them out of sight. Instead of lounging in front of the fire, we check our guests are warm enough. Rather than over-indulge in the spirits of Christmas past, we seek out and fill dry glasses. No arriving at the table with nothing but faithful anticipation and an empty stomach, only the serving up of what we know to expect because Zoë's been preparing it for days.

Seeing it all from this perspective, it makes me question why our parents put themselves through it, not only indulging us so generously but making it all seem so effortless. What was in it for them? Even the can of Strongbow, left out after Dad thoughtfully suggested that Santa might like something a little stronger than a glass of milk, was offered up from his own supply.

But the answer lies in Zoë's bump; it makes us imagine Christmas through the younger eyes of another, someone for whom the lights will just twinkle never mind the electricity bill, for whom Santa will be a jolly, rosy-cheeked giver of gifts rather than a tiresome trawl around the shops, for whom it will only be natural to be surrounded by family regardless of the miles between them, and for whom the cold and dark outside will create an exciting world full of possibility. In a world that has dissected all the colours of the rainbow, there remains one night at least where magic – for some – is still considered possible.

And so no doubt, bolstered by nostalgia for our own childhood Christmases, we'll continue the indulgence year on year, again and again. The real test will come when one day, perhaps, we'll visit our child's home to eat their turkey and drink their wine. If they've reason to be as grateful to us as we now are to our parents, we'll have done something right, and all the effort and organizing – as much a part of the Christmas tradition as Santa himself – will have proved itself worthwhile.

Monday, 25th December – 31 weeks, 3 days – Christmas Day

One hour before eleven guests are due to arrive for lunch, three generations of Zoë's family are fussing in the kitchen over a roast turkey when the lights fuse.

'It says here,' points out Rob from behind yesterday's paper, 'that stress during pregnancy doubles a child's chances of a lower than average IQ while increasing their own tendency towards stress, hyperactivity, disobedience and emotional problems.'

'Very helpful, thanks Rob,' I say, heading off to the fuse box.

'Well at least you can now blame it on the electrician.'

Thursday, 28th December – 31 weeks, 6 days

It seems as though half the country has had the same idea as us, to swoop on the Christmas sales in the hope of getting a good deal on a pram. The baby seems as reluctant to be there as its father, and kicks and squirms as we fight our way from shop to shop around Oxford Circus. Finally, after what seems like hours of debate, we agree on a sale-price Mamas and Papas Pliko Pramette, and approach the shop assistant, wallet in hand.

'You're in luck!' says the shop assistant. 'That's the last one.'

'Oh, quick!' says Zoë. 'Can you go and get it before anyone else takes it?'

Soon the boxed pushchair and a bagful of accessories are beside us, and the assistant is back at the till.

'Oh,' she says, staring at the screen. 'I'm afraid we don't have any more car seats for that model.'

'What about that one?' Zoë points to a demonstration seat on the shop wall identical to the one we're after.

'That's actually a different shade of grey. It would work fine, but it's meant for a different line.'

Zoë shakes her head angrily. 'That's no good. The whole point is that it's a set.'

I struggle to contain my impatience. She must be at least as exhausted as I am, yet after hours of shopping Zoë would have us return home empty handed – and I can't even tell the difference between the colours.

'I'll tell you what,' says the assistant. 'Seeing as it's the last pram in stock, I can probably give you some money off if you'll take that car seat with it.'

Very reluctantly, Zoë agrees. Minutes later, laden with boxed-up pram, car seat and accessory bag, we're heading for the door.

'We've just saved £75 – on a half-price pram!' I say, delighted. 'I can't believe you were planning to leave with nothing!'

'*I've* just saved £75. I don't give a shit what colour it is. I just wanted to see if we could get a discount.'

For many women, 'pregnancy brain' causes forgetfulness. In Zoë, it seems to exhibit itself as rare streaks of practicality and devious cunning. I like it.

Friday, 29th December – 32 weeks pregnant, 8 weeks to go

Zoë returns from her routine GP check-up with tears streaming down her face.

'I've got gestational diabetes!' she cries. 'A routine urine test showed high sugar levels, so I went to my own surgery to do a more accurate blood sugar test. A normal reading is somewhere between 5 and 7.8; mine was 15.' The result, she says, sobbing, is irrefutably diagnostic.

I grab our hefty pregnancy guide and look it up, my confusion immediately picking out the most dramatic phrases. 'An inability to process glucose leading to higher blood sugar levels ... a larger baby with a higher risk of jaundice, obesity and diabetes ... can require a caesarean to avoid nerve damage, bone fractures or even brain damage ... serious consequences ... higher risk of future strokes, heart disease and diabetes for the mother.'

I look at the risk factors – a family history, high body mass index, poor diet, lack of exercise – and I shake my head; Zoë has not a single one of them. I look at the symptoms – tiredness, thirst, increased urination, irritability – and I close the book. Who would settle on a diagnosis based on that? Then I look at my wife, curled on the sofa in tears and cradling her belly, and I wonder how I can reassure her on a subject about which I know nothing. It's like warming up for an argument with Newton about gravity. In an orchard.

'OK,' I say, 'even if we assume that you *do* have diabetes, we can live with that, can't we?'

'It's not just that,' she answers. 'I'm 32 weeks now. In some hospitals, they routinely test for this at 26 weeks. I *know* that; I should have tested myself. So for six weeks I've been unnecessarily exposing our baby to high levels of sugar. God, think of all the chocolate and sugary stuff I scoffed over Christmas!'

'But you have been eating more healthily. We both have.'

'But I've still eaten a lot of stuff I shouldn't. If I've harmed the baby...' she weeps, as laden with guilt as with shock. 'I don't understand it,' she says, at last. 'It's the last thing I'd expect.'

From what I've learnt in my crash course on gestational diabetes, it's the last thing I'd expect as well. Fortunately Zoë has brought home the blood sugar monitor along with the necessary needles to prick the finger and summon up the blood, so we begin to test her again.

The first result, while she's still wiping away the tears, reads 5.5. Within five minutes, that has dropped to 5.3. After an hour her fingers are full of holes and the reading has levelled at 4.7.

As the night progresses, tearful misery slowly becomes doubt and confusion, and she at last falls asleep with the monitor on the bedside table.

Month Nine

Saturday, 30th December – 32 weeks, 1 day

By dawn, Zoë's cautiously optimistic. As soon as she can, she takes herself off for a more conclusive hospital blood test. It's afternoon before we get the results. Gestational diabetes: negative. As we lie on the bed in an exhausted fog of relief and confusion, we piece together what must have happened. About half an hour before her GP check-up, Zoë remembers, she scoffed the last of the Christmas mince pies, giving her a temporarily high urine sugar level.

When she then rushed to her own practice intending to take charge of her own diagnosis by pricking her finger for a 'reassuring' blood test, the machine either registered some sugar still on her finger or still in the machine from the last person tested. The aberrant reading only seemed to confirm the previous, very generalized urine test that, had she gone later in the afternoon, would have shown nothing out of the ordinary.

Were Zoë anything other than a doctor, she'd have done as her GP suggested: waited for the hospital blood test and been reassured, without a single finger being pricked. But because she has the means available to investigate further, she did – making matters worse when she got a second misleading result. Her guilt at not putting her clinical knowledge to use earlier allowed her too easily to shake off the reassurance that would have given a patient relief. Which is why I've been catching her since, secretly pricking her finger with painful regularity.

I never appreciated how much Zoë prides herself on a healthy pregnancy, nor recognized the pressure she puts on herself. Nor have I given the relative ease of it to date the appreciation it deserves; I somehow simply expected it to run as smoothly as everything else Zoë does.

But when you can't tell if reports of a medical problem come from a doctor or patient, you're left stranded in confusion, for how do you gauge its seriousness? At what point does a professional response become an individual's dramatic reaction? I've a feeling our child may be asking that question in a few years' time, when one casual cough could lead to Zoë chasing them round the house with a sample bottle. But who's to say if she really will be taking the piss?

Monday, 1st January – 32 weeks, 3 days – New Year's Day

A cottage by the coast, full of new parents and babies, the same place we were staying when our baby was conceived. A good location and a good time, then, to look forward into the year in which we're to become parents.

From the top of the year I can peer out and see the view is bright. There remain inescapable patches of cloud, brief moments of grief for a lost father and lost home that distort the landscape beneath their shadows and require a conscious act of will to overlook. And, as in any view, some areas are still out of sight, unknown hillsides yet to reveal if they're steep or gently sloping. But, above all, I know that Zoë stands alongside me sharing the same view, and for that I appreciate how lucky I am. For one who, at heart, often feels as bewildered as my early teenage self, I can only be grateful that I've found a woman willing to take my hand as we go.

Monday, 8th January – 33 weeks, 3 days pregnant, 6 and a half weeks to go

The final scan. Our baby's now chubby face looms out of the darkness, eyes rolling in sockets as though already exasperated by all the attention.

'The placenta's shifted well away from the cervix,' says the sonographer, 'so she should be fine.'

She? The fear of having such a blatant revelation confirmed one way or the other holds my tongue until we're leaving the ward.

'Did you hear that?' I ask Zoë. 'She said "she"!'

'I know, but let's not draw any conclusions. She knew we didn't want to know. I still think we need to be prepared for either,' she says, prompting another 20-minute argument over our shortlist of names.

Our visit coincides with an official tour of the maternity ward, so we join a small crowd of anxious couples blocking the corridors. Apart from lots more waiting for lifts and one messy bath that's out of order (no one dares ask what might be blocking the plughole), we're pleasantly surprised by the cleanliness and relative normality of the delivery rooms. For a process that's often overly medicalized, the sight of a comfortable room not cluttered with equipment is reassuring, and altogether helpful in eliminating from our fears one more unknown.

I drive home self-consciously. It feels like there are three of us in the car, and it's long been the case that even the smallest cry from Zoë over a stubbed toe or itchy back results in me running up to ask, 'Are you all right? Did you fall over? Did you bump the bump?' With each day, we grow more and more aware of what dangers Zoë's belly may be subject to as, inevitably, it arrives first into every situation.

Friday, 12th January – 34 weeks pregnant, 6 weeks to go

'What about James?'

Zoë shrugs noncommittally.

'Jonathan?'

Another shrug.

We're standing in the supermarket queue. And like any

supermarket queue I've ever joined, there's a woman up ahead who's now decided she'd rather have the 'low fat' version instead, so half a dozen frustrated shoppers wait while she ambles back to the dairy aisle.

She's gone so long that, by the time she gets back, Zoë and I have actually tentatively agreed on a boy's name. It's one we both like and, suitably, is also a family name: Jack. Feeling very pleased with ourselves, we turn to girls' names.

'Amelia?'

'No,' says Zoë. 'It would get shortened to Millie and that's too similar to Katie's daughter.'

'Isabella?'

'That would be Bella, and my aunt had a cat called Bella.' We shuffle forward a few feet. 'How about Emily?'

'I like it, but isn't there an actress called Emily Watson?'

'Lara?'

'My uncle had a dog called Lara. What about Sophia?'

'Too grand.'

The elderly couple in front have at last made it level with the checkout and begin to empty their trolley for scanning.

'Claudia?' I try.

'Too German.'

'Catherine?'

'Too normal.'

I turn to the magazine racks alongside for inspiration. 'Gwyneth? Jennifer? Angelina?'

'No...'

'What about one of those Gaelic names that are spelt so differently from their pronunciation? It's like getting two names for the price of one – like Ailidh, Siobhan or Niamhe?'

'No.'

'Something Shakespearean, then? Juliet? Olivia? Viola?'

Zoë wrinkles her nose. 'No.'

'Biblical: Judith? Mary? Rebecca?'

'I don't think so.'

'Something artistic?' I suggest, wracking my brain to remember my art history A level: 'Venus? Ariadne? Mona? Lisa?' I'm getting desperate, and in my frustration begin listing every girl's name I can think of. 'Justine? Natasha? Antonia? Jane?'

'No … no … no.'

'Melanie? Eliza? Yoko? Polly? Wendy? Matilda? Anna?'

'Wait a minute! What was that last one?'

'Anna?'

'No, before that.'

'Wendy? Matilda?'

'Before that.'

'Polly?'

'Polly … Polly.' It's like she's tasting the word. 'Polly Watson. Yes. Polly Watson! I like that.'

At her words, the elderly couple in front turn to face us with beaming smiles. 'Polly's a lovely name,' says the woman, clapping her hands as though to congratulate us on the choice. Beside her, her husband nods in enthusiastic agreement.

Five minutes later, we walk back to the car, laden with baked beans, frozen chips, toilet roll, and – one way or the other – a name for our baby.

Saturday, 13th January – 34 weeks, 1 day

Exploiting the post-New Year lull, we've grabbed a bargain couple of nights at a hotel in the Cotswolds for a last break before two becomes three. The idea is to eat well, wander the grounds if the weather allows, and generally wallow in bed. Little do we know – until the concierge informs us – that the marketing people have already slapped an expensive title on our weekend away: it seems that Zoë and I are on 'babymoon'.

Lounging over an immense plate of fried breakfast, we decide to draw up a birth plan. After three cups of coffee and as many sausages, we've got what actually amounts to little more than a few sentences: Zoë wants a 'natural' birth, with as little intervention as possible. Because of the risks involved – and the seriousness of any situation that might lead us there – she's desperate to avoid an unplanned caesarean and, for pain relief, she wants to avoid taking anything. Although if it gets too much, she will opt for an epidural – nothing half-hearted like pethidine, which can then affect the baby. And, of course, the bottom line is that she'll do whatever we're told is best for our child.

But wouldn't anyone? I can't help wondering whether all the choices, from differing painkillers to differing birthing positions, offer only an illusion of control. Yet I'm jealous even for that. It's seems my options revolve only around which end of Zoë I want to share the experience with: the tears and exhaustion, or the blood and the shit.

Having their breakfast at the table alongside are a father and son, the latter no more than about ten years old. Together, they're setting the world to rights, and for the first time I consider the appealing prospect of being a friend to our child as well as a father.

Wednesday 17th January – 34 weeks, 5 days

Zoë's worried about breastfeeding. Will she have enough milk? Will she be able to do it at all? And if not, will that irreparably damage her bond with her baby?

With no experience beyond my own distant past, I simply assumed that it was something all mothers do, albeit for varying lengths of time. So while Zoë worries about the whole issue, I'm more concerned about Zoë herself. In my flitting perusal of the literature piled up by the bedside, it's clear that the best way to maximize a mother's milk supply is a state of total relaxation – the more a mother stresses about her breastfeeding, the worse it's likely to get. Only when she's comfortable, calm and collected will the 'let down reflex' really kick in, causing the tiny muscles around the nipple to contract and eject the breastmilk.

The problem with this, I realize, is not just that Zoë has an appetite for anxiety rivalled only by her mother, but there's nothing guaranteed to get her back up more than telling her to 'relax' – a word I long ago learnt to treat with all the caution of an angry wasp.

So, in the hope of avoiding a vicious cycle of tension and drought and to allow me to offer a few credible suggestions should I ever have to tell her what she's doing wrong, I accompany her down the A3 to sit in the front room of a Raynes Park semi. There, as the only male in a room full of heavily pregnant women, I share in the dark secrets of breastfeeding.

The teacher is authoritative, confident and comprehensive. Although I make sure to say the word 'breast' twice within the first five minutes just to show I'm not daunted, two hours later I'm slipping into a state of shock. Rather than revelling in an array of photos that would do a teenage porn stash proud, I'm gaining a whole new appreciation of aversion therapy.

After telling us all there is to know about pumps, leaks and the colour and consistency of human milk, the teacher finally stops to take questions from the floor.

'What happens,' asks one worried mother-to-be, 'if I can't produce any milk?'

'Oh, you will,' replies the teacher with encouraging verve. 'The shape or size is irrelevant,' she declaims. 'A breast is a breast and where there's a nipple, there's a way. I've never met one yet that hasn't given up the goods.'

Perhaps goaded on by her own rhetoric, she turns to me with a pump in her hand and a glint in her eye. 'I could milk you, if you want,' she says.

A small part of me is curious. And it does seem only a kindness to grant my nipples a greater sense of purpose in life. But given the size of the bottle onto which her pump is attached, I think it wiser to politely decline and instead edge towards the door.

'Feeling better about it all now?' I ask Zoë as we head home.

'A bit. But I'm still not convinced that just because I've got breasts, it'll all work out fine. After all, I've got two eyes, but I still have to wear glasses. If it was all so simple, I wouldn't see so many mothers at work who've found it so hard.'

Thursday, 18th January – 34 weeks, 6 days

The realization that this evening is our final NCT class spurs on last preparations. Leaving Zoë to pack her hospital bag before heading off to work, I 'temporarily' fit the car seat to check it'll be OK and then, after wrestling with seatbelts and clasps for half an hour, decide it will remain fitted.

Zoë, who can now barely get out of bed without help, let alone dodge city-centre tourists and shoppers, uses her lunch break to trawl Mothercare and John Lewis, debating the difference between babygrows, sleepsuits and jumpsuits. She finally opts to phone a friend before declaring she's returning to the surgery to draw up a list for her hospital bag.

I drive to Kingston to buy more baby bits and am peeved to notice that, when a mother's angry shriek of 'Jack!' echoes around the store, four different kids come running. Leaving with a changing table, I then swear liberally when I try to put it in the back of the car and find a baby seat in the way. On the road back, I find myself crawling along behind a hearse. In the back is a tiny coffin. As the traffic in my wing mirror grows impatient, I pull out just far enough to block them from overtaking.

Zoë gets home and, instead of packing her hospital bag, puts the baby clothes and sheets in a wash, then directs me in the hanging of pictures in the nursery. We compile a list of DIY jobs that will never be finished in time, discuss who we should list in our new wills to be our baby's legal guardians in the event of our deaths, and argue some more about boys' names.

We arrive at the final NCT class to find that two of the six women have already given birth. The news brings home to us what we'll soon be bringing home with us, especially when we all go our separate ways at the end, each with a horrible sense of: 'Is that it? Does this mean we should feel ready?'

Finally, in an awesome display of denial given the size of her bump, Zoë admits she hasn't yet packed her hospital bag.

Thursday, 25th January – 35 weeks, 6 days pregnant, just over 4 weeks to go

As one who views our current drastic refurbishment of the planet with real trepidation, I'm delighted to get a commission to write an article comparing disposable nappies to washables, and to be paid for doing research I'd have willingly done anyway. I put my fiction book aside and spend the morning emailing my questions to everyone involved, from the small, independent reusable nappy makers to the PR managers for the multinational disposable brands.

It's mid-afternoon before I manage to get hold of the man at the Environment Agency who chaired their study into the environmental impact of both washables and disposables, finally concluding – to much controversy – that 'there was little or no difference between the different types': disposables impact in manufacture, transport and disposal, while washables impact mainly in the course of their use, through the energy required to wash them.

'Admittedly, though,' confesses the chairman, 'the data we used was historical before the report was even published. The only figures we could get for the energy consumption of washing machines were from almost ten years ago, and in the two and a half years it took us to compile the study, there were huge advances in washables.'

Yet although this study's own chairman admits that the conclusion is founded on outdated information, it has still been published, misinforming the debate and allowing a wave of resentment to break on proponents of washable nappies.

But even were the study accurate, to infer that it justifies the use of disposables is to overlook the fact that, whatever the environmental impact, we still have to find space in the UK for the 7.5 million disposable nappies thrown out every day. If our baby's bowels are up to the national average, he or she will get through an estimated 5,400 nappies, some of which will be incinerated while most will be preserved for ever in a hole in the ground.

It's actually possible, I discover, to buy biodegradable nappies (and a large amount of a disposable nappy is biodegradable). The problem, though, is that unless you're going to pile them up at the bottom of your garden and lovingly turn and air, water and care for your nappy compost, your only option is to send them to landfill. And to biodegrade effectively, organic matter needs ventilation of the sort just not found in landfills beneath thousands of tonnes of household waste. In fact, the anaerobic environment of a landfill merely mummifies, to little benefit beyond the archaeological. Most importantly, EU directives demand that we *reduce* the biodegradable element of our landfill waste, because it's through biodegrading that we add to methane emissions and thus the greenhouse gases in the atmosphere.

Unhappy with the tone of my questions and the suggestion of an article questioning their environmental credentials, a representative of one of the disposable nappy companies contacts my editor. Mindful of their contribution to her advertising budget, the editor then instructs me to play down the environmental aspects, and to emphasize instead that 'it's a matter of individual choice and lifestyle'.

Having spoken to both sides of the debate, it seems bizarre how inflammatory it can be, especially since, on average, disposable nappies account for only 2–3% of household waste. Yet as an argument, it seems indicative of why the world remains as it is. Aided by the moral cowardice that makes us reluctant to question the individual consumer's right to choice, it's too easy for those whose interests it serves to obfuscate the facts. And so we continue as before, blissfully ignorant or, worse, consciously uncaring of the repercussions of our actions.

I end the day convinced, zealously spouting facts and figures across the dinner table in self-righteous indignation, determined that our baby will wear washable nappies.

Month Ten

Tuesday, 23rd January – 36 weeks, 3 days

'Zoë, why are we having a baby?'

She turns from the curry simmering on the stove and looks at me like *I'm* the baby. 'Well, Andrew, do you remember about nine months ago when we had that very special cuddle?'

'Yeah, I get the mechanics of it, thanks. I got that around five years old when Dad first tried to introduce me to the subject and I had to crawl under the coffee table to hide my hysterics. What I mean is why exactly do we *want* children? What made us want to create another human being?'

'Isn't that question a bit academic now?'

'Maybe. But it's still relevant. It says here in the paper that, nine months ago, you and I were acting under a papal blessing. Apparently the Pope thinks that anyone who declines to have children is selfish.'

'But he's meant to be celibate!'

'Yes, but he'd claim we're all his children. Even you Jews – you just don't know it yet.'

She smiles. 'So why does he think it's selfish not to have kids?'

'He's saying that by not having children, you deny them the opportunity to live, because you want it all for yourself.'

'Hmmm.' She looks out a couple of trays, and some cutlery. 'Do you agree with that?'

'I guess it depends on your view of the world. You could just as easily argue that you're being selfless *not* having kids, by saving them from any pain. Besides, if they've never been conceived, then they're not going to know either way. I don't think there's anything selfish about deciding not to have kids.'

'Why not?'

'Is it selfish to want a peaceful, tidy home without brightly

106

coloured lumps of landfill fodder littering the floor? To want the freedom to travel and live spontaneously without the responsibility and the worry and the sacrifice? And it's not selfish to feel threatened by a changing body, or the loss of time and privacy. If you're happy without kids, who does it harm to maintain the status quo?'

'Because if everyone chose not to have kids, the human race would die off.'

'Have you stood in a supermarket queue recently? There's no shortage of people out there. And wouldn't it be more selfless to try to get this little planet in order before we invite more people on board?'

'OK,' says Zoë, though I can see her patience wearing thin. 'Maybe you can't rationalize it. Maybe we're all tricked by our genes into breeding against all common sense.'

'That's possible, I guess. The urge to procreate has nothing to do with practical debate – that's why the withdrawal method is so impractical: when you're building up steam, clear-minded thought just doesn't get a look-in. But surely, thanks to the intellect and other more reliable forms of contraception that don't require deliberate thought when no thought is possible, we should be capable of defying the dictates of our genes? And who's to say that wouldn't be for the best? For all we know, the happiest of hominids managed just that, actively choosing to pass into extinction with big smiles on their faces.'

'People say that having kids gives their life meaning or fulfilment.'

'Maybe, but parents don't have a monopoly on either, just as the child-free aren't the only ones to feel discontentment.'

'Andrew, you do *want* a baby, don't you?'

'Definitely,' I say, with absolute confidence. 'I can't wait. I don't think I've ever anticipated anything quite so much.'

'All right,' she says, obviously intending to bring the discussion to a close as she dishes up our dinner. '*Why* do you want a baby?'

I can only shrug. 'I don't know. I suppose it's for all the vague reasons you'd expect: to cement our relationship, to express it through the creation of another whose life we can share. Because I want to play cricket with my son the way Dad did with me, or dance with my daughter at her eighteenth birthday party.'

'So what's wrong with that?'

'Nothing. But all those reasons are about me. They're all selfish!'

'Fine,' says Zoë, heading for the sofa with a trayful of curry. 'So succumb to your selfishness! Surrender to the irrationality! But just do it quietly so I can watch *EastEnders*.'

Thursday 1st February – 36 weeks, 6 days

The baby's head has engaged. The idea that some people at this stage have two or three or even seven kids in there is mind-boggling.

Zoë seems pleased. 'Don't you resent it,' she asks smugly, 'knowing that you'll never be pregnant?'

I think of the symptoms of her pregnancy: the headaches, the bloating, the trips to the loo at all hours, the nausea and the tiredness, let alone the fact that *that* has to come out of *there*, and I wonder why anyone would ask such a question. I've never believed the claim that a bed you've made yourself is more comfortable; nor do I believe that I'll have less of a bond with our baby just because my body won't have split with pain at its arrival. Whatever the problems of being a mere bystander, there are definite advantages as well.

Like all the amusement that comes from trying to induce the birth. Dan tells me he finished his NCT course having written down only one thing, 'Nipple-tweaking, curry and sex', all of which can apparently be used when approaching a baby's due date to hurry it along.

'It's true,' confirms Zoë. 'Curry and semen contain ingredients that can help stimulate labour. But nipple-tweaking works best if you only go for a single nipple; then the body reacts as it would to breastfeeding and the uterus starts to contract. If you tweak both nipples, you can overwhelm the baby in a flood of hormones.'

So when dinner is suggested with the remaining survivors of the NCT class, we all agree on a curry house at the bottom of the street. Looking at the four bulging women around me as they pass heartburn tablets round the table like after-dinner mints, I wonder if any ambulance would be big enough to cope.

Friday, 2nd February – 37 weeks pregnant, 3 weeks to go

Zoë's ready to burst. Having been forced to sleep all night on her back, letting rip snores of such ferocity that I've barely dozed, she then wakes up with another cold sore on her top lip. When she sticks out her lower lip in her typical pout of complaint, the swelling on top makes her look like a botox victim.

'If this is still infectious when the baby's born,' she says, 'there's a risk of encephalitis. I won't even be able to kiss my own baby. I couldn't bear that.' The box of raspberry leaf tea is banished to the back of the cupboard and she pats her belly. 'Hang in there! At least ten more days, OK?'

Mum calls. Finally, almost three years after Dad's death, she's found a new house. It's great news, although the only date she can move is the exact day our baby's due. So not only is Rob planning to be on holiday at that time, but Mum will be tied up with moving house. Zoë's family and friends will be all over our baby before one of mine has even had the chance to say 'hello'.

Tuesday, 6th February – 37 weeks, 4 days

I dream that the builders have moved back into the loft, that they're attacking our house with their tools, sawing away until the roof's fallen in on me and I'm trapped beneath collapsed rafters and piles of bricks, pinned to the floor by their immense, breath-denying weight. And I wake to find Zoë strewn across me, the bed quivering with her snores.

The unanimous advice from our few friends with young babies is to sleep while we can, as though we can store it up and approach the birth in credit. But the truth is that it's just not that easy for either of us. Unable to sleep on her front and with a nose that blocks up the moment she's horizontal, Zoë hasn't slept properly in weeks. And since she's still at work, yawning her way through all-day surgeries, I find it hard to justify waking her when she does finally drop off, no matter how much it affects me.

But having been roused now by the equivalent of a WWF super-hold, I almost have to chew my arm off to escape to the bathroom. My temporary absence is obviously taken as a weakness; on my return, I find Zoë more on my side of the bed than hers, having invaded westwards with all the efficiency and speed of the Third Reich. I actually have to lift her leg and climb under it just to reclaim a thin sliver of mattress.

Realizing I'll never get to sleep like this, I roll out my arsenal of combative techniques. I try the wriggling arm scratch, the leaning cough and – if I've been left one to operate with – the pillow fluff, all of which are intended to cause 'accidental' noise sufficient to rouse her to shift into a non-snoring position.

But, perhaps testament to how much she needs her sleep, my petty retaliatory efforts are exhausted within half an hour, around the time that my willingness to allow her a good night's sleep fades.

'Zoë!'

'Hmm?'

'Can you move over?'

'Hmmm.'

'Can you move *over*?'

A grunt, then a sigh, then, 'Can you push me?'

Given that the nation's experts with a sophisticated get-up of harnesses and barges couldn't nudge a whale back into the deeper waters of the Thames some time back, it's no surprise when my shunts fail to shift her, particularly since the only real area to push against is her belly. Finally I surrender and head for the stairs to sleep in the loft. Behind me, Zoë's soft palate beats a steady drum roll of victory.

Wednesday, 7th February – 37 weeks, 5 days

Zoë arrives back from work with an apologetic face and a gift – a pack of earplugs. And since her waters could theoretically break at any moment, day or night, she's also decided that some sort of mattress protector would be a good idea. Living under the influence of a Scot, she's decided against paying £30 for a plastic undersheet, opting instead for a £2 dustsheet from Homebase.

A false economy, it soon becomes clear. I collapse into bed around ten o'clock and find myself sliding across and nearly knocking Zoë out the other side. With every move, the sheets crackle like breaking ice – even through my earplugs. Finally we settle on a compromise: a double layer of 'pregnancy mats' of the same sort that cover her car seat and anywhere else she might find herself sitting when the time comes. Unsure whether amniotic fluid will show up on a cream sofa, there's a third mat for *EastEnders* viewing.

This three-hour cycle of sleeping, feeding and changing we're told to expect when the baby's here terrifies me. It usually takes me at least half that time just to get to sleep. At last we get comfortable, and then the race begins – can I start snoozing before Zoë starts snoring? Thoughts that during the day tug me from one task to another are forced to skulk back into the dark corners of my mind as metal hatches slam down tight, enforcing total blackout. I will sleep to sidle closer. But then, far off down the A3, someone lightly kickstarts a motorbike. It gathers pace as it draws closer, finds a rhythm, then revs joyously as it turns into our street, batters down our door and pulls up beside the bed.

I do appreciate that any complaint from me is more than a little self-indulgent. Zoë, after all, is the one who needs her sleep. She's the one who's off to war – I'm barely a water-carrier. But is it wrong to admit that I'm quite looking forward to that first night after the birth, when she'll stay in hospital with the baby and I can come home to a great big empty and luxuriously peaceful bed?

Friday, 9th February – 38 weeks pregnant, 2 weeks to go

Zoë's folks come round for dinner to celebrate the end of her last day at work. I'm amazed she's lasted so long. Her dad kisses her hello and, with the best of intentions, says, 'Oh, you don't look big at all. Mum said you'd put on weight around the face but I don't think so.' Such was the crassness of the comment that her mum escaped all retribution.

They head home an hour later, leaving me to pick up the pieces by reiterating how great she looks, and how clever she is to have restricted her pregnancy to just her belly rather than allowing it to spread everywhere else as well.

It's not all lies. Her feet are swollen and her belly's like a torpedo, but tuck that out of sight beneath a jacket and you wouldn't know she was pregnant at all. At least I presume that's the excuse of all those guys on the tube who pointedly fail to offer her their seats.

Monday, 12th February – 38 weeks, 3 days – Zoë's maternity leave begins

I get up at the usual time leaving Zoë in bed, theoretically making the most of her free day. So she takes a bath. She irons some clothes that don't need ironing. And 15 minutes before her maternity leave even officially starts, she complains that she's bored.

Too big to do anything but wallow and too used to being active to sit around, she huffs and puffs her way through the day, willing something to happen.

'I want a show!' she cries, as though impatient for our baby to appear tap-dancing in a top hat.

I grow increasingly grateful for the loft, into which I barricade myself to work.

Tuesday, 13th February – 38 weeks, 4 days

An elderly neighbour catches us in the street to ask if Zoë can please give birth this week because she's off on Saturday for a month with her son. Then, in a misguided effort to reassure Zoë that she'll soon return to her normal weight, she tells us how easily she lost the extra pounds. 'After I had James,' she says, 'I walked out of hospital in my skinny jeans.'

'Yeah, more than a week after the birth,' replies Zoë, but only once we've parted and got back home. Her annoyance is cut short by a sudden attack of diarrhoea, as though her insides have decided to play their part in shifting the weight.

With her typical disdain for the closing of bathroom doors when it's just the two of us in the house, I can easily hear her groaning.

'I feel a bit fluey,' she says. 'Maybe I caught something from one of my last patients.'

I find a thermometer but her temperature is normal. Her belly has firmed up; the baby's squirming around more than ever, just beyond the skin, kicking at her bladder and keeping her within reach of the loo. And then the contractions begin.

Suddenly, reality dawns. On a bigger picture, I'm quite calm, but little things remind me that I could be more prepared: it's night time so I won't need money for a meter, but is the iPod charged so she can listen to music? Do we have all we'll need? What *do* we need? And why didn't I get more sleep last night?

It's already nine o'clock at night. Zoë goes for a bath, feeling uncomfortable and a little nauseous. Half an hour later we're lying on the bed timing the contractions. They're not painful, she says, but they're evident even to me with a hand on her belly. About five minutes apart, each wave seizes her stomach tighter than anything I've achieved in two years of gym visits.

She reads a book to distract herself, and I prepare to try to gather what sleep I can by her side, ready to head to the hospital as required.

I go to brush my teeth and find myself staring into the mirror. *Good,* I find myself thinking, surprising even myself with my vanity. *Not too many spots for the photos. But what can I do about my hair?* I nod approvingly at what seems a level of stubble befitting a father.

'I can see the attraction of a home birth now,' says Zoë around ten o'clock, as the contractions grow stronger. 'The last thing I feel like doing is going to hospital.'

By half past ten, the contractions are no more frequent but getting more painful, and the baby is squirming madly in between, rippling her stomach like a sheet in the wind.

For the next few hours we walk around the room, we lie on the bedroom floor in front of the fire, we hold each other like we're dancing as Zoë wiggles her hips from side to side, and we count off the contractions, pulsing every 4–6 minutes without effect. Around one in the morning, Zoë decides to try and get some sleep.

Wednesday, 14th February – 38 weeks, 5 days

I wake soon after six and find Zoë watching TV, her stomach still throbbing but far more gently than last night.

'What's going on?' I ask, but Zoë's got no more idea than me. We guess it's either a stomach bug that's brought on mild but ultimately ineffectual contractions, or early labour that's now died back.

'I've not had a show,' she says, 'just continual nausea.'

I try without success to get her to eat something. Finally, mid-afternoon, she falls asleep for a few hours. It's all such an anti-climax, yet I'm grateful for it, and hurry to complete a long list of chores while I can, in the shadow of a reprieve. All the mundane intricacies of life continue, while all we can do is wait...

We celebrate Valentine's Day with a takeaway pizza. I spill sauce on the white sofa cover, and Zoë manages only a few slices. Maybe we should have got another curry.

Thursday, 15th February – 38 weeks, 6 days

While Zoë goes to have her hair done ('Highly important,' says her mother. 'She's going to have so many visitors over the next few weeks'), I sit upstairs and try to maximize on a few hours of work. Instead, I find myself watching from the window as a skeletal crane effortlessly swings impossibly large loads of concrete back and forth above south-west London. Jumbo jets weighing over 400 tonnes are somehow circling the sky and a thick layer of dew has appeared out of nowhere on my neighbour's garden.

Everywhere I look, I see things that I'm not entirely sure I could explain. And as a very-soon-to-be infallible and omniscient father, I begin to realize that there are lots of things I need to learn about this world around me before our child is old enough to question me directly.

Instead of working, I waste a whole hour looking up answers on the internet. I'm amazed. So many things I've taken for granted I now see as inspiring tributes to man's ingenuity, from radar and two-stroke engines to biros and septic tanks.

When Zoë returns from the hairdresser, I head downstairs and enthral her with a lengthy and detailed explanation of how toilets flush. Naturally, she's in awe and hangs on every word.

This sudden awareness of my lack of knowledge is symptomatic; I just don't feel old enough or wise enough to be a father. I think that's always in the back of my mind when I'm presented with a forbidding form, from work contracts to mortgage agreements, and I sign away my life with the same signature practised on the back of my geography textbook – ultimately it doesn't really matter, because I'm not really old enough to be held accountable anyway. In fact, the only mature quality I can relate to is forgetfulness as, by evening, all I've learnt has leached away, the fine detail dripping all too easily through the coarse netting of my brain.

But knowing I could become a father any day makes me stop and, as I brush my teeth for bed, take notice of what's really in the mirror: a few bulges that demand more effort to shift, lines around those bags beneath the eyes and, unmistakably, a forelock of pure, white hair. A cruel state of affairs for one still barely capable of growing stubble, to be sure, and yet this year I'm turning 30.

I've heard it said that you don't really grow up until you lose a parent. In which case, I should qualify. I should be facing this world with rock-like confidence as an oracle of truth, as tireless and dependable as the tide, with every right to be looked up to as the definitive 'grown-up'.

If anything, though, losing Dad has only confirmed what I'd always suspected and would rather not have known: that life doesn't just click into place and there are no easy answers, that we're not all unfazed and unwavering, and that our fears can grow with us. Is that what an adult is, then – just a person who's better at pretending to be grown up?

In which case, I already know the answers I'll give my kid: cranes lift using anti-gravity podules, aeroplanes are shot into the air by big catapults, and dew is just a sign that it rained overnight. And if you don't believe me, go ask your mother.

Friday, 16th February – 39 weeks pregnant, 1 week to go

It seems appropriate that this pregnancy should be book-ended by my contributions in bed, from the pressure to conceive at the start to, nine months later, the pressure to prod and prompt the baby to emerge.

Feeling slightly better thanks to a good night's sleep and impatient to meet our son or daughter face to face, Zoë reckons it's worth seeing if there's any truth to the claim that sex induces birth. And so, before heading upstairs as usual to the loft, I slip between her sheets and do my duty before retiring to my own quarters, like a Victorian patriarch, for another undisturbed night's sleep.

Saturday, 17th February – 39 weeks, 1 day

My bedroom efforts prove ineffectual – not for the first time, Zoë might argue. The kettle is warm when I come downstairs the following morning, the TV is on and, when I turn on my laptop, I find a couple of emails forwarded from her at 5 a.m., so she hasn't had a trouble-free night. I assume, however, that her absence means she's in the bath and not the hospital.

'Your TV series was on this morning,' she says when I find her almost jammed into the tub. 'That should mean more repeat fees for you, shouldn't it?'

I nod, pleased, but distracted by the sight of her body. I know some view their pregnant partners as a turn-off, their bodies become nothing more than incubators, but fortunately I've only ever found this fuller version of Zoë infinitely sexy – even if she doesn't herself. For the last few months she's avoided tight tops, embarrassed to be exhibiting a popped-out belly button, and she can't stand the sight of her swollen feet – not really a problem as they're so obstructed by her stomach that I have to help her with her shoes and socks every morning. But so far she's avoided stretch marks and all the other joys that pregnancy can offer, from varicose veins to piles.

'Look at this,' she says and firmly squeezes an enormous breast. A thin squirt of bright yellow pools on her front.

'I was just thinking,' she says, 'that all the big decisions, like buying property or getting married, they're all reversible. But having a baby, that's irreversible.'

Eventually we go for a walk around the block, hoping to get things moving. I even manage a jocular nipple tweak, but induce only a shriek and a slap in return.

She collapses in front of the telly. 'Will you sit with me?'

These days make irreconcilable demands; I'm desperate to get some work done while I can, but want to support her and share our last moments of peace.

'It's like waiting for the summer holidays knowing we've got exams to do first,' she says.

For the first time in weeks, we fall asleep together in the same bed.

Sunday, 18th February – 39 weeks, 2 days

Or, rather, Zoë sleeps – I lie listening to her snoring for 15 minutes then resort once again to the earplugs. As a result, when she calls from the bathroom at two in the morning to tell me her waters have broken, I sleep on, oblivious, waking finally to see her looming over me, just as when she woke me to tell me she was pregnant, with that look of controlled terror.

I watch as Zoë, still gushing amniotic fluid, struggles to pull on a pair of disposable knickers that look more like waders than lingerie. Having called the hospital, it's about 2.30 a.m. when we leave. It's not a dramatic rush, despite the adrenaline, and I gather her bags with relative calm, ticking off items from her list. One thing I want for myself is a notepad to record her progress, so I grab one from a deep drawer in Dad's desk. As I throw it on top of a bag, it falls open on a page of his writing, an old list of items for one of his last trips to hospital, written in a weak and jagged hand. It stops me short, tingeing my excitement with heavy regret and a dawning appreciation of my impending change of status. I even lay a hand on the desk, exactly where he sat the night he died, as though I can physically draw strength for the hours and years ahead from the memory of his example.

Somehow, despite having prepared our route and agreed a parking strategy, I drive the wrong way down the hospital's labyrinthine, one-way roads and, dumping the car in the A&E ambulance bay in desperation, am chased away by a territorial receptionist. At last, we find the car park and head towards the labour ward entrance. It's the middle of the night and I'm accompanied by an obviously pained and full-bellied woman, yet the jobsworth security guard still stops us.

'And you are?' he asks, as though the wrong name will have us kicked back out onto the street.

At last, having negotiated endless corridors and been shunted from room to room, examined and wired up to monitors and had cold water sprinkled on her belly to rouse the baby further, Zoë is told she hasn't even begun to dilate.

'Go home,' says the midwife. 'Call us if there's any change.'

The endurance test has begun. To gather her strength, Zoë wants something to eat. She asks me to take her to the 24-hour McDonalds by Wandsworth Bridge before the thought of future ridicule makes her settle for something at home, so, by four in the morning, she's munching on toast with ham and melted cheese while, for want of anything else to do, I empty the dishwasher. Twenty minutes later we decide to go back to bed, but Zoë's still gushing amniotic fluid so we lay out some towels. By six, we've given up trying to sleep. She gets into the bath; the pain's better, but she still needs to breathe through each contraction.

By seven, she's back in the bedroom and I'm trying to rub her dry with a towel, but every three to five minutes she's incapacitated with contractions lasting anything from 30 seconds to one minute. I strap a TENS machine onto her back and she kneels in front of the fire.

'You forget in between how bad the last contraction was,' she says, during a break in the pain. 'They come so quickly, it's quite a shock. I guess I could go back to the hospital, but I'm not going to.'

I know what she's saying; she wants to avoid being turned away again with the disheartening news that this has barely begun.

But by 9 a.m., she's changed her mind. We've tried the TENS machine; we've tried breathing exercises; we've tried an arsenal of positions, both lying and sitting, but nothing will touch the regular bursts of pain, the mere prospect of which fills each respite with dread.

Grateful for the quieter weekend traffic, we're soon back at the hospital. And less than half an hour later, having been told she's still not dilating, Zoë's back home and back in the bath, a warm flannel laid across her taut belly. In the three-minute windows between each contraction, I book a flight down from Edinburgh for my mum, dashing back and forth between the computer and the animal cries of agony.

With midday as the goal before we return to the hospital, we start to get her ready. Sitting on the edge of the bed, she rolls and moans as the pain grows worse.

'I can't do this,' she wails.

It's then that, as I'm bending over her and she's in thrall to the agony, she tries to sink her teeth into my stomach. I have to wait until she's able to speak again before I can ask her what she thinks she's doing.

'I don't know,' she says. 'I thought I might be able to transfer the pain to you. It seemed to make sense at the time.'

It takes over half an hour to dry and dress her, so it's just past noon when we leave for the third time. From the start of this pregnancy, Zoë has been clear that she wants to try to get by without an epidural. As with a caesarean, she sees it as a potentially avoidable surgical procedure, and therefore a risk she's keen to dodge. Now though, despite still being at home and two miles from the hospital, she's begging me to administer an epidural myself, and promising with every breath that she'll henceforth show nothing but intense sympathy for every pregnant patient who walks through her door.

Despite the pain, she bravely insists on remaining upright and mobile for as long as possible to lend gravity a hand, so I feel the stares and hear the comments of those who see me walking my suffering wife down miles of corridors, straight past large numbers of available wheelchairs.

After nine hours of contractions, Zoë is finally admitted, five centimetres dilated and in so much pain she can barely ask for the epidural. She sucks on the gas and air while she waits, with little effect, but ten minutes later, after one quick injection into her back, she's more her former self, chatting and laughing and even singing along to Take That on the iPod – a sure sign of my compassion, that I'd risk them heralding my child into the world.

After another examination, the midwife wonders if the baby isn't facing the wrong way, forward rather than backwards, but doesn't seem too worried.

'It's called an OP: occiput posterior,' Zoë tells me. 'It's not unusual, and there's still time for the baby to turn.'

The midwife agrees and, by five o'clock in the evening, reckons we'll be parents before she's finished her shift at eight. We text the grandparents-to-be and, buoyed by the war cries of the woman across the corridor, wait for the word to start pushing.

By this time I'm already feeling utterly drained by the plodding relentlessness of the process, neither frantic nor panicked but grinding, like the movement of a glacier. I've watched my wife go through the worst pain she's ever experienced, and the shared relief of the epidural has left me near total exhaustion. Every minute has been filled with fetching and carrying to the point that I've eaten nearly nothing since early last night, and all of this on two hours' sleep. As Zoë manages a brief doze, I collapse in a chair, staring at the jagged line on the monitor that represents our baby's heartbeat, munching on crisps and wondering at my wife's ability to endure. And thinking that, in just a few hours, we'll be holding our child.

An examination at 7.30 p.m. shows that Zoë is now fully

dilated. Everything has gone so smoothly, I begin to suspect that Zoë and the baby have sat down together with a birthing textbook to confirm the details in advance. And when the midwife tells us that the baby is only half a finger's length from crowning, we see the end approaching.

But then, two and a half hours later, Zoë's contractions still aren't intense or regular enough to allow her to push. She herself is still composed enough to remind the new shift midwife that, as it's now been over 18 hours since her waters broke, she's due some antibiotics, so by ten o'clock she's on three drips: fluids as part of the epidural (along with a catheter), antibiotics, and oxytocin, a hormone designed to strengthen the contractions. But after another hour of pushing to the sound of a newborn baby crying across the corridor, ours hasn't moved.

'Keep breathing! That's it! Breathe!' is all I can offer, but it sounds so hackneyed and useless that I feel stupid even saying it. As the midwife unconvincingly smiles and nods her own encouragement, I can see Zoë's strength fading with each weakening effort.

Finally, sometime around midnight, the midwife slips away, her face a mask, to find an obstetrician.

And that's when the trauma really begins.

Monday, 19th February – 39 weeks, 3 days

A few years ago my wife gave birth to twins. It was a near effortless home birth in the front room of our north London townhouse, surrounded by designer furniture and expensive upholstery and attended by a pair of glamorous private midwives. The only concession to the pristine nature of our surroundings was that my wife leant on me for support rather than the ludicrously overpriced sofa.

The babies, looking nothing like either of their parents, were passed straight to me, spotless and already swaddled, and I never did discover if they were boys or girls. Of course, there was music playing over the few mild groans, a song intended to be poignant yet soothing enough to carry those watching through a blissfully brief period of pushing. And then there I was, juggling a baby on each arm, overcome with emotion as I kissed my wife's artfully beaded brow.

Until this moment, that's the closest I've ever come to experiencing childbirth: a short scene in an ITV drama. The mere idea that I could have owned such a home should have suggested that it wouldn't be a wholly realistic portrayal. Even my reactions on seeing my 'children' for the first time were themselves gleaned from countless films where, if the father's in the room at all, he's simply there to hold a hand, lend encouragement and – if it's a comedy – pass out on the floor.

Now, as I watch my wife fading before my eyes, I begin to appreciate how large the gulf really is between drama and reality, and recognize that all TV and film has taught me about childbirth is how unrealistic they've been. In fact, the only point at which their portrayals overlap with our reality is in how close I am to fainting.

Within minutes of our midwife's disappearance, I'm following Zoë's bed in a rushed surge through double doors and dead corridors as she's trolleyed to theatre. They've given me a blue gown to wear, plastic slippers to put over my shoes and a paper hat. Zoë is trembling in the bed, partly an effect of the epidural, partly an accompaniment to the tears as circumstances lurch way beyond our expectations. The doctor confirms that our baby is facing the wrong way and gains consent for a rotational ventouse – they plan to attach a suction cup to our baby's head and pull it out, twisting as they tug to turn it as it comes.

In contrast to the soothing delivery suite, the lights are stark and the room is a flurry of noise. A second obstetrician appears. Together the doctors consult, undecided as to whether what they feel alongside the baby's head is an ear or a hand. Their deliberations are cut short by an alarm from the monitor – the baby's heartbeat is dropping and the ventouse is immediately rejected in favour of forceps.

'We have to get this baby out *now!*' someone says. As they rapidly erect a sheet to screen us from the action, I catch sight of the doctor raising the forceps – gleaming clamps, big brutal things as forbidding as garden shears.

While Zoë's worst scenario is a caesarean, I've been secretly dreading a forceps delivery. Courtesy of our antenatal classes, I know that forceps were originally used to extract babies that had already died, and are now used so infrequently that training in their use has actually declined. And while I know many who have been delivered successfully this way, I've also known people who have suffered, from the loss of fingers to the severing of facial nerves. If it *is* a hand rather than an ear that they're feeling alongside our baby's head, who knows what might happen now?

But when the professionals tell you something is necessary, you can do nothing but take that leap of faith, trusting that they know best. So I sit at Zoë's head, stroking her face and telling her that it's forceps and not a caesarean and that everything will be all right. She seems comatose with terror, withdrawn into herself perhaps to avoid understanding too much of what's being said; all I can recognize is the doctors' new sense of urgency and the pressure to act, emphasized by the fact that they no longer have the privilege of time to keep us informed of what's happening.

With the forceps clamped around our baby's head and who knows what else, the doctors hurriedly try three times to wrench it out. Despite having lost all sensation to the epidural, Zoë pushes gamely but, as the baby's heartbeat continues to drop, the doctors give up. One begins to shave her pubic hair and yellow her stomach with iodine while another manually pushes the baby back up the birth canal in preparation for an emergency caesarean.

Having never thought of myself as squeamish, I feel confident that my stomach can stand the sight of hers, so it's curiosity and a foolish sense of bravado that prompts me to peek around the low screen as a scalpel hovers above her belly. And it's a horrifying wave of reality that makes me very quickly turn back.

The rapidity with which our textbook delivery has gone wrong is overwhelming. The phrase 'sick with fear' suddenly takes on a very real meaning as I'm engulfed by nausea. The blood rushes from my head, and I have to clench every muscle against the churning contents of my stomach, a mixture of adrenaline and the debris of our well-intentioned curries.

Wanting to be only a comfort to Zoë, I lean in, telling her she'll be fine as I wipe away her tears, then I turn out of her sight to collapse my head on the pillow behind her, the scenario that's haunted me since the beginning rearing up with terrifying solidity: how can it be that, in a matter of minutes, the promise of three has become the threat of one?

The anaesthetist works to engage us in banal conversation as the doctor dives in and begins to pull with all his might, tugging so hard that he leans back and almost smothers Zoë who is whimpering, begging for our baby to be OK. His movement drags down the screen that should have kept us from the worst – Zoë can't see because his body's in the way but, as the monitor continues to sound the alarm, I get a full view of the blood-soaked sheets and her insides, crimson and torn. Beyond the bulk of his body is hidden whatever it is he's tugging on and I collapse back into my chair, their urgent shouts and the sight of so much blood making my head spin. I try to ask the nurse discreetly for a bucket without alarming Zoë, but at the sight of my white face one of them rushes over with a glass full of water and sugar.

A huddle of people dart to the side of the room. Zoë and I strain to hear signs of life above the doctors calling to each other as they try to stem the bleeding from her uterus that's been torn by the sheer force of ripping our baby free. There's not a sound. And still not a sound. I'm close to retching, desperately trying to control my breathing, unable even to turn my head in the direction of the baby. Zoë's similarly silent, trembling, waiting.

And then a cry. It's 1.19 a.m. on Monday, 19th February.

A baby-shaped noise is held up before us. 'You've got a baby girl,' the midwife says. Zoë and I stare, unable to respond. Until a few moments ago, we'd expected a smooth delivery to give us a boy. The news only throws me even further off balance. I turn back to Zoë. Beyond the screen, her lower half seems to float in a bed of blood. A nurse carries away red-stained sheets as the doctors continue to stitch inside and out, to flush and to wipe, but the urgency has gone. And Zoë is beaming.

'Andrew,' asks the midwife, 'do you want to come and see your baby?'

I struggle even to speak. 'I can't,' I manage, my embarrassment forcing a smile. 'I'm not sure I can even stand up.' Another glass of sugared water appears, and then they bring over a swaddled bundle and, at last, we meet Polly, our daughter. She lies beside Zoë and we coo and ahh, each of us thinking – as every parent must do – that she's perfect and that the world has changed for ever. Because of course she is and it has.

PART TWO

The First Month

Despite being, in effect, born twice – squeezed along the birth canal, forced back up and then tugged out the top – Polly looks only a little swollen. The forceps have done nothing but waken her, and she stares silently, totally alert, examining us both with big dark eyes.

There's no immediate skin on skin, no textbook rush to the breast. As they continue to stitch Zoë up, our baby is taken aside for a standard vitamin injection, then weighed. Peeing all over the scales in what I hope is relief rather than terror at the first sight of her parents, she's finally swaddled and laid down next to her mum.

As I follow Zoë's bed round more corners towards the surreal calm of the post-op room, we're both too shocked to speak. She lies totally prostrate, still linked up to drips and catheterized, our new baby resting in her arms.

A nurse points me in the direction of the labour ward and tells me to collect our bags, and by the time I've broken the happy news of their first grandchild to our nervously waiting parents, I return to find Polly happily breastfeeding, soothing Zoë's anxieties with every strong little suck.

Minutes later, my girls are wheeled into the curtained corner of a darkened ward. Both are well, with help already fretting around the bed. We stare at our daughter who stares sweetly back, looking so unlike either of us that it's hard to believe she's ours.

Zoë seems ready to pass out with exhaustion, as am I. When a nurse asks me to leave, I'm too shaken to do anything other than obey. I pick up what's no longer needed, kiss my wife and daughter goodbye, and somehow find my way back home.

On my first night of fatherhood, returning alone and traumatized at four in the morning having walked away from my post-op wife and baby daughter less than 30 minutes after her birth, I step back through our front door to find the day's post on the mat. Among the normal stack of bills, takeaway menus and estate agents' flyers, there's a payment slip from my agent: the ITV drama in which I fathered twins has been broadcast on cable, providing me with another effortless repeat fee. After only two hours' sleep in the last three days, I pass out on the bed before I can verbalize the thought that if the profit of the experience is proportional to the pain, we're going to be rich indeed.

Monday, 19th February – Week One

Three hours later, I'm woken by a text from Zoë: 'Will you call me when you wake up?'

Before I can rouse myself, there's a flood of further messages either hungry for news or offering congratulations. I hunt down some painkillers for a growing headache, and dial the ward.

'Can you get me a few things?' asks a sleepy voice when I'm transferred.

Within half an hour I'm pinballing frantically around the shopping centre with an eclectic shopping list that includes jumpsuits (the few Zoë has are already posset-stained) and almond oil (to moisturize Polly's skin).

Thanks to a broken car park ticket machine and a supermarket conveyor belt that pushes my bag onto the floor, smashing the oil all over the new jumpsuits, it's already four minutes into visiting hours when I run down the hospital corridors and tap impatiently at the elevator button, desperate to meet my daughter properly.

Zoë has been wheeled into a private side room with her own toilet and shower, in deference as much to the horror of her experience as to her position as a fellow medic. She looks up with a tired smile from where she's perched on the edge of the bed, and I can see immediately that the trauma of the night before has left her swollen all over. But with Polly sucking greedily from a breast, she looks every inch the natural mother and the sight – the most effective balm imaginable – makes me infinitely proud.

'I changed her into fresh clothes for a proper introduction to her dad,' she smiles wearily. 'But just five minutes ago she possetted a big yellow smear down her front and demanded more to eat. Sorry.'

The feed over and dutifully recorded in a notebook by Zoë's side, I hold my daughter properly for the first time, reeling not only at her absolute perfection but at the realization that she'll soon be coming home with us. Every blink and twitch seems magical, every rise and fall of her chest: she's alive and she works and she's ours.

Polly herself stares up at her new family as though to reassure us, and my eyes never leave hers until they flutter and close and she falls asleep in my arms. Between more phone calls and messages, Zoë manages to doze as well, and I sit with Polly beside the bed, staring in awe at my two girls. I'm ecstatic, and totally in love with them both.

Time passes, and soon the three grandparents arrive, tears in their eyes as I lead them into the room to greet their first grandchild, and soon it's like every bad baby film I've ever seen – all three line up around the cot, cooing and gurning, their cameras flashing. Polly withstands the onslaught well, barely murmuring as, with hands washed against MRSA, they hold her to pose for photos.

'It was a roller coaster,' Zoë tells them.

I think again of the frustration of helplessness, and the fearful, stomach-churning physicality. I think of the minutes that crawled, full of nothing but pain, and then the sudden lurches, when all was change, and I think of the utter exhaustion in the face of the relentless inevitability that something had to happen, for good or for bad.

'More like a thick-brushed, open-topped car-wash,' I say. 'On a roller coaster.'

But already I can sense my mind colluding with my exhaustion to shelter me from the worst. Seen in hindsight through bloodshot eyes, the experience is already growing distant, like the memory of something I once read.

Polly has barely murmured by the time the grandparents leave around 6 p.m. Zoë still has her catheter and saline drip and, mindful of the swelling, vetoes any photos taken from wide circulation.

Then, barely 19 hours old, our daughter squeezes out her first poo. Unable to do much more than sit up, Zoë watches while I change the first nappy, scraping at the tar-like meconium. Having seen my daughter wrapped up tightly all day, it's a shock to see her full body again, the slimy green slug-like umbilicus, the thighs like underfed chicken drumsticks, and her feet like monkey's, each toe so active and independent. Her intense stare makes her seem almost capable of communicating, but the best she can manage is to squeeze my finger as she lets out a fart.

Though giving the impression of coping perfectly, as it gets closer to 8.30 p.m. and the end of visiting time I notice Zoë stealing mournful glances at the clock.

I try to reassure her. 'It's great having the midwife station right outside.'

She pouts. 'I'd rather be coming home with you.'

With stitches that forbid her from lifting Polly in and out of the bedside crib, it'll be another few nights at least before she's allowed home. And there's a clear benefit to having a team of experts by the door. But we're both impatient to get the family home, as though we'll only really become parents when we start to make decisions for ourselves, without instructions from nurses and midwives.

By nine o'clock I'm back in the house. I scoff a dinner kindly supplied by Zoë's mum, then answer a few more calls before putting on a wash that includes an impossibly small white jumpsuit. Soon after, I collapse, at last, in bed.

Tuesday, 20th February

The jumpsuit is still spinning when I come down the next morning, the washing machine jammed.

Back in the hospital, Zoë's sitting up on the edge of the bed, her catheter and drips removed and face less swollen. And Polly, again feeding, is even more gorgeous than I remember. I want to send everyone photos, as though what will appear to the recipients as just another Churchillian snap can really communicate the strength of our feelings.

Grandparents come and go, there's tearful talk of Dad, and at one point I wheel Polly to another room for a hearing test: as soft clicking sounds are made in her ears, small electrodes record her brain's reassuringly normal response.

'There'll be more tests to come, because of the family history,' says Zoë. 'But I'm not worried – a door slammed earlier and she jumped out of her skin!'

By 8.30 I'm flagging and am kicked out soon after, amazed at how Zoë's managing if, as her detailed notes suggest, she's never getting more than 45 minutes between feeds. The regular latching on seems to be as much for their mutual comfort as any actual sustenance, as Zoë stares at Polly for hours on end. And I just can't blame her.

Back at the house, I think about taking a shower but don't want to wash the smell of Polly from my hands. I'm impatient to get her home, to start our new life together.

Zoë calls from her hospital bed. 'I miss you,' she says. 'And Polly misses you. We're missing the man of the family.' It's bizarre to think that I now have a family of my own, and I resolve then and there to organize my life to ensure worthiness.

Wednesday, 21st February

Zoë texts to say she's received her discharge papers so can leave at any time. I run around the house preparing for their return, rush out to buy more food for the fridge and some flowers, then hurry to the hospital.

The scrupulously filled notebook supplies a detailed report on the night's poos and feeds, and fills me with admiration for Zoë who, again, has been up most of the night. And all after months of discomfort, the terror of the birth and serious surgery.

After a brief struggle to get a sleeping Polly safely fitted inside the car seat, we leave for home. Those long sterile corridors I'd resented for every metre when Zoë was reeling in pain now just aren't long enough. I carry Polly through the crowds like a trophy, a tiny scrap in a pristine white jumpsuit swamped in her seat, as small and fragile as a bird, and I try not to block the way with my grin. Zoë follows carefully behind, her legs and feet still so swollen she's wearing only socks.

Thanks to a well-planned feed and nappy change, our daughter never wakes, and remains oblivious to her first car journey as I drive away at less than half the speed with which we arrived, Zoë bracing herself over every bump for her own sake as much as our daughter's.

Outside the house, despite all the preparation, the car seat's straps and levers force me to refer to the instructions. And then at last I'm carrying my daughter into our home. Cards and presents block the door, and only when we're inside does it finally sink in: this baby is ours and will be part of us to the end. I feel an enthralling yet vertiginous sense of responsibility for the life stretching ahead of her.

Polly's first bath highlights again the disadvantage of growing up a boy in a household without sisters as, not for the first time, I lament my life's minimal exposure to female genitalia. When it comes to cleaning between her legs, I'm forced to refer to an authority beyond my experience.

'Using fresh cotton wool,' reads Zoë from our parenting manual, 'gently wipe the outer lips of the vulva – but don't clean inside.'

I try, but the result is an untouched smear of white castor oil and zinc cream, obstinate stuff that by design is resistant to wiping with water. With no real option, I dig tentatively deeper and, as my daughter stares up at me from the bath, my over-active imagination wonders if what she's seeing now will resurface decades from now in her therapist's chair, at which point my door will be kicked in and I'll be carted off to a pervert's prison.

It's absurd, and a sad sign of the times: already I'm wondering if the mass of photos we've taken of Polly's naked body will get us into trouble when we have them developed, the ones that show her little belly and everything beneath, entirely innocent, entirely chaste, and entirely naked.

Thursday, 22nd February

The house is swamped in flowers. With any luck, it'll be weeks before we smell the content of Polly's nappies. While Zoë rests upstairs, our daughter is passed out in her Moses basket, unintentionally out of sight behind the coffee table. And despite the tiredness, the hundreds of cards covering every surface, the balloons and the humbling mass of gifts, I forget that she's there. For perhaps ten minutes, as I sit quietly working, everything is as it has so often been – just Zoë and I alone in the house.

And then, with a little sniffle from a few feet away, it all comes flooding back – the positive flip-side, I guess, to that terrible sinking feeling of loss on waking soon after the death of a loved one, waking to remember the world you now face is that much emptier.

Before she can settle herself, the girls are roused by the doorbell and another delivery for Polly Watson. She begins to cry, stretching in her Moses basket like she's performing t'ai chi. By the time I'm back, Zoë is already leaning over her adoringly, insistent on doing all she can despite the stitches.

As I watch them together, I begin to understand why men so often feel cut out of the equation, almost superfluous. For nine months and several excruciating hours, we're mere bystanders while it all happens right before our eyes to the one person we care most about. And throughout it all, there's just no way of being directly involved. Nor can we compete with the sheer physicality of our baby's arrival or the intimacy and fundamental importance of its feeding. And any attempt to do so can feel like an intrusion into this symbiotic and strongest of relationships – because nothing comforts our baby like a nipple in the gob.

Instead, it seems that my job is to float around the touchline, to do all the things Zoë can't because she's too busy feeding, too tired or too sore: managing our meals, washing and cleaning, or heading out to register the birth and getting my head in a spin when I venture deeper into the alien world of baby clothes shopping. I do all these things so that Zoë can fight her private battle over the breastfeeding, a campaign that, despite the relative ease thus far, is so laden with expectation that no amount of success can pacify her.

Friday, 23rd February

'Would you mind massaging my breasts?' asks Zoë. 'It's meant to guard against the risk of milk clots and I'm too tired to do it myself.'

Had I but known, I could have consoled my early teenage self for hours with just the thought of this request. But the reality is strangely anti-climactic, because these beautifully rounded, firm obtrusions are no longer here simply for my benefit and admiration. They're functional, tools with a very specific job, and a job of such importance that I can't give vent to my jealousy.

'It's the latching on that's worst,' she says. 'This nipple ointment helps, Lansinoh, but they're getting engorged now as well. What have we got in the fridge? Cabbage leaves are meant to help.'

When all we can muster is the stump of an old cabbage and a few carrots, she nods enthusiastically. 'Lucy used carrots – let's give it a go.'

Dutifully, I grate and pack them into an old bra then wrap the moist mess tight against Zoë's body with clingfilm. And, unbelievably, she's soon collapsed in front of the telly with a grin of relief, her entire front stained an indelible orange.

It'll be a while before I eat coleslaw again.

Saturday, 24th February

Having done my now daily Mothercare raid – this time to *return* a load of previously misjudged purchases – I pop into the chemist to stock up on painkillers: Zoë's been staring down at our daughter so hard and for so long that she's jarred her neck.

I get home just in time to conspire in burying our exhaustion beneath a perfect front of domestic bliss as a stream of friends and family arrive, each bearing an embarrassing pile of gifts.

Sunday, 25th February

Rob comes round to meet his niece. Polly takes one look at him before puking down the front of his designer t-shirt, an impressive blast that splatters over them both and leaves her staring in confusion, like the victim of a custard pie ambush. She should be used to it by now: post-feed possets have become pretty standard as she erupts like a creamy geyser in streams of lava-like, yellowish yack.

My aunt drives up to visit from Kent, and we ask her to call when she's about 40 minutes away. But who could have guessed that 40 minutes wouldn't be enough time to feed Polly, clean her, clothe her and then wash and dress ourselves in preparation?

After just a bowl of cereal for dinner, we're both in bed by eight o'clock, but the time is as irrelevant as any hope for a good night's sleep is absurd; we're living in a detached time zone of our own that consists only of three-hour cycles.

Monday, 26th February – 1 week old

As the excitement subsides, everyday life begins to resurface, like mud-topped mountains after the Flood. That pile of correspondence can't be put off for ever, those builders still need chasing, and then there's real work to be done of the sort that'll actually pay for all these trips to Mothercare.

Zoë's mum continues to do all she can to help. She's turned up at the door with so many meals, from enormous beef joints to chicken soup and fish pie, that it'll be weeks before we have to risk the food I prepared for Zoë's return. And unaware of my efforts to tidy the house for my family's homecoming, she even sends round her cleaner, forcing us to search the house desperately for something for her to clean before sending her home an hour early, a joint of roast beef tucked into her bag.

Tuesday, 27th February

Bundled up beneath several blankets, Polly's first outing firmly establishes her as a citizen of this country, embroiling her forever in the inevitable bureaucracies of life. Thanks to a cheque from her great-grandparents, we open a bank account in her name. Then, in preparation for a friend's wedding in France in May, we book flights and pick up a passport application form.

Since Her Majesty's government seems to suggest that the appearance of a supportive hand in our daughter's passport photo could imply terrorist yearnings, Zoë and I waste several ponderous minutes wondering how to persuade Polly to sit up straight, only to be ridiculed with the simplest of moves when the photographer lays her down on a white sheet and takes the shot from above.

Now that she's officially registered, I wonder how long it'll be before Polly's name finds its way onto marketing lists. How long until letters fall through the door offering her interest-free credit or a great deal on double-glazing? Or until someone calls from India asking if she fancies faster broadband speeds?

Wednesday, 28th February

My role here, undoubtedly, is to manage the outside world. I feel like a master of ceremonies, standing by the front door to announce each new visitor's arrival, offering up yet another account of the birth as the kettle boils, guarding Zoë's energy and time with Polly as our desire to let her sleep struggles with the need to pass her around.

So when just the threat of a friend arriving late for a brief visit pushes Zoë to tears, it's clear that the necessities of keeping an open house and cheerful front amidst so much turmoil have pushed her too far, and I issue the edict banning all visitors until further notice.

We take a bath together, and Polly floats happily between us, her right arm waving, her left hugged close in to her chest in what's becoming a typical pose.

While drying her afterwards, her umbilical stump falls free to sit on her changing table like a blood-encrusted booger of gargantuan proportions.

Thursday, 1st March

With Polly taking her morning nap, I'm passing through the front room en route to making another coffee when I find Zoë on the sofa in tears.

'What's wrong?'

'I don't know,' she says, with a smile.

We sit together, holding each other in silence. A minute passes.

'I'm feeling a bit overwhelmed by the enormity of it all,' she whispers, sniffing.

'You really needn't,' I tell her. 'You're doing brilliantly. And Polly's doing brilliantly.'

Our daughter snorts and mews, whimpers and farts. She stares intently with serene calm, poos and pees plentifully, cries only when in need, and settles immediately when those needs are met. So far, she couldn't be kinder to us. So I suspect Zoë's tears are more to do with breastfeeding pressures, hormones and/or sheer fatigue.

'Honestly,' I say, 'you've got nothing to worry about.'

A few seconds later, an idea comes to Zoë. 'Maybe this is just baby blues,' she says. Consoled by the idea, she smiles again, lets out a big sigh, and then picks herself up to get on with her day, as though glad that's one more thing she can tick off her to-do list.

Friday, 2nd March

'She's got lovely skin colour,' says the midwife.

'Everyone keeps saying that.' Zoë's response to what was obviously intended as a compliment is surprisingly prickly. 'Do you think she could be jaundiced?'

The midwife just chuckles and shakes her head and, as Zoë rubs her now stitch-free belly, weighs our daughter.

Our NCT teacher told us that breastfed babies can't overfeed, that any surplus is simply excreted. It's a claim I find hard to credit and one that Polly herself is doing all she can to debunk: in under two weeks, our baby has not only regained her birth weight (normally expected by day ten) but put on a huge amount more, growing from the 6lb 5oz when born to 7lb 4oz.

So for all the torrential possetting and Zoë's concerns about breastfeeding, Polly has proved herself more than capable, sucking with such strength it's as though her whole body is one single muscle intent on the task.

Aside from feeding, she doesn't do much. I rub my nose against hers and she chews her sleeve. I tell her I love her and she chews her sleeve. I hold her up, burbling in a way only fatherhood could allow, swearing she's the most adorable thing in the world, and she turns her head, farts and chews her sleeve. She doesn't do much, but it's enough. I feel such unconditional love, she could pull a knife on me and I'd only coo over her co-ordination and strength.

Day by day, she becomes more and more of this world, for good or for bad. Her velvet skin, previously so smooth and untainted, is starting to flake, and developing little milia, those tiny whiteheads that should resolve themselves with time. Her face is streaked in scratches from flailing fingers, themselves no longer looking so manicured, as she struggles to co-ordinate. And the distinctive baby smell is disappearing beneath that other common babyish whiff, or just the fragrance of whoever cuddled her last.

The tar-like meconium that in the first few days took half a field's worth of cotton wool to scrape off has been replaced by a relatively mild, all-too-fluid splattering of what look like tiny yellow mustard seeds.

'Her poo won't be properly shitty till she's off the breast,' says Zoë, removing the nappy. Seconds later, she dives for cover as Polly perfects a high-speed, parabolic arc that clears the edge of the changing table and lays a line along the floor.

In almost two weeks, Polly's experimented with a whole range of noises that vary in volume and pitch, from 'the choking seal' to 'the wet sponge on glass', from 'the frightened puppy' to 'the squeaking hinge'. Some of them are hilarious and, in the middle of the night when worst-case scenarios lurk beneath the bed, all are reassuring.

While her lungs are still too small to give the neighbours much more than polite notice of her existence (or so they kindly tell us), there's nothing wrong with her neck muscles: at four o'clock in the morning when I'm holding her in one hand en route to the changing table, she twitches violently, like a learner breakdancer, causing my heart to backflip as the weight of her head leads a leap for freedom.

Saturday, 3rd March

Polly lunges for the breast and is jetted in the face by a forceful stream of milk. Her response is heroic: she throws herself at the nipple like a fireman wrestling down a dangerously flailing hose, lapping loosely to stop herself choking, masterfully taking off the worst of the flow until the mass of taut flesh subsides and she can clamp her jowly chops around it to assume full control.

When she finally comes up for air – to give and to take – she unlatches herself like a thirst-quenched limpet, the nipple ejected from her boneless gums to reveal suction lines on her cheeks flashing red like the scars from a well-won battle.

And no matter how gently she's handled, no matter how soft the rub on her back to help that wind on its way, she grins cheerfully as a tidal wave of semi-digested milk streams over her chin and down her front, splattering over everything and everyone. Not even the built-in pouches in the plastic-backed bibs are up to the task of containing the flood – it's like holding back the tide with a bucket.

Finally, her hunger sated, she slumps back, eyes rolling as she slips off into sleep.

Sunday, 4th March

The books tell me that she can't yet smile, that it's an accidental alignment of facial muscles, bound to happen if you leave her for long enough, like those monkeys locked in a room writing Shakespeare. But, as I'm changing her nappy, her face bursts into a broad-faced grin, like the sun emerging from behind the clouds. My heart soars – until I realize she's not expressing her overwhelming love for her father but admiration for the nursery curtains that, in her line of vision, lie just over my head. Either that or she's laughing at my haircut.

It reminds me of a camping holiday 18 years ago in France, when I saw a shooting star and, for just a moment, was touched by something mystical – until the 'star' started flashing and extended its landing gear.

Monday, 5th March – 2 weeks old

With Polly asleep in our bedroom, Zoë surprises even herself as, against her better judgement and probably all medical advice, we find ourselves rolling around, very carefully and very gently, on the floor of the nursery.

'I was worried I'd never want to have sex again,' she says afterwards, thrilled to have proved herself wrong. 'I feel like I've reclaimed my body. And I've got to say, I'm loving these great tits.'

That makes three of us.

Tuesday, 6th March

Polly has brought into this tainted world a little of the perfection that, as the tenant of her mother's womb, she's so obviously been accustomed to. She cries only when hungry, wakes according to Zoë's diarized expectations almost to the minute, and is as generally well behaved as we could hope for, having extended her cycle to sometimes as much as four hours.

And yet, for Zoë in particular, every waking minute is now pregnant with worry. Every gained ounce of adoration is matched by an equal weight in terror, with no state offering comfort. If Polly cries, something is wrong, but if she doesn't cry, it could be worse, so every blissful second of silence screams a threat.

If she sleeps all the time or doesn't sleep, if she eats too much or not enough, if she's too hot or too cold – it's all cause for concern.

The tests and her own obvious response to noises confirm that our daughter isn't deaf. And though her eyes at times seem to flicker independently as they struggle to focus, she doesn't have a squint. But still the slightest thing can knock Zoë's confidence.

'Did you hear that?' she asks.

'What?'

'Polly grunted.'

'So?'

'Grunting is a medical term. It shows that Polly's having difficulty breathing.'

'It's also a normal, everyday sort of term. It means I'm clearing my throat, or trying to get your attention, or just making a noise for the hell of it.'

'But what if Polly *is* having trouble breathing? Do you think she's too hot?'

Seconds later, Zoë's in what's now a typical pose, wandering the house with a beeping digital thermometer held out in front as though monitoring for radioactivity.

Wednesday, 7th March

Zoë's relief that Polly has taken so naturally to breastfeeding is almost tangible. As a doctor, she's met lots of mothers who've likened the process to stabbing their nipples with needles.

'Those who don't give up entirely persevere in pain,' she tells me, 'or express the milk instead – but that can double the time it takes. You've got to sterilize all the equipment, pump out every drop, and then feed the baby from a bottle. But as long as the baby's ultimately getting its mother's milk, it's getting all the antibodies, proteins and other goodness it needs.'

Aside from the extra time required to express, this suggests to me that breastfeeding concerns are based less on issues of health and more on the threat of guilt. If I've followed the reasoning correctly, it's this: if you can't breastfeed then you're a bad mother and you'll never properly bond with your baby and it'll be your fault when they grow up painting their initials on bus stops, taunting pensioners and torturing stray dogs.

With Polly proving herself so adept, Zoë decides to heed the practical advice of friends and experts and introduce our daughter to the bottle so she'll be used to it from the start. But with the change, the terror resurfaces.

'What if she *prefers* the bottle? What if she won't go back to the boob? And when am I meant to express anyway? If I pump it out *before* feeding, will there be enough left for Polly? And if I express afterwards, will my boobs recover in time for the next feed, or will I over-stimulate them and have too much?'

'What do your books say?'

'Some of them say express *during* the feed, but you've got to be an octopus to manage a hand pump at the same time as a baby. And how much do I express off anyway?'

Still undecided, we turn to the microwave sterilizer, itself a provider of ample opportunity for stress.

'These instructions say that, as long as we keep the lid on, everything will stay sterile for three hours. But what if I open it to take out just one bottle? Do I have to resterilize the other stuff before we can use it later?'

It's 11:30 p.m. when I give Polly her first bottle, laying her down on my lap, proud to be offering views marginally more stimulating than Zoë's armpit or a smothering bulk of boob. But Polly's eyes remain resolutely closed as, in a textbook 'dream' feed, she guzzles greedily through 3oz.

I'm finally in bed myself and drifting off when a text message comes through from a friend who *doesn't* have kids. 'Thinking of you and your family today,' it says. 'Can't believe it's been three years.'

Only then do I realize that, in my fuddled state, dislocated from the turnings of the real world, I've lost all track of the date: it's three years to the day that Dad died.

In the last few weeks, Nathan's got engaged, Mum's got a new home, Rob's had an offer accepted on a flat, and I've become a father. Platitude or not, life marches on – a fact for which I'm both resentful and grateful.

Thursday, 8th March – 7lb 13oz

In just 17 days, Polly's gained a quarter of her birth weight. Although I'm forbidden from using the word, there's no doubt the girl is growing podgier, so much so that often I don't know which chin to kiss. And she's lost a lot of that fragility, no longer fluttering in my hand like a captured bird but lolling like a Rubenesque beauty ornately decorated with necklaces and bracelets of spare skin.

As Polly's put on the weight, Zoë's lost it – she's being sucked thinner by the day, to the point that I think she's now skinnier than she was when she fell pregnant and has the perfect excuse for gorging on the mass of chocolate biscuits supplied by our still frequent visitors.

'Polly's going through a growth spurt,' Zoë tells them, a kind way of saying our baby's a greedy tubster. It's certainly an excuse I'll be remembering next time I reach for the biscuit tin, unless by then I've given in to my curiosity over that breastfeeding teacher's claims and am milking off my extra weight.

Friday, 9th March

Desperate to get mobile so she can show off our daughter, Zoë speaks to her car insurer about driving again and is told she needs her GP's approval. The danger is that an emergency stop could cause the uterus, not yet fully contracted, to rupture.

'Don't be ridiculous!' her GP says. 'The guidelines say four to six weeks after a caesarean. What sort of doctor are you?'

Zoë comes home furious with herself, her professional pride clearly dented. 'I *knew* it was four to six weeks!'

'So why did you think it would be any different for you?'

'I don't know,' she sulks. 'Because ... I don't know.'

I know what she was going to say. She was going to say, 'Because I'm a doctor.'

Somehow the extra pressure she feels to be good at mothering simply because she's a medic has blinded her to the realization that her body works like anyone else's.

Monday, 12th March – 3 weeks old

Polly's playing her favourite game: she latches on and off the breast, cooing in between to get Zoë's attention, then offering up an enormous smile before the game starts again.

'Apparently breastmilk changes flavour according to what I've eaten,' Zoë says. 'I like the idea that I'm giving Polly a little variety.'

As she notes down a change of breast in her little book, she sighs. 'Not having a gauge on the side of the breast to tell you how much your baby's fed is a real design flaw.' She looks down at our daughter. 'Who do you think she looks like?'

I shrug. This is a game played with depressing regularity by one and all, depressing because the answer is never 'her dad'. And while in other circumstances I might be grateful that my daughter has gained a fortunate start in life, I do find myself wondering if *anyone* in my family has bright red cheeks, a dribbling smile and podgy knees. I guess Polly has to have *had* hair before she can exhibit a receding hairline.

Wednesday, 14th March

Day and night blur around the edges as life rolls on in a relentless cycle of feeding, changing, winding and washing, with only the phone and the doorbell to link us to the pace of the outside world.

The deluge of presents so generously given come mostly in the form of parcels too big for our letterbox. When all we really want is sleep, we're woken daily by requests for signatures by an amused and infuriatingly fresh-faced postman.

We wade through the days feeling permanently like it's the evening after a big party: bone tired and fuzzy brained, counting on collapsing within hours to sleep the sleep of the dead. But of course we can't. Because as soon as you've fed, winded, changed and settled a baby, tidied up the strewn blankets and dirty nappies, put on a wash, had something to eat, showered and settled into bed with the alluring fantasy of eight solid hours, there's a squeak that becomes a moan that grows into a cry that develops into a wail, and the cycle starts all over again.

As I head upstairs after the late-night bottle feed to collapse in the loft for the third night running, I know it makes sense to have at least one parent well rested and capable of supporting the other through the day, but I feel guilty accepting that role – like a deserter sloping away from the front line under cover of darkness. But the alternative is to wake dutifully as Zoë answers Polly's cries, then to chase sleep around the pillow for the next half hour.

A recent survey suggests that new parents can lose up to 90 minutes of sleep each night, resulting in a total loss of two months' worth in the first year. Already, then, Polly owes us almost 36 hours of solid sleep. And it's the cumulative effect that's most devastating: after less than four weeks, my eyes are itching, the left one twitching. On several occasions my head has spun and I've found myself breaking out in a cold sweat, while what was just one grey-white tuft of forelock has sent out runners in all directions and, having encountered no resistance, is establishing an empire around my temples.

The lack of sleep makes me so incapable that I can almost understand why some new parents are willing to fork out as much as £200 per night for a maternity nurse. And it's no real surprise to read that '52% of dads sleep through their baby waking – *or at least pretend to*'.

Fortunately, unlike what the survey claims is nearly half of new parents, Zoë and I are not yet displaying signs of 'competitive sleep syndrome' by arguing over who's had the least. Because I know that, however exhausting it is for me, however much I may try to play my part in changing, washing and winding, it's the feeding that's time-consuming and literally draining – it's a challenge just to keep Zoë's weight constant. Yet she continues, unwavering, hauling herself from bed at all hours with no complaint, with only her natural determination always to worry about something blinding her to how well she's doing.

Thursday, 15th March

Zoë and I are chatting together in the nursery as Polly breastfeeds, guzzling as much as ever, and it's a while before we realize that our daughter has stopped breathing. She's red in the face and trying to cry but no sound's coming out. And then she starts turning blue.

Zoë freezes, horrified, her hand supporting Polly's head from behind so I can't reach to thump her on the back.

The world really does go into slow motion as, before our eyes, our daughter begins to suffocate. At last, Zoë wakes from her fear and slaps Polly between the shoulder blades, hard enough to prompt a long intake of breath and then a terrified howl that floods us both with relief.

Polly outsucked herself. And within seconds, as her little round face purpled like a bruise, we realized again how fragile she is, and how quickly her brief life could be snuffed out.

Friday, 16th March – 8lb 8oz

When it came to sleeping, I always thought of Dad as an expert. It wasn't unusual to find him dozing at his desk of an evening, or kneeling by the fire as he snored quietly in front of 'the box'. And he could be an exceptionally heavy sleeper – unless, of course, there was something on another channel that we wanted to watch, in which case he'd instinctively wake as we stalked the remote, spluttering adamantly, 'Oi! I'm watching that!'

At times it seems that Polly's inherited that same gift. She can be doing anything, anywhere (although her preferred locations are the buggy and car – when there's no risk of us being able to catch up); when sleep comes calling, she obeys instantly, as though a switch has been flicked. In conjunction with her supernatural ability to sense the instant our heads touch the pillow, the relative ease with which she can drop off seems downright unfair.

Or – worse – she'll take the best part of an hour to settle and then finally drift off, an enormous smile flickering across her face as though an invisible someone is whispering into her ear the greatest secret in the world. And I'm torn between finding it utterly endearing and, given how hard I've worked to get her there, totally infuriating that she's sharing her smile not with me but with a dreamy world where I can't follow.

In order to escape the worst of our daughter's gorilla-like grunts, the phantom umbilical cord is unravelled just enough to relocate the Moses basket to the nursery. But although the doors between us are left open, Zoë insists on using the monitor as well, with the result that, although she's further away, Polly's every noise is actually amplified. Only when she's woken us for the second time with a casual cough do my negotiations over the volume button become more insistent.

As Zoë jumps at every imaginary sound, I sink gratefully into the folds of our bed, wallowing in the silence.

The Second Month

Tuesday, 20th March – 4 weeks, 1 day old

Travelling with kids, someone once told me, is best done when they're still breastfeeding and sleeping through large parts of the day. That way, they said, you don't need to worry about their meals and you can shove them into a sling and take off. As long as you've a spare nappy and a couple of boobs, the world awaits.

Our journey to King's Cross with the mass of luggage apparently required for our brief trip to Scotland, from suitcase, rucksack and bags to car seat and baby herself, I feel conclusively contradicts such an optimistic suggestion.

As official porter, I'm slowly following my wife down the aisle of the train, efficiently blocking its use for anyone else, when Zoë, who has now found our booked seats, glares back at me. 'I told you to ask for a table.'

'I did.'

'Well, we haven't got one. I'm going to look for some free seats with a table.'

Dumping our things, I wait until she's found two seats back by the door, then laboriously relocate all our belongings.

'Actually,' says Zoë when we're finally settled, 'if I'm going to be feeding her, maybe those booked seats are a little more private.'

One might claim it was beneficial, then, to have accidentally left Polly behind in our original seats. When we return, she's silently rolling her eyes like an embarrassed teenager.

I look around. Two businesswomen across the aisle are chatting happily – until one of them glances across and recognizes the bundle on Zoë's lap as a baby. Her lips purse, she nudges her companion and, together, they stare ahead, their thoughts visible: 'Of all the seats ... *How* long to Doncaster?'

In fact, drugged up on milk, Polly sleeps peacefully all the way, and is admirably placid for her first introductions to the wider family.

Wednesday, 28th March – 5 weeks, 2 days old

Apparently, while babies can see in colour from birth, they can't distinguish between similar tones. High-contrast colours are best, like the book kindly given by our neighbours showing simple black-and-white faces labelled 'Mummy' and 'Daddy'. I suspect, however, that Polly's stimulation comes less from the pictures and more from Mummy and Daddy's highly competitive tendency to fight over which page it's open on.

Walking back through our front door after a few days away makes it clear what colour our life has become: the whole building is pink. It's as though a glutinous wall of crimson lava has passed through our home, leaving its pale residue to drip from every surface, our daughter included. With that in mind, I set out for Mothercare before it closes and deliberately – almost defiantly – buy Polly a set of blue babygrows.

With two brothers, I grew up in a house full of tattered *Commando* comics, racing cars and rugby balls. No doubt, with her two brothers, Zoë experienced the same. Which is why she's now aiming to cram two generations of girliness into one. I picture the scene, five years from now, our house still blushing from floor to ceiling as lace-covered dolls are thrown down in tutu-clad tantrums, watched over by posters of boy bands, ponies and sickly sweet kittens. It's a million miles from anything I ever knew, and I fear the unknown.

Sunday, 1st April

People and books say a baby is disruptive – they just don't say *how* disruptive. They mention the extra stuff needed to care for them; they just don't mention *how* much extra stuff. And, above all, they say it's tiring. They just don't say *how* tiring. Instead, they say it casually and without impact, in the same way they might mention that their dog's got a bout of halitosis – a little unpleasant while it lasts, perhaps, but essentially to be expected.

Yet merely hearing the problem reiterated is in no way an introduction to the reality. Feed that dog garlic and coffee, strap it to your chest and shut yourself in an airtight room and you might be getting closer.

'It's like being on call again,' says Zoë, 'when any second my bleep could signal a life-threatening situation. It left me permanently edgy and unable to settle. But at least back then I could hand the bleep to someone else at the end of the day. In all those years of 36-hour shifts, I've never been so tired as I am now.'

My own need for sleep blankets everything, stifling all energy, making a trial of the simplest of tasks, and wearing my patience paper thin. Just coming upstairs to work is a challenge, like wading through treacle. Everything requires twice as much strength and gumption, from washing the ever-constant pile of posset-soaked muslins to filling the fridge.

And this fog of fatigue breeds an army of morbid imaginings. When I do finally sleep, I dream I'm by the roadside, powerless, as Polly is run over by a car. The scene is punctured by a crying baby and then I'm in hospital, in a bed beside a bundled daughter that squeaks and mews, and the rest of the ward are telling me to shut up because they're trying to sleep. And, as I wake in tears, my lingering rage and despair make me realize the depth to which I've already identified with this little girl. Above and beyond an instinctive desire to care for something so helpless, in just a few weeks our lives have entwined ever closer.

I sneak next door, careful not to wake my wife or daughter, and peer through the low light first at Polly, and then at all her belongings, both functional and frivolous, and I imagine them as the debris of a life stolen from us. And I marvel at how such a small thing can demand so much stuff, can carve out such an intrinsic role and make such an impact on our lives.

Thursday, 5th April – 6 weeks, 3 days old, 10lb

In total contrast to her usual unquenchable appetite, Polly starts pulling off the breast in tears and spewing copiously down a selection of bibs as she wriggles desperately, her back arched and face red, to escape every offered nipple.

Obviously, it's not much fun realizing your baby isn't retaining any food. And naturally, as both a concerned mother and an individual with an uncanny ability to ferret out even the slightest cause for concern, Zoë is fretting and getting nowhere.

'Am I overfeeding her?' she asks, as though I have the answer. 'Maybe the possetting is a form of self-regulation?'

'I thought it was impossible to overfeed a baby.'

'Well, maybe my milk flow's too fast, then?'

'Surely your breasts are designed to feed babies, not choke them?'

We've already learnt not to wind Polly over the shoulder, but now we go out of our way to keep her upright during and after feeds. We even wipe her bum by turning her sideways rather than pressuring her stomach by bending her at the waist, but still the fountains of yacked milk continue skyward.

'I'm not enjoying this at all,' Zoë admits, staring down at our daughter with a frown of worry. 'I don't know what's wrong with her.'

Friday, 6th April – Good Friday

The weekly baby clinics are stressful in themselves, as Zoë struggles to find a health visitor who doesn't know she's a GP so she can ask questions without fear of reproach. But this afternoon, when

Polly's weigh-in reveals a gain of only 3oz, Zoë's common sense – already adrift in a sea of worry – is almost capsized by the tempest of her terror. By the time she gets home her practical doctor's brain has all but leapt overboard and faces a tidal wave of irrational babbling. Fortunately, just as it threatens to submerge for ever, it makes one last effort and catches hold of the flotsam of a firm diagnosis: reflux.

'The little ring of muscle that's supposed to close off the oesophagus between feeds isn't yet fully developed,' she explains, now in full doctor mode with a plan of action before her. 'So any feed is free to shoot straight back up, bringing the stomach acid with it.'

It's hardly a pleasant sensation for an adult, let alone a sensitive little baby, and obviously an experience capable of causing extreme discomfort and tears in the baby and then, soon after, in its mother.

'We need Gaviscon,' she says. 'It thickens the feed, so it's less likely to be regurgitated.'

Luckily the treatment is available over the counter so Zoë doesn't face the ethical dilemma of writing a private prescription for her own daughter, or the worry of waiting over the Easter weekend.

'Right,' she says, after a trip to the chemist. 'Will you give it to her?'

Accepting my role as bad cop to her big-breasted good cop, I look at the packet. A 10lb baby, it says, should take two sachets, each diluted in 15ml of sterilized water. That's a total of 30ml (1.5oz) of fluid which, for a baby's stomach with space for only a few ounces per feed, leaves a lot less room for milk, risking a lot less sleep for us all.

'We'll just give her one sachet first,' decides Zoë. 'It says here we're to give it *after* the feed, but let's try now – she's always asleep afterwards.'

Trusting to the instructions, I try to give it from a bottle, but Polly twists and kicks her little legs, spitting it out. I try a spoon but she pushes it away and then, when I persevere, the liquid runs straight into her lungs, causing her to choke through her tears.

Meanwhile Zoë's hiding in the next room, hands over her ears and almost in tears herself. Her worry that Polly will come to associate the trauma with normal feeds is distracted only by the worry that, by the time we're done, the sterilized water we're using to mix up the medicine might no longer be sterile.

Finally we hit upon a successful strategy, tearing Polly off the breast mid-feed and using a sterilized syringe to squirt small, easily swallowed amounts of a more concentrated mix into the corner of her mouth. By staggering it through the feed, it also helps wake Polly each time to take a little more milk.

And it seems to make a difference – she stops vomiting almost immediately, and gives every sign of enjoying her feeds once more. But it'll take proof positive of continued weight gain before Zoë will breathe freely again.

Saturday, 7th April

Zoë's folks arrive for lunch laden with presents, including some enormous, heart-shaped pink glasses for Polly. It doesn't take us long to discover the pleasures of dressing up a baby for cheap laughs.

Late afternoon, Polly begins to cry without stop, desperately trying to poo. The Gaviscon has made her constipated.

'But it says here that it's a laxative,' reads an exasperated Zoë from the packet.

By nightfall, Polly's found apparent relief despite passing only a few pellets. But in a bid to trade off the posset prevention for poo, we reduce the Gaviscon dose.

Sunday, 8th April – Easter Sunday

As though the constipation weren't enough, Polly's scalp begins to flake. Rather than be horrified, Zoë seems almost grateful to have something else to focus on.

'I tell my patients to rub in a little olive oil,' she says. 'If we leave it overnight, we should be able to scrape away the flakes with a brush tomorrow morning.'

Within minutes, Polly's sporting a tiny, greasy quiff and her milky baby smell is drowned beneath the stench of olives. Yet despite her sluggish guts and singular fragrance she continues unperturbed, feeding as ever with single-minded ferocity, slurping and belching like a banqueting boar, then smiling serenely on the knee like a post-feed Buddha, a dribble of milk drying on her chin.

Monday, 9th April – 7 weeks old

I've got a cold. What started as just a tickle in the throat has grown into a full-blown steamroller. And ever conscious that I don't get sick pay, I've not given myself any slack and have driven an already exhausted body into the ground.

In the chemist for some flu medicine, I spot a bottle of cradle cap shampoo called Dentinox. Since large chunks of skin are still lifting from the top of Polly's head and I'm sick of the stink of olives, I grab it. I think about getting some baby laxative as well, but since it's Zoë who's suffering from Polly's constipation far more than our daughter, I head home without.

Breathing infection, I'm banished to the top room, giving me the most guilt-free night since Polly arrived, because this time it's for *their* good rather than mine. And I'm forbidden from cuddling my daughter – probably just as well because, having still not shat, she'd probably explode.

I'm also forbidden from cuddling my wife – a cruel quarantine given how magnificent her cleavage has become. Yet even were I allowed, when would we ever find the time or energy to exploit it?

Tuesday, 10th April

Mothers are expected to be protective of their young, of course. It's natural. They're programmed to look out for their children and do all they can to save them from harm. So close is the bond that they actually have a physiological reaction to the sound of their baby's cries, making some form of response almost irresistible.

This intimate connection I understand. I admire it. But what I'm wondering is how exactly it differs in nature to the way I feel for my daughter. Does it mean I love Polly any the less simply because I don't leak into my t-shirt the moment she starts to scream? Or because, as long as Polly herself seems happy, I don't spend every spare minute waiting for her to poo?

I don't mean to belittle the difficulty of having to listen to one's baby crying as they strain their guts, or watch as they regurgitate their feed, obviously in pain. I would, though, like to be able to belittle the reaction to such a situation. After all, ours is not the first baby ever to face these problems.

So what is the nature of the difference in our connection with Polly that allows us to react so differently? And why does it seem that those different reactions are expected? Fathers, it seems, are supposed to remain stoical and hard headed in the face of their baby's pain, while a mother is forgiven for crumbling or even deserting her post. But why should the father be any better at facing his child's grief? Or more suited to imposing the necessary treatment?

Whatever the reason, it does seem to be the case that they can. I do feel I can step back a little to observe from a slightly more objective perspective, and act accordingly. I can hear Polly crying furiously upstairs and still finish my chicken and chips without immediately running off to comfort her. I don't feel the need to constantly count the minutes since her last shit, or pause the DVD when the baby monitor's sound meter hits the red – I simply turn it down and give her a few minutes to see if she'll settle herself. Does this make me a worse parent? Is it proof that I do, in fact, love our baby less?

Wednesday, 11th April

'Five days without a proper poo!'

As Zoë's wail rings through the house, I'm hoping the neighbours realize who she's talking about.

'I know that two weeks without a poo's not abnormal,' she says, 'but *still*! Five days and only a few pellets!'

Seeing an opportunity to blame herself, Zoë grabs it with both hands. 'Maybe I was too quick in prescribing Gaviscon,' she says. 'Maybe it wasn't proper reflux. But the volume of posset, and the way she was pulling off the breast...'

Eventually, with Polly peacefully at rest, Zoë agrees to try to get some sleep herself. But our daughter soon has other ideas, and wakes within half an hour, demanding attention. Only by carrying her around from room to room can I calm her, a solution that doesn't lend itself to much work. And then I remember the dummy lying unused in the kitchen, so far studiously avoided by Zoë.

Five minutes later, Polly lies back in her seat, slowly dropping off as she sucks silently on a big plastic nipple, and I'm wondering what anyone could ever have against them.

A few hours later, I'm walking back from recording a voice-over in town when I pass a kid who must be at least five years old, leaning against a shop window like he owns the world – in his mouth a red-tipped dummy.

Thursday, 12th April

Polly lies on her changing mat, her parents staring down at her as she grunts and strains.

Buoyed by the fact that she seems ready to produce anything at all, Zoë is cajoling and shouting encouragement as if her horse is leading the last lengths of the Grand National. And, through her tears, Polly finally comes up with the goods. It's like fudge ice cream from a Mr Whippy dispenser delighted to be back in action.

'Oh my God!' cries Zoë, delighted. 'Look at that! Look at that! Good girl, Polly! That must feel so good! *Good* girl, Polly!'

But as her daughter continues to leak onto the mat, Zoë now spots another opportunity to worry: Polly's plentiful performance could compromise her later when the time comes for weighing at the baby clinic. Not even Zoë's usual trick of feeding her just beforehand could compensate for the contents of our nursery floor.

As I wave them out the door, I try to sound encouraging. 'Whatever the result, she's still got plenty of chub in reserve.'

Half an hour later, they're back, and Zoë is beaming. Despite the possetting and faecal explosions, Polly has put on 10oz and is continuing exactly as before: a healthy, beautiful, noisy, well-cared-for little baby.

The biggest consequence of Polly's recovery is Zoë's happiness. The confirmation of both podge and poo in one day makes her smile as though Take That have called to say they're popping round for dinner.

Friday, 13th April

Unlucky for some. A helicopter circling endlessly overhead warns us something's up, then Zoë and Polly are out for a walk when they're almost run down by a busload of police. There's been an armed robbery at the local bank. Meanwhile the news is full of the six teenagers stabbed here in London in the last two weeks alone.

I feel strangely nostalgic for a time I never knew: our grandparents' day, when the world seemed simpler, less frantic. Certainly all the properly good things in life were around then, and more noticeable for the lack of clutter.

And I feel more and more that this city is far from representative of the world in which I'd hoped to raise my children.

Monday, 16th April – 8 weeks old

Nathan comes to stay for a few nights and hands over an old box of Dad's letters written to his mother 20 years ago. I'm alone on the sofa when I read through them for the first time, long pages detailing everyday life at Ardburdan: the trees that have fallen, the local illnesses and deaths, his trips with Mum to visit us at boarding school and our rugby match results. Reading the banality of a life I failed to appreciate fully at the time, I feel once again close to the place and to him, as if it's one of those late-night fireside chats. I can hear him in his words and picture him in my mind, and I miss him.

The letters are in random order, but it's the very last one in the whole box that stands out. In it, he notes his exhaustion as he struggles to harvest the annual Christmas tree crop while caring for Mum, who's fallen ill. And then, at that critical point when he's rushing to get the cut trees to the shops in time, I fall ill as well, in a school at the other end of the country. After half a day in the fields, he's forced to drop everything to drive a round trip of a thousand miles to bring me home.

'After all,' he writes, 'Andrew means more to me than some Christmas trees.'

The ludicrousness of the comparison, so typically understated, makes me weep, and rouses in me a determination to say to Polly what Dad so clearly felt but found so hard to put into words.

The Third Month

Thursday, 19th April

'For the purpose of this,' says Zoë as we step into our local GP's surgery, 'I'm not a doctor, OK? I'm just a parent.'

It's time for Polly's eight-week immunizations and, in preparation for the possible feverish side-effect of a cocktail of vaccine, Zoë's had Polly on a preventative course of Calpol since early morning.

After a brief wait, we're ushered into the nurse's room; Zoë has insistently handed Polly over to me and, having forgotten to bring any teddies of our own, is trailing instead an enormous, bedraggled pink elephant from the reception toy box.

'It's to distract her afterwards,' says Zoë, as I take up the single seat by the desk.

With a welcoming smile, the nurse begins questioning me to confirm Polly's identity and age. From somewhere near the door, Zoë answers.

The nurse asks me about Polly's general health; Zoë answers.

The nurse asks about allergies and family history; Zoë answers.

The nurse asks me to verify the date on the vaccine; Zoë steps forward, squints at the label, then approves it with a nod.

The nurse shows me how to hold Polly, pinning her arms across my chest and her head against my front; Zoë checks I'm doing it correctly then scuttles back out of Polly's eye line. 'I don't want her to associate me with the pain,' she explains, as though it's perfectly reasonable that the words 'Daddy' and 'evil' should forever be entwined in our daughter's mind.

'You wouldn't think she's a GP, would you?' I say in cheerful retribution, and immediately feel a finger stabbing me in the back.

'It's just that ... But ... I don't do the immunizations,' flusters Zoë. 'The nurses do that, so ... I just don't want to have to see her in pain.'

162

'Don't worry!' smiles the nurse. 'I remember how I was with my own kids.'

But Zoë only takes such sensitivity as further permission to fret and, at the first sight of the needles, she turns away to cower by the side of the bed.

With the first quick jab, Polly twitches in surprise, then her little mouth curls at the corners as she sucks in a lungful of air and begins to bawl. Above the cries, I can hear Zoë hyperventilating behind me as the second jab is given, immediately after which she leaps forward and scoops our daughter from my arms.

Instantly, Polly stops crying, distracted as much by the look of terror on her mother's face as by the ragged bulk of dangerously flailing pink elephant being thrust in her direction.

Friday, 20th April

It's no wonder we all grow up so confused – already Polly has started along a path of contradictory expectations. We wake her when sleeping and want her to sleep when she's awake. We laugh uproariously at her farts and belches but will soon be scowling in disgust. We act as though her poo is the most interesting thing in the world, though it won't be long before we'll never want anything to do with it again.

In a year or so we'll demand that she starts talking, just before we start telling her to be quiet. We want her to smile and coo at every face into which she's proudly thrust, but the minute she does so uncoerced we'll be telling her not to speak to strangers. We revel in every ounce she gains, though soon she'll be pressured from all sides to conform to a particular shape of underweight beauty.

And the strain of abiding by such conflicting wishes isn't confined to the children. Parenthood is beginning to look like a lifetime of opposing emotions that threaten to tear holes in places we didn't even know we had. Zoë and I swing from a slow, deep-set sense of comfort to total paranoia. We want to settle Polly when she cries, but know she should be left to settle herself. We want to show her a world that offers nothing but happiness, yet not be utterly bewildered when that world turns nasty. We want her to think others will be as considerate, warm and friendly as we want her to be, but not have her foundations rocked when others treat her differently. We want so much for her without dictating what she'll want for herself.

Sunday, 22nd April

Zoë goes to the shops, leaving me to keep an eye on Polly while I work in the garden. Pretty soon I track down the dummy, and all it takes is for me to replace it each time she makes a noise. Parenting suddenly seems easy, and I can't understand why a dummy can be such a divisive instrument – it turns a bellowing, unsettled, grouchy little noisebag into a sweetly placid cherub.

But when the ferocity of her sucking causes the dummy to pop out and disappear between her arse and her seat, I begin to wonder at what point it needs to be sterilized again. When it's caught amongst her chins, still tantalizingly out of her reach? When it falls briefly to the floor? Or when it rolls through the doorway onto the patio? And am I meant to just bung it under boiling water every time? Or pop it in the microwave for another four minutes?

I decide to try to bypass the problem by demonstrating the delights of thumbsucking instead. 'Polly,' I say, grabbing her hand. 'This is what it should feel like.'

But sucking her tiny thumb only gains me a grin – when I try to get her to copy me, she obstinately refuses to separate the thumb from her fist, trying instead to cram the whole thing into her mouth. The result is a brief and frustrating smooch of her knuckle, which she soon rejects in favour of the dummy again.

'I'm worried that will put her off her food,' says Zoë on her return. 'And I don't want her using it when other people are around.'

'Why not?'

'It just looks terrible.'

'You think they'd rather hear her screaming?'

'If we're going to use it, Gina says we shouldn't let Polly fall asleep with it, otherwise she'll be unable to settle without it, and wake up when it falls out.'

I've heard the phrase 'Gina says' so many times now, I may as well be raising Polly with her. Who'd have thought there'd be so many rules? I guess it's like anything else – the more you learn, the more you realize how much more there is to learn. The instruction to 'Use a dummy to settle your child' is as over-simplistic as the claim that 'Cricket's about hitting a ball with a bat.'

Monday, 23rd April – 9 weeks old

Preparing to give Polly her late-night bottle, I suggest trying a faster-flowing teat – given that she's usually too sluggish to get in more than 2 or 3oz and Zoë's expressed over 6oz, it seems a good idea to maximize on Polly's efforts.

It's a vain hope that a bigger feed will give us all a better night, but I'm up for trying anything, even squirting an extra half-ounce into her when she refuses to take more from the bottle, force-feeding her like a goose. It's an excess of zeal aroused by Zoë's nightly question as I finally crawl into bed afterwards: 'How much did she take?' An answer of anything less than 4oz gets a moan of apprehension for the night ahead.

So, with the faster teat attached, I begin the feed. And six minutes later I'm standing, amazed, in the doorway of our bedroom.

'She scoffed the lot!'

Zoë's face appears from beneath the duvet. 'All of it?'

'Six and a half ounces. In six minutes!' I'm grinning, so proud of myself for having suggested the faster teat. 'It disappeared from the bottle like a plug had been pulled! Maybe she's been ready for this for ages. Maybe she'll start sleeping through the night now!'

I leave Zoë to sleep and go back to the nursery to change Polly, a slow and careful process involving trying not to wake her or prompt a cascade of posset all over her and her sleeping bag. But before I've even undressed her, she starts crying. And won't stop.

When I pick her up again, I realize why: she's sodden. Despite my looking for it and neither seeing nor hearing it, Polly seems to have yacked everywhere, as if the entire feed has come back up to soak through to her vest.

Calling for help, I begin to change her clothes while Zoë dashes off to raid her enormous supply of frozen breastmilk for the first time; after all, Polly's lost most of her feed and Zoë's breasts are now empty.

Finally changed, Polly stops crying. She's now wide awake, and probably a lot happier than the neighbours. Zoë arrives with more milk and only when I start to feed Polly again does it become clear what's really happened.

She hasn't possetted at all – she hasn't had the chance. Because I haven't pushed the new teat firmly into its surround, over 6oz of breastmilk have spilt all over her.

Tuesday, 24th April

A meeting at the house of our local Lollipop representative, a group dedicated to giving impartial advice on washable nappies.

I'm so exhausted that I begin to fall asleep as soon as I've sat down. That we're there largely at my instigation only consoles me that I've done my part, and thankfully Zoë's far more on the ball.

Half an hour later, impressed at the wide range of modern

options, we leave having ordered the full pack, from liners and nappies of varying sizes to inserts and covers. Costing around £300, they should still be cheaper than disposables – all the more so if we can reuse them with a second – and, given that we're on a green electricity tariff, use ecological detergent and are lucky enough to be able to hang-dry them, there's no doubt they're better for the planet.

'Sure, that's important,' says Zoë on the way home. 'But most importantly, they just seem so much better for Polly.'

Saturday, 28th April

A friend's stag weekend gives me my first time away since Polly came home from hospital, and that means Zoë's first time holding the baby alone, something that everyone else seems to know she's more than capable of, even if she doesn't realize it herself.

'You know,' she says as I'm packing my bags, 'apparently wives with husbands who work from home are more prone to postnatal depression, because they've always got someone around to lend a hand.' Somehow, she makes it sound like a threat.

'Then this'll be a good opportunity for you to prove you don't need me, won't it?'

A few hours later, I'm sitting in a pub in Brighton. Out of a dozen, I'm the youngest one here, and the only one with a wife, let alone a child. That I have a child is a fact no one doubts as I face a worrying inability to talk about anything else. I've become a cliché, a baby bore detailing every moment of her growth, increment by increment and excrement by excrement.

Sunday, 29th April

Zoë and I measure out our lives in fluid ounces of breastmilk and regimented sleep, in bathtimes and nappy bins filled to the brim, in grabbed dinners serenaded by the churning and spinning of bibs and babygrows in the wash. So away from all of that, I find myself settling back into the pace I knew before, slipping back so naturally that at times I forget it's not just one I've left behind, but two.

Then I catch sight of another baby, or a rising thought of Zoë reminds me, and instantly I think of my daughter's smile, I pull out the photo of my family, and my stomach twists with the excitement of the memory and in anticipation of my return.

Since my only exercise these days is in rushing upstairs to grab every minute of work, I'm out of breath by the time I've run down the street and straight up to Polly's room to catch her before her bedtime. Maybe it's the timing – she's just had a feed – but my arrival is rewarded with an enormous smile of recognition, a beam that tells me all is right with the world.

Not long after, Zoë and I have just sat down to dinner when Polly begins to cry. Instead of moaning that she's still wide awake, I find myself putting aside my spaghetti and running upstairs to comfort her, grinning proudly all the way.

My weekend away has broken the baby bubble. It's rubbed away the tarnish of the sleep-starved nights and the relentless routine and granted a refreshed perspective, a more generalized view that informs the specific. In a way I could never have foreseen, I realize that every moment contains not only its own present, but also the excitement of future promise. Smile or cry, my daughter's every second is heavy with potential for our years ahead as a family. And I can't wait.

Monday, 30th April – 10 weeks old

One of those many activities casually squandered in my former life but now appreciated as a luxury is reading. Now, holding every spare minute so precious, I choose my reading material with greater care.

Beside my bed now is a book in which the author makes the point that we're all, each and every one of us, the products of awesome success. Not only have we individually developed against all the odds into capable human beings, but our parents did as well, and their parents, and theirs. If survival is the name of the game, then we're all descended from a long line of successful parents. As qualities that might endanger offspring are naturally sieved out by evolution, our DNA represents the ultimate parental distillate of millennia.

And now I've passed it on to the next generation. In purely evolutionary terms, as long as Zoë and I can keep Polly fed and watered, I am a success – my role on earth is fulfilled. I've peaked already and I'm not yet 30. I should take early retirement, be put out to pasture. I'm an over-achiever.

Tuesday, 1st May – our second wedding anniversary

Our first night out since Polly's arrival is more perfunctory than romantic, and everything I'd have imagined: the frantic last-minute instructions to all three grandparent babysitters as she attempts to cover every aspect of everything that could possibly go wrong, the repeated reminders that she'll have her phone (even if mobiles are banned from the restaurant), the self-consciousness that comes from finding oneself back in adult society wearing clothes that aren't stained in baby yack, the weary chat and regular exchange of yawns across the table exacerbated by her first glass of wine in months, the nervous examination of the watch between courses wondering if we'll make it back in time for the 10.30 p.m. feed, the glances to check for missed calls and the jumping in the seat at imagined vibrations from the phone that's at last been negotiated into 'silent' mode and, finally, having grown accustomed to eating all meals as though sitting astride a ticking time bomb, the rapid scoffing of the *hautest* of *cuisines* with the sort of casual insensitivity for price more usually exhibited by Russian oligarchs.

Thursday 3rd May – my thirtieth birthday

Today I crawl from my twenties to my thirties. Already I've been a father for two and a half months, and still I can't get my head round it. The title of 'parent' seems too laden with responsibility, too alien from the life I knew before Polly arrived for me to accept it immediately or instinctively just because there's now a baby in the house.

We push through the days without the time – or often the energy – to consider our new roles, until now and again a jolt of realization forces me to recognize it. It's like catching sight of myself in a new school uniform after a long summer of rolling around in t-shirts and tracksuits – I can't help wondering if I shouldn't now be acting differently and filling my time with weightier matters.

Surely I should be casting off the frivolities of youth? Scorning the Playstation for the *Financial Times*, twiddling the dial from pop to politics and nodding sagely to the Radio 4 commentary, knowledgeably comparing 4x4s with MPVs, and declining that bottled beer because, after all, it's not yet six o'clock, at which point I'll sip it respectably from a glass? Zoë and I are responsible for the existence and future well-being of an entirely new human being. Given the enormous implications, it's strange – and oddly reassuring – how easy it can be to forget and continue as before.

Until I find myself saying 'my daughter'. I was only just getting used to using phrases like 'my wife' without chuckling at the inferred maturity of it all. It still comes as a shock to see Zoë signing documents with my surname instead of hers. And yet now we've celebrated our second wedding anniversary. Busily dealing with the minutes, I never noticed the passing of the hours, and now I look up at the clock to find myself a married, 30-year-old father.

So is this a precocious mid-life crisis, the point where I start pining for a sports car or smuggling hair dye into the bathroom? No – it's not a yearning for some ill-defined goal or nostalgia for younger days, just the realization that, in another few years, I'll have travelled halfway along my expected path. It's recognition of where I am, not a moan that I don't want to be here.

But such a barrage of benchmarks – birthday, anniversary and parenthood – is enough to make me take stock and consider the answers to a few questions. What have I achieved with my time so far? Am I heading in the right direction? And am I the person I always wanted to be?

Now that my life with Zoë is no longer just about us, there are additional thoughts as well. Will I be giving my child the life I want for her? Is there anything I can do to better this world for her? And how can I be more deserving of what I have?

Expecting a calm evening befitting my newly mature status, I walk into the kitchen to find my whole family gathered round the table, come down from Scotland to surprise me and take me out for a birthday dinner. After much discussion, we opt to take Polly with us – her first night out.

'What do we do if she won't stop crying?' wonders Zoë, fearing the worst. 'And will she sleep properly through the night if we upset her routine now?'

It's the fear that, by not taking her with us, we might never again be able to socialize in the evening without a babysitter that convinces her.

Fortunately Polly behaves perfectly, dozing for most of the meal and only waking towards the end to smile serenely at the waiter as though wondering what time he clocks off.

Monday, 7th May – 11 weeks old

When Zoë points out that Polly's nearing the three-month peak danger point for cot death, I track down and read out the supposedly reassuring statistic in our parenting manual. 'If you had a baby every year for five hundred years, only one of them might die of cot death.'

'But that only confirms there's a risk!'

It's true – it's the sort of claim that relies on a level of rationality difficult to achieve when it comes to your own kid. And cot death is such an insidious scare, a little reminder that, in our sanitized civilization of progress and medicine, space flight and nuclear power, babies can still die young without any real explanation.

There's suddenly so much more to fear from life. I feel more and more that every minute and every action, whether it's acknowledged with Polly's smile or not, is an investment of emotion. As the attachment grows and grows, the more we give, the more we stand to lose. And such a loss would tear us apart more than anything I can imagine. I wonder if anything would survive what it would do to me.

Tuesday, 8th May

Polly wakes with a sodden nappy. Even with an insert to soak up the excess, the washables don't seem up to the task of keeping her dry overnight.

'Let's compromise,' says Zoë. 'We'll use washables during the day, then stick with the disposables at night. That way we're only using one disposable nappy a day.'

In the afternoon, her NCT girlfriends come round for tea and chat about nurseries and schools. By the time they leave, Zoë is thoroughly spooked and spends what little of the evening Polly has left her sitting on the computer, researching.

Here we are, still getting to grips with the soggy nappies and lack of sleep, and we're already having to think about schools. It's insane.

Thursday, 10th May

'Have you booked the car park?' asks Zoë.

'Yes.'

'And you're sure we'll arrive in time to heat the milk for her bedtime feed?'

'Yes.'

'Did you reserve plane seats on the aisle? We might need to walk her around if she's fractious.'

'Yes.'

'And did you check our baggage allowance? The pushchair's not included, right?'

'Right.'

'Did you order a car seat from the hire company?'

'Yes.'

'And a cot for the hotel room?'

'Yes.'

'I've got her swimsuit and a sun shader for the pram. Oh, did you confirm the villa has a washing machine? If she's still possetting, we'll definitely have to wash her vests and bibs.'

'Yes.'

'And did you ask them if there's somewhere nearby we can buy nappies?'

'There's a *supermarché* a couple of minutes away.'

'OK. Um...' she walks in a small circle around Polly's room, wondering what she's forgotten, and I know already that we're going to need a holiday after this holiday.

I also know now why we've worked so hard to establish a routine – it's for us, not for Polly. It's so we feel we're in control and know what needs to be done and when. And that's why the total disruption threatened by our week away terrifies Zoë so much.

Friday, 11th May – Polly's first trip abroad

When Rob mentioned the other week that he'd be happy any time to take Polly for a walk in the park because it's a great way to meet girls, I wasn't convinced. Naively, I imagined that the presence of a child would only scream unavailability.

Now, as we bundle Polly from car to bus to plane to bus and back again, Rob's claim is only confirmed: a baby seems to endow whoever accompanies it with an air of accessibility that no amount of committed scowling can puncture, effortlessly inviting advances from one and all. A sign around my neck shouting 'Ask me her age!' couldn't have prompted more inquiries. And at every response the women cluck and twitter before talking about their own children, while the older men just nod knowingly with a sympathetic weariness before recounting the grief of their daughter's teenage years.

But as we walk through the airport, it becomes clear that there's one section of the population visibly repelled by Polly: young men. Spotting her a mile off with a practised sensitivity I once knew well, they act quickly to herd their girlfriends or wives in the opposite direction.

Yet Polly loves all the attention. Those who get her early in the day are rewarded with the sweetest of smiles and the grabbing of her hands across her chest as though to stop herself exploding from the merriment. As the journey wears on, though, her response wanes to a glassy stare and a tight pursing of the lips around a generous bouquet of bubbles – still infinitely more tolerant than I'd be if strangers were reaching from all sides, uninvited, to stroke my legs and rub my cheeks. By the time we arrive at the departure gate and the BA stewardesses ask Polly's name and chorus at my now automatic reply, I can't help rolling my eyes in anguish.

But Polly does give us the ability to skip queues. Shoving her pram down the luggage shoot with a brief prayer, we grab a complimentary newspaper and board the plane.

Hard though it is normally to read a newspaper on a plane, it soon becomes clear that it's near impossible with a wriggling baby on my lap. Especially when I'm juggling a glass of water and a sandwich.

Seeing my struggle, Zoë wolfs down her own lunch then offers to take Polly off me. In an effort to free my hands for passing her over, I foolishly opt to use my mouth to hold the water glass, gripping its plastic edge with my teeth.

With a chicken and ham sandwich on your lap giving you the come-on, it's easy to be blinkered to your own stupidity. Needless to say, my eyes are opened a moment later when the full glass falls, emptying its contents all over me. Having been airlifted out of the danger zone only seconds before, Polly looks on smugly, smiling as if to suggest I should give those nappies a go myself.

For the next 40 minutes, I sit in a puddle of icy water, cradling the torn and soggy remains of my sandwich, until our landing in Nice and an embarrassed waddle down the aisle allows my grateful escape into warmer air.

There we're delighted to discover that most of the pram has arrived with us. Somewhere, unknown to anyone, circling the globe in the bowels of a BA airbus, is a piece of Polly's pram – the button on the side that should allow me to extend the arms so I don't look like an arthritic question mark as I push it down the street.

Zoë's plan to keep Polly on British time works a treat – we're in our hotel room in plenty of time for her feed, then back out for a feed of our own, throughout which Polly ridicules our own worry over the disruption to her routine with nothing but a smiling and totally calm curiosity.

Saturday, 12th May

The Moro reflex: a baby's instinctive response to an unexpected loud noise or the sense of falling, exhibited by a startled expression, the spreading and unspreading of arms and, sometimes, tears. It's used by doctors to evaluate the integration of a baby's central nervous system and, in Polly – where the reaction is anything but tearful – by fathers in search of a cheap laugh.

Every time I blow on her face, she lets out a sudden gasp, her arms shoot up beside her head as though she's surrendering, her eyes close dreamily and her mouth widens in a tight smile. She seems to love it as much as I do.

Having bust a gut blowing up her inflatable pool seat, I'm determined to get her swimming. As I lower her carefully into the pool, she shoots me a stabbing look of betrayal but then, as I hold her tight against me, slowly calms.

Beginning to play with her, I have a go at instigating the Moro reflex, not by blowing in her face but – as Zoë does with babies in the surgery – by pretending to drop her. To be fair, I assume Zoë gives the babies' mothers more warning.

Seeing her daughter apparently about to be dunked underwater, Zoë screams and slaps me full strength across the back.

'Pick her up!' she screeches, so loudly that Polly inhales a heaving gasp, stretches her little arms wide and then, instead of grinning as usual, begins to destroy the siesta with a loud bawl.

Ten minutes later, by which time I've a hand-shaped burn across my shoulder, Polly has at last settled again, so much so that she's fallen asleep. Not quite the family album memory I'd been hoping for.

The wedding we've come to attend is in the afternoon in a neighbouring hilltop village. Polly looks sickly sweet in a bright pink dress for all of five minutes before the heat gets to her, so she witnesses the exchanged vows of eternal love stripped to her nappy, slurping greedily on a dummy. Perhaps it's the heat rather than the champagne that makes her sleep cheerfully through the reception, dinner and speeches without so much as a mew. Her behaviour is noted and, as though Zoë and I have some kind of influence over it, earns us many compliments. Someone, no doubt a victim of the surplus of alcohol, even goes so far as to congratulate Zoë for being 'relaxed'.

Aware that, unlike the rest of the dance floor, we'll be woken a few hours later by a baby, Zoë and I show restraint when it comes to the drinking and follow the pram off to our room around midnight.

Sunday, 13th May

When Polly greets us and the day ahead with such a welcoming grin, it's difficult to begrudge her the perceived restrictions on the night before – 'perceived' because, if you wouldn't want to be anything other than shackled, it can't really count as a restraint, can it? In exchange for dancing the night away or emptying the cellars, it's clear that we're getting something far more valuable. Plus, there's nothing like getting to the breakfast buffet first.

Another advantage is that, when I go looking for the bride's parents to thank them with a bottle of whisky, I'm not suffering from the traditional post-celebration hangover. So there's really no excuse for standing by their breakfast table and instinctively jiggling the bottle in my arms to keep it quiet, caressing it as though it's the most valuable thing in my life.

We drive on to our 'holiday village' in the hills above Cannes, where we're to share a villa with Al and Lorna for the week. Five minutes away, Zoë leans over Polly with a look of horror. Meanwhile Polly herself seems really quite comfortable. And brown around the edges.

Minutes later we're storming into our villa like Secret Service agents bundling the president under cover after an assassination attempt. Holding a dripping Polly at arm's length, we make straight for the nearest bath. A quick hose down and change of clothes, a brief dab of the hired baby seat and hire car interior, and we're free to settle in.

Wednesday, 16th May – 12 weeks, 2 days old

Holidays with a baby aren't that different from weekends at home; at best, they simply offer a different environment in which to provide stimulation. And I don't know who that realization is disappointing more: Zoë and me, because there's not much lounging in the sun when Polly's demanding to be entertained, or Lorna, whose plan has utterly backfired.

She and Al are engaged and she'd imagined that a few days' exposure to a baby would raise his broodiness levels to the point that he'd agree to start trying for a family soon after the wedding. Instead, she's now decided they can wait a few years after all.

So while they wallow smugly by the pool, Zoë and I take it in turns to walk a suncream-smeared, wide-hatted daughter around the shaded parts of the garden. And instead of reading our books, we sit beneath the shader and nibble her fingernails – her face is covered in so many self-inflicted scratches it's beginning to look like negligence.

Friday, 18th May

Perhaps it's the Mediterranean air, perhaps it's all the canapés that she's ingested indirectly through Zoë, but Polly has definitely grown longer and heavier while we've been away.

Back home, the Moses basket and a bag of culled clothes are buried in the loft and, having first evicted a menagerie of cuddly toys, we place her in her cot. Now, once again, she looks tiny. But the upgrade reinforces how fast the days are flying.

And it's Zoë who decides the time has come to turn off the monitor overnight, so now the neighbours will learn that Polly's awake when we do.

A week of firsts for her, then: her first flight, luxury hotel, swimming pool and wedding. Her first (indirect) taste of champagne, her first car-based bowel explosion, her first nail trimming and, finally, her first unmonitored night in her cot. And far more than her parents, she's taken the whole thing in her stride.

The Fourth Month

Monday, 28th May – 14 weeks old

Just as I'm changing her nappy, Polly lets rip an impossibly wet fart, propelling a thin squirt of molten poo all over my hand that, with my flinching reaction, is then fanned all over the room. The subsequent desperate attempt to dodge the falling drops reminds me of that slow-motion scene in *The Matrix* when Keanu Reeves bends backwards at an impossible angle to avoid a hail of bullets. Except Keanu doesn't put his back out as a result.'

Thursday, 31st May

Our first tour of a nursery, a few miles away on the other side of the park. It's in the grounds of a church and surrounded by a graveyard, but Zoë has spent hours researching on the internet and reckons this is the place. I'm hoping so – it's a minimum £25 non-refundable deposit at each nursery just to get on the waiting lists.

Luckily Zoë is, as ever, on the ball with the questions, because I'm immediately out of my depth. The place is a riot of bright colours, screaming kids, snot, sand and plasticine, tubs of water, paint, glue and paper. It all looks great and I can imagine any kid having an amazing time, but as the woman in charge lists the variety of other parents, I begin to feel more than a little daunted.

'It's a wonderfully diverse environment. We've got Germans, South Africans, Italians, Spaniards, some Japanese, even a few Arab-speakers. And we love birthdays: most parents like to treat everyone to something extra on their child's birthday.'

I nod, reminded of my schooldays when a birthday meant

handing out a chocolate biscuit to all your classmates, but what she says next gives me a whole new respect for inflation: 'Nothing too grand,' she tells us. 'For instance, last week we just had a bouncy castle in the garden.'

I'm still wondering what she might consider 'too grand' when we finally leave, information pack and fee details in hand, and make our way past a pavement straddled by lines of mums waiting in double-parked 4x4s.

I can't help voicing the old concern. 'Even just two mornings a week is extortionate,' I say to Zoë. 'If this is the kind of lifestyle we want, I should be working in the City like all the other dads.'

'That's ridiculous!' she answers. 'If you were in the City, then Polly would be here every day, 8 a.m. till 6 p.m. five days a week. I'd much rather she was brought up at home by her parents.'

I agree with her. But I can't help feeling we're still accumulating all the expenses as though we did both work full time.

I glance at the local parking restrictions – dropping off and picking up just two mornings a week will cost a fortune itself – and make a mental note to search for a gravestone with our surname. That way I should be able to park in the churchyard for free and claim to be visiting.

Saturday, 2nd June

As so often, it's three steps forward and two steps back. After a succession of nights when Polly has settled so easily that I've forgotten the oppression of total exhaustion, she begins to cry with all the strength her little lungs can muster. We decide to adopt the hard-hearted Dr Spock school of thought and let her cry it out, a method that involves shutting the door on her bawling, then standing guard so her mother can't get back in to comfort her.

Unable to bear having the monitor's desperate wails within earshot, Zoë curls up in silent pain on the sofa. And though I may not express it with the same wailing and gnashing of teeth, I'm also feeling the inner strain that comes from leaving her to cry when we know how easily we could calm her just by picking her up.

Monday, 4th June – 15 weeks old

'I'm bored of watching TV,' says Zoë, who has admittedly spent an inordinate amount of time sitting on our couch staring at a screen, to the point that I'm already worried about Polly's TV exposure.

'Let's play a game, then.'

Zoë inspects the games drawer and settles on the one she has the greatest chance of winning, and soon we're sitting at a table, alternately staring and yawning at a Scrabble board. Between us on the table, like electric timers at those Grand Master chess championships, is Polly's monitor, counting the seconds until the next bout of screams that will send either one of us running upstairs.

'Does this mean we're mature and intellectual?' I ask. 'Or just boring and prematurely aged?' As words and thoughts flitter through my mind, flighty as butterflies with nowhere to settle, latching on to nothing and wafted ever onwards by a fog of fatigue, I know the answer already. My brain, vague at the best of times before, needs only a mild distraction or the briefest of interruptions to be thrown off track, and I wonder if I'll ever recover or whether this will become a perennial excuse.

I thought having children was supposed to keep you young. I'm not sure that arguing over the existence of a three-letter word denoting an East Indian shrub simply because we're both too tired to walk upstairs to bed is a sign of youth.

At the point we decide to give up at last, Zoë is winning – or, rather, she's the better loser. Just as well, or else her competitive streak would have had us up all night.

Wednesday, 6th June

Polly wakes on and off from around 5 a.m. Rather than bringing her straight into bed with us, we simply shut the doors between her room and ours, and try to get back to sleep. Beside me, Zoë quivers in time to each little whimper from next door.

But the whole crying-down approach seems to be working, as each successive bout of crying becomes shorter and shorter. And then we bump into one of the neighbours.

'You've found your lungs, haven't you?' the woman says to Polly in her pram, and suddenly we're paranoid parents again, realizing that the cot is probably no further from our neighbour's bed than it is from ours.

Instantly regressing, we revert to charging into Polly's bedroom at the first sign of trouble, with the inevitable result that all our previous efforts are negated – a particularly foolish response given that the neighbour is herself pregnant and due to burst any day, at which point she'll have her own wailer to point in our direction.

Sunday, 10th June

A moment to remember, to be stored safely and aired frequently, and brought out in the balance against those indulgent moments of self-pity.

As I sit upstairs at work, the sun burning through the open window, the infectious giggling of my wife and daughter float up from the lawn outside, and at the sound of their chuckling I feel a happiness that's recognizable only as a distant cousin of anything I've felt before.

Monday, 11th June – 16 weeks old

'Polly's in a good mood today.'

I stop en route to the kettle and peer more closely at my daughter. From her perch on Zoë's lap, Polly peers back. 'What parental instinct am I lacking, then?' I ask. 'She doesn't seem any more or less cheerful than any other day.'

'That's because she's about to have a sleep.'

'Now?' I gesture at our daughter who, as though trying to fly away from my scrutiny, has begun to flap her arms exuberantly. 'She doesn't seem very tired.'

'I know,' says Zoë, checking her watch and standing up. 'But it's time for her nap.'

And no sooner is she zipped into her sleeping bag than, to the predicted minute, Polly's eyes begin to droop and, as if a button has been switched, she's asleep.

'It's brilliant, this Gina stuff,' whispers Zoë, as we shut the nursery door, and off she goes to run a bath, confident that – thanks to the routine – she's got a clear half hour to herself.

For one used to marking off her days on a rota weeks in advance, laying them out before her like items to be ticked off a list, I can see the appeal of the routine. And for one who's so successful in her work, so in control, I can appreciate how reassuring it must be to have found a book that hands control back to her just as she's under threat of taking orders from a crying baby.

Not only that but, by strictly standardizing each day, it becomes easier to make comparisons, thereby charting progress or highlighting problems. With no live-in grandparents or experience of their own, it's no wonder so many first-time parents grasp at Gina Ford's books like life rafts. And when the routine works, it's great.

But routine can be a curse as well as a blessing. After all, we're trying to impose a pattern on something that's – thankfully – ever changing. In the face of such rigidity, the most natural inconsistencies can begin to suggest that something's wrong, either with the mum or the baby. If, despite what we're told is the optimum routine for her, Polly doesn't seem hungry when she's meant to be eating, or decides she's not tired when it's time for a nap, Zoë's instant reaction is to question her own abilities as a mother, or to wonder what's wrong with Polly. In trying to discover that magic formula of snack and snooze, bath and playtime that will work the same every day in getting her to sleep at the same time every night, such dependency on routine can backfire.

After all, is there anything more wonderfully, frustratingly or irrationally capricious than a human? And, being human, there are times when Polly doesn't respond robotically; sometimes she just has a bad day or a sleepless night.

To grasp that is in itself the exciting realization that we're now sharing our home with a real little person.

Tuesday, 12th June

Zoë's role as primary carer gives her a burden of responsibility that I escape; she leads the changes while I just follow up behind, trying to lend support but wondering if all the stress is really necessary.

'Surely if she doesn't need changing, feeding or sleep, then she's fine?'

'It's not that simple!'

So while she worries, I get the best of both worlds: I can escape by heading upstairs to work, yet still nip down for frequent cuddles, bringing to our daughter all the appeal of novelty.

When Polly sees me, she offers up her feet again and again for a flurry of kisses, causing her brief chuckles – really no more than a couple of hoops strung together – to erupt for the first time into a full-on giggle.

At the sound, Zoë's competitive streak flares up. 'It's not fair. Why does she laugh more for you than for me?'

I manage to draw it out several hours before admitting that my stubble offers a tickly advantage, at which point I'm immediately sent to shave.

Thursday, 14th June

'I hope you didn't think I was complaining when I made that comment about Polly's lungs,' says our neighbour. 'My husband hasn't been disturbed at all, and I can't sleep so I'm awake early every morning anyway.'

We're victims of our own over-sensitivity. Like the majority of our fears, they're shadows of ourselves that, when seen in the clearer light of day, prove to be nothing but empty air.

Saturday, 16th June

Polly sleeps badly, waking with a right eye that's swollen and red. All morning she rubs at it, restless and miserable, both eyes squeezed tightly shut. At one point, lying on my knee, she looks up and smiles a brave and heart-melting smile, like a patient of infinite courage managing a grin for the benefit of others.

'Conjunctivitis,' declares Zoë, volunteering herself for a run to the chemist and me for the infliction of the antibiotic eye drops. Throughout the day, I terrorize our baby, forcing the drops into her face.

By lunchtime, the eye is already looking better and, by late afternoon, Polly is more herself. I'm working upstairs when Zoë sidles up, looking sheepish. 'Conjunctivitis wouldn't clear up that quickly,' she says quietly. 'Maybe I was a bit quick with my diagnosis.'

'But the drops seem to have worked,' I say, not wanting Polly's screams to have been in vain.

'I washed her hair last night. I think she must just have had shampoo in her eye.'

Sunday, 17th June – Father's Day

With typical self-effacement, Dad was always dismissive about

Father's Day and the artificiality of just another opportunity to line the pockets of card manufacturers. Taking his apparent disdain to heart, I seldom gave him more than a card. But when I wake to find a beribboned package on the pillow beside me and consider anew the sanctioned circumstance that allows children to freely express their love and appreciation, however artificial the excuse, I wonder if I should have made more of those opportunities regardless.

'Happy Father's Day!' says Zoë, holding Polly out for a kiss.

Inside the box is a plaster-cast relief of a tiny hand and foot, and a small blue rosette for 'The Greatest Daddy in the World'.

When our planned lunch with Zoë's folks is cancelled on hearing that they have colds, we face the unusual prospect of an entirely free day.

'We could go swimming?'

'There won't be time after her sleep.'

'We could go round to Rob's?'

'Polly doesn't like being stuck in the car.'

When every suggestion is rebuffed by a minor complication, we settle on another slow stroll around the park and then a collapse in front of the telly.

And just as I regret having been persuaded in the past not to exploit all that Father's Day traditionally offers, I'm slightly ashamed of our inability to *carpe* the *diem* today, as though we're waiting for an imaginary future of greater opportunity, in which life will be easier.

Because soon Zoë will be back at work, at which point we'll only be more shackled. And you don't need to have dug your father's grave to know there isn't always another opportunity.

Monday, 18th June – 17 weeks old

I pick Polly up for her dream feed and she immediately begins to scream – neither bottle nor dummy will soothe her. Zoë comes running through and only by rocking her slowly manages to get Polly back to sleep.

I try again to feed her but she takes only 1oz before refusing any more, so reluctantly I put her down again, fully expecting to be woken a few hours later by a hungry little baby.

Instead, Polly wakes as normal around 5.30 a.m. before settling herself for another hour and a half. When Zoë goes to fetch her for the standard morning cuddle, she's bounding with excitement.

'This is the third night running she hasn't had a wet nappy, so maybe we don't need to change her last thing. And she only took 1oz! Maybe we can cut out the 10.30 dream feed?'

Unfortunately there's no gauge we can refer to that will confirm we've moved on a stage. Instead, we have to ease ourselves into the water bit by bit, all the time being prepared to jump back out.

The Fifth Month

Tuesday, 19th June

'I'm dreading the goodbyes each morning, but at the same time I'm actually looking forward to going back to work,' admits Zoë. Her confession comes as a relief. Although I'm dreading the day when I take over the Polly-care, I've also been worried Zoë won't want to leave her at all – which would only have exacerbated my guilt at making it necessary.

'Polly's getting more and more demanding – the instant I put her down she starts moaning because she wants to be stimulated, but can't yet stimulate herself. It's exhausting! And every day is just the same. I feel like I'm just treading water between feeds.'

I can see the idea of regaining her previous high level of efficiency is clearly appealing – there's a limit to how much satisfaction even Zoë can get from plucking boogers out of Polly's nostrils in front of *EastEnders* repeats, or copying out and learning every nursery rhyme ever written, as though she's writing a thesis on the preferred trajectory of bovine lunar leaps.

Perhaps it's only because there are two of us at home that she's lasted so long without outside stimulation. But her response to the frustration is admirably practical: she embarks on a sustained campaign of organized 'fun', from music and play groups to the local kids' activity centre.

Even with me in the house, even with her many friends with babies of the same age and their regular coffee gatherings, even with her maternal ease and boundless energy for her daughter, she's finding it hard: tiring and tedious. So how will I cope when it's my turn?

Thursday, 21st June

At bathtime, Polly and I have our first fight – over her Beatrix Potter mug. I'm trying to wash away the dried milk from her many neck folds and, while I want the mug to rinse her, she wants to eat it. Fortunately she's easily distracted, especially in the bath, where her favourite pastime is to curl up like a hedgehog, freeze for a few seconds of anticipation, then slam down her legs in a divebombing splash. She's not yet worked out why it doesn't have the same effect on the changing mat. Soon, given her ever-increasing length and strength, that sort of behaviour will have her backflipping off the changing table to cartwheel across the floor.

Monday, 25th June – 18 weeks old

Zoë and I have one of those increasingly frequent conversations that, a matter of months ago, I'd never have foreseen myself having.

'What word are we going to use to describe Polly's ... you know ... bits?'

'Vagina?' I suggest, but Zoë rules it out – too medical. 'The bits between your legs?'

'Too lengthy. What about fanny?'

'Might cause problems with my American cousins.'

'Crack?'

'Horrible. What about front bottom?'

'Too twee.'

The options are plentiful, but we want one that's tame without being dainty, specific without being offensive. As the minutes roll by and suggestions are summoned and discarded, it reminds me of playground games from 25 years ago. I feel I should be keeping a watch over my shoulder for approaching teachers.

Monday, 2nd July – 19 weeks

Polly sits in her bouncy chair, grabbing awkwardly across her chest at her fingers that meet only in a crooked jumble. And then, for the first time, her fingers interlock properly. Immediately, she gains a pensive air, a look that's almost intimidatingly superior. With her balding head (these days her pillow is a blanket of small brown curls), she's like a wizened old man smiling calmly at life's foibles.

It's her total honesty that's so appealing. Soon this world will dull her transparency of expression as she learns to hide her thoughts and feelings behind a tarnish of civility, but for now it's a refreshing delight, from the moment she greets us in the mornings with a grin of infectious enthusiasm for the day ahead to when she yawns with fading interest as we sing her to sleep.

What's so human about it is that so often she clearly doesn't know herself how she feels. As she looks down at her bundled hands and the evidence of their new-found dexterity, the corners of her mouth flitter from north to south and back again within seconds. At last, she settles for a look of contented pride that, only moments later, gives way to frustration, and then squawks of annoyance. She may have mastered the art of interlocking her fingers, but she hasn't yet learnt to separate them.

Saturday, 7th July

This morning Rob's in Pamplona running with the bulls, ticking off another box in those lifestyle magazines suggesting that, unless you've jumped out of a plane, been arrested or had a threesome, your life has been wasted.

'Are you jealous, then?' taunts Zoë. 'Even I've done a parachute jump! Wouldn't you like to be dodging bulls instead of projectile poo?'

'I don't think so. Maybe a few years ago, but it doesn't seem right to willingly place yourself at risk once you've got a family.'

'That's just an excuse, isn't it? You're chicken, aren't you!'
'I'm still open to the threesome idea, if you know any models.'
'Now you *are* putting yourself at risk.'

Sunday, 8th July

At lunchtime, our NCT group joins us for a barbecue. As ever, Zoë over-prepares with buckets of coleslaw and several dead cows' worth of meat.

True to form, the men gather around the barbecue to discuss the relative merits of gas over charcoal before retiring to watch the end of the Grand Prix and Wimbledon final, while the women sit around the table outside, jiggling babies (all with names ending in the obligatory -ie or -y) and discussing weaning and timings and ounces and the myriad things I can't seem to rouse much interest for. My brain goes numb at such talk, while Zoë seems to have an endless energy for it, backed by hours of research.

I eavesdrop on the chat outside, a comparison of this book to that, the science of clock-watching and routine, all dominated by the oft-repeated phrase 'Gina says', and I try to imagine myself in just a few months' time immersed in such a world. Will I ever feel comfortable there? Or will I get *too* comfortable, and emerge the other side talking cheerfully about making bread, darning socks and whether the cushions go with the curtains?

Monday, 9th July – 20 weeks old

Zoë has become the perfect housewife. Whenever I summon the courage to scoop out the contents of the laundry basket, I find it's empty, the clothes already hanging up to dry. If I venture to suggest an idea for supper, I learn that Zoë's already planned the week's menu, not only with old favourites but with a few adventurous experiments as well. With her daily pram walks, I've not had to visit the shops in weeks. And when the weather allows, she deliberately takes Polly out during the day, giving me time and a little quiet to get on with work.

But in about two months, all will change. No longer will I be able to enjoy the peak of parenthood, where all the household chores are done while I pop in and out of Polly's life with stolen minutes wrestled from my conscience, sneaking downstairs for coffee breaks to blow a quick raspberry on her tummy, then disappearing off again when she starts to get grumpy. Soon, Zoë will return to work and the scales will tip sharply the other way. And while she knows what she's leaving, she also knows what she's getting into. I have no idea.

At times, I tell myself that I can't wait to be sharing my week between work and my daughter in what could be the perfect work-life balance. At other times I breathe in dread, wondering if I'm really cut out for it.

Even now, after four months, I hear myself asking Zoë what's next in the routine. Is this the time Polly sleeps, or feeds? When is she due a nappy change? Does that noise mean she's hungry, or just missing *EastEnders*? And why can't I sing her some of the songs I like instead of 'Two Little Boys' every two little minutes?

Naturally, I blame Zoë. She's so organized and gives the impression of having everything under such control that I've never felt the need to bother myself with it. And now that I try, I just can't get the routine into my head. Even 'bathtime' – which actually equates to a two-hour procedure of which a bath is only a small part – is at a fixed time every day. Yet I can't be sure now if it starts at 5.30 or 6 p.m. And then what time does she get out? Is that when she gets more milk?

Why can't I get these boringly everyday timings into my head? It's not a simple matter of brain drain – Zoë seems to have effortlessly assimilated every detail. It feels like something more fundamental, something to do with my attitude or outlook to parenting. I can't put my finger on it, but it doesn't bode well.

Thursday, 12th July

'I'm going to need your help, Andrew,' says my enormous-breasted wife. 'I think we should set aside 24 hours to wean Polly onto the bottle.'

So, the battle is set. Reluctantly. Since we'll soon be dumping Polly on my mum as we head off to Al and Lorna's wedding in Perthshire, since Zoë's managed five months of breastfeeding already, and since her breasts will explode if they get any bigger, ballooning as they are to keep pace with Polly's growing appetite, now seems a good time to wean our daughter onto the bottle.

'Set aside a day and a night and prepare for a war of attrition,' advises Zoë's latest book *du jour*. 'Your baby won't starve to death in 24 hours, so harden your heart against the tears.' Easily said, I'm thinking. But *whose* tears?

Friday, 13th July

Polly's attitude to feeding seems admirably practical: she doesn't really care where the milk comes from, just as long as she gets it. And if she doesn't, she's sure to let us know.

So when offered her first feed from a bottle, there are a few initial grumbles of surprise and some early chewing as she unexpectedly finds a rubber teat in her mouth rather than a tautly quivering boob, but by her second feed she seems quite at ease with the new set-up – to the point that I'm wondering what all the fuss is about.

What I never realized – though the lengthy discussions should have warned me, if nothing else – is that moving from breast to bottle is about so much more than just waiting until Polly's hungry and then giving her something to drink. And that's because, perhaps more than most things to do with parenthood, the whole breast-to-bottle issue is inextricably bound up with a heaving mass of maternal emotions, the greatest of which is guilt.

As I walk around the kitchen with a bottle-slurping Polly in my arms, my struggle to find new songs to sing for her brings to mind a perhaps horribly inappropriate comparison that nevertheless strikes a chord – I find myself thinking of Cosette in *Les Misérables*. When her mother, Fantine, becomes destitute, the young girl is handed over to the care of a crooked landlord. Fantine reluctantly considers it's for her daughter's own good; she has convinced herself that it has to be done, that it's for the best and that her daughter will be well looked after. But at the same time she's naturally torn apart by the loss and the guilt and the pain – after all, who can better provide for a child than that child's own mother?

As Zoë silently eyes me walking our daughter round the kitchen, I'm convinced that she sees herself in a similar role. No doubt, as I self-consciously coax Polly to take a little more, I'm the crooked landlord, watering down the breastmilk and giving her only 4oz when I claim she's taken 5oz.

'Maybe I should give her a final feed from the boob this evening?'

'Why? The milk's still milk. Polly's doing fine.'

'Maybe. But we want to make sure she gets enough to see her through the night.'

'Look at her! She's getting plenty.'

Zoë pouts her frustration, and I realize she's only hovering to witness Polly's betrayal in the hope that our daughter will show a moment's refusal to take anything but her mother's boob. This is nothing to do with Polly's willingness to be weaned and everything to do with Zoë's inability to let go.

Saturday, 14th July

Since Zoë has approached every previous bottle-induction deadline only to shift it back yet further, I'm doing all I can to encourage her. 'That's 36 hours without so much as a lick of breast!' I say. 'How's she doing?'

Zoë looks shifty. 'Fine,' she says. 'But I looked it up and the new guidelines say breast is best for the first six months.'

'Maybe, but...'

'And it's such a faff, all that pumping and sterilizing.'

'I know, but...'

'So I've decided to go back to breastfeeding.'

'I can't believe...'

'We can still give her a bottle of expressed milk twice a day to keep her flexible,' she says loudly, making it clear that objections based on practicality hold no sway in this discussion. 'There's no harm in that.'

Monday, 16th July – 21 weeks old

I'm beginning to realize that we won't know where we're going wrong in raising Polly until it's too late. Because there's no going back, no reversing the accumulated effect of the everyday decisions we're forced to make as parents, from the simplest (do I pay her enough attention or too much?) to the more complex (how long should I hide from her the fact that this world can be pretty mean?).

If I actually ever did any baking, I'd guess it's not dissimilar – only once it's finished do you realize where you've gone wrong, by which time it already tastes strange. All that's left to do is apologize and have another go – at which point you're handed a whole different set of ingredients.

Tuesday, 17th July

It's 5.30 a.m. The nursery is sweetly silent, but we still wake to the muffled sound of a baby crying, as though Polly's nipped downstairs for a coffee and had a breakdown over the kitchen table. It takes us a few dazed minutes before we realize the noise is coming from next door: our neighbours' baby has arrived. And only now do I appreciate how nine inches of brick just isn't that much when it comes to soundproofing.

Mid-afternoon, they're in the garden, jiggling a little bundle in their arms. On their faces is a look I recognize, of utterly exhausted bewilderment. Zoë and I head out to congratulate them and, as we're cooing over their daughter, I wish there were some words of wisdom we could dispense over the fence, but it's hard to muster the arrogance to assume that our few months have made us expert, or even to think of any advice that isn't simple common sense.

'It helps to work in shifts,' is all I can come up with, remembering that once the initial amazement and desire to be with Polly every minute had worn off, it took us some time to overcome the guilt that stopped at least one of us resting while the other looked after her.

'And don't worry if you don't enjoy bits of it,' offers Zoë. 'For the first four to six weeks I was just permanently exhausted. It's relentless. I still loved Polly utterly, of course, but there were times when I felt I just couldn't cope.'

We wish them luck, leaving them looking even more shell-shocked than before.

Wednesday, 18th July

'We've got a problem,' says Zoë. 'I express off enough to fill a bottle up to the recommended dosage and Polly gulps it all down. But then she wants more. And I don't think my boobs are up to the task.'

'But they're enormous!'

'I know, but I keep having to raid the freezer to thaw out some of the expressed milk.'

'Good job it's so well stocked.' It's been a running issue of contention for months now, as each shelf is jealously guarded against the introduction of frozen food in preference for row upon row of carefully weighed bags of breastmilk.

'We're getting through at least one bag a day. But the increased intake does make a difference. Don't you think Polly seems happier?'

It's true that she did sleep better last night, and that makes us all happier. But the confirmation that her breasts are lagging is clearly hard to accept. Soon Zoë's not only going to have to face the pain as they deflate, but she'll also have to deal with the loss of dependency and that close connection that she loves. Polly's going to lose that irreplaceable intimacy with her mum, and I'm going to have to kiss goodbye to the biggest boobs I've ever had the pleasure of knowing.

The Sixth Month

Thursday, 19th July

Polly is five months old. Naturally, she couldn't care less about the date and is far more interested in the pink rabbit hanging over her playmat and its length of string, a tug of which triggers a burst of mechanical laughter that's meant to be endearing but conjures up an image of an overworked clown whose heart's not really in it.

'Congratulations!' I tell Zoë over breakfast. 'Despite all your worries, Polly's had five months of breastmilk.'

But judging by her lower-lip pout, the milestone obviously prompts mixed feelings – she's allowing the usual dosage of guilt to overshadow the achievement. 'The World Health Organization recommends six months. That's what I should be doing, especially as I'm a GP. Otherwise what will I tell my patients?'

'We've been through this, Zoë. That WHO guideline is an ideal. It doesn't necessarily relate to our reality.'

'It still feels too early.' She shoots a stare in the direction of the corner cupboard, where a box of baby rice is sitting ready for next week. 'And it's six months for rice as well.'

'She took that peach quite happily, didn't she?' Two days ago, Zoë offered Polly a skinned slice of ripe peach wrapped in muslin to suck on.

'Yeah.'

'And you said then that judging from her reaction she's ready for something more solid than milk.'

'Yeah.'

'So it's for her own good.'

And, although I don't say it, I'm hoping it'll be for our own good as well, not only because the introduction of solids should give us all longer nights, but for the very reason that Zoë's

198

simultaneously lamenting the demise of the breastfeed: independence.

No doubt there'll be increased complications over bottle-warming and sterilizing, but no longer will everything have to be planned around the regular union of Zoë and Polly. Zoë will at last be able to reclaim a life of her own and I'll be equally capable of taking our daughter out for the day. And I definitely won't miss those awkward public breastfeeds as I hover over them both to protect Zoë's modesty, holding up a muslin like a magician's handkerchief.

'We should try her with some solids,' I say. 'What's the worst that could happen? Even if Polly spits out the rice and refuses the formula, even if your breasts fall off sometime this afternoon, thanks to your meticulousness there's still enough breastmilk stockpiled in the freezer to keep Polly going until her early teens.'

Monday, 23rd July – 22 weeks old

We're on the train back to London after the Perthshire wedding when Polly begins to get hungry.

'Don't worry about a thermos,' I'd confidently told Zoë as she was packing for the journey home. 'There'll be hot water on the train. We'll use that to heat Polly's milk.'

So when the guy with the trolley comes round, I ask him for a cup full of hot water. It's pretty obvious what I want it for; I'm jiggling a screaming Polly in one hand and holding up the bottle with the other, while the people in the carriage around us stare, tight-lipped, out of the windows.

'I can't give you any hot water. I'm not allowed to.'

'Excuse me?'

'You can ask at the buffet car. But I don't have the facility to pour you hot water.'

'What about that?' I ask, pointing at his hot water dispenser, from which he's just poured hot water for someone else's cup of tea.

'I can't give you any hot water.'

'All right, can I have a cup of tea, then? Without the teabag?'

A mere £1.30 later, the trolley dolly has a spare teabag and I have a cup of the train company's best hot water – in a cup that's far too small to heat the bottle.

Giving up, I trudge half the length of the train to ask for a larger cup of hot water from the buffet car.

'No,' says the man behind the counter immediately. 'I'm not allowed to give you any hot water.'

'But you can give me a hot coffee or tea, can't you?'

'Yes.'

'So what's the difference between hot water and hot coffee? I'll even carry it back to my seat in one of your paper bags.'

This suggestion seems to stump him and he goes off to get the customer service manager, a woman who's soon insisting that she's got kids herself so knows how difficult it is, but for her own sake and the sake of her crew she isn't going to give me any hot water.

The lack of simple humanity stuns me into temporary silence. It's like someone standing guard over a fully functioning toilet, refusing to allow anyone inside while happily agreeing that 'Yes, diarrhoea really is terrible, isn't it, and I should know because I had it once.'

'If we know the water's for heating a bottle,' she says, 'we're not allowed to give you any.'

'But what's the difference between giving me hot water and hot coffee?' I try again.

She thinks for a while, then has a go. 'It's because we can't guarantee the final temperature of the milk when you give it to your baby. You might burn your baby and then blame us.'

'But you'd sell me a hot chocolate for my child, wouldn't you? Do you guarantee the temperature then?'

'I'm sorry,' she insists, loyally avoiding logical discussion. 'I can't give you any water.'

All the time this conversation is continuing, I'm aware of Polly no doubt still screaming in our carriage at the other end of the train, to say nothing of Zoë needing to get to the loo to express.

Finally, as I'm on the point of buying three cups of coffee to pour into our travel sterilizer, the woman agrees that if I bring the bottle to her, she'll 'take the chill off it' for me.

So back I go down the train, where I collect both the bottle and a now starving Polly, and then, hurdling suitcases and dodging swinging rucksacks as people stretch out from all sides, despite my daughter's tears, to tickle her feet or stroke her cheek, I hand over the bottle of cold milk.

Eventually I have a tepid bottle in my hands and, in a pique of furious retribution, I bring Polly back to life by singing as I feed her, standing by the doorway of the buffet car, not only frightening off their customers but subjecting them to three whole rounds of "Two Little Boys'.

When I get back to Zoë, still furious at the stupidity of this world, she reminds me of a lecture she received when graduating from medical school, in which she was advised never to operate on a passenger taken ill on an aeroplane without getting a signed waiver first. In other words, doctors trained over a process of many years to treat ill people are being warned off treating ill people.

Life outside our front doors is now a series of Health and Safety misdemeanours waiting to be blamed on someone else. Beneath the constant clamours for compensation, only insurers and lawyers are laughing. No hot water is to be given to warm milk on trains because the milk might get too hot. Every hot drink sold must be served in a paper bag in case the drink is spilt and the people who sold that drink are blamed. Isn't that like blaming the chicken when we drop our shopping bags and break the eggs?

We've done that. We've made this modern world what it is – it's our fault.

So when something goes wrong, is it old fashioned simply to accept it and admit that accidents happen? To put it another way, shit happens; must we always try to track down the arsehole responsible?

'We should have just brought a thermos,' sighs Zoë.

'A little hot water!' I'm still ranting. 'Is that such an unreasonable request?'

'Forget about it. What can you do?'

'I can write to them,' I say. 'And demand compensation for the emotional distress.'

Friday, 27th July

The temptation to video Polly's every second is enormous. As she spots another teaspoonful of baby rice and puréed pear flying through the air towards her, she lunges towards it with wiggling tongue, grabbing it to guide it into her eager mouth, her stare intently following its progress to the point that she goes cross-eyed. Much is dribbled liberally down her front, to be scraped from her chin and finally swallowed, reappearing not long after in luminous colours in her once-white nappies.

This feed marks the end of the previously enormous supply of frozen breastmilk. I'd never have thought it before, but now I recognize the event as a major milestone – and not just because I'll now be able to treat myself to an ice lolly without turning on the kitchen lights.

It's because, just as Polly now often settles better in her cot than in our arms, she's proving without a doubt that she's ready to progress, at times even fighting the boob but surrendering to the bottle.

Understandably, as her breasts fall from grace, Zoë finds it difficult. Wiping tears from her eyes, she tries to overwhelm the sense of betrayal with a frenzied assault on a pile of courgettes, carrots, pears and apples, filling the freezer with ice-cube-sized portions of puréed food.

Personally, I'm in two minds: the end of breastfeeding should bring a greater balance to our care for Polly as I play a greater role in the feeds, but that in turn means less opportunity to work.

Monday, 30th July – 23 weeks old

'Look at me!' wails Zoë, standing naked before the mirror – an invitation that doesn't need repeating.

'Your scar's fading.'

She runs a hand over the thin line through which Polly was tugged into the world. 'Yeah, but the sensation's returning, so it's really itchy. And what about this?'

Although her former washboard-flat stomach is returning, she's still able to grab a handful of loose skin. But much as I loved her flawless, straight-edge belly, I'm also proud of what it's become, because I've seen this woman's insides – literally. I've seen what her body is capable of producing, both good and bad, and so find myself judging its outer covering by different criteria. Easy to say, admittedly, when she's still a beautiful woman.

I look at her breasts, one obviously larger than the other, each of them prominently veined, but both undeniably shrinking. And as I salute their passing, I can't help realizing that my own physical transformation since her pregnancy is going in the opposite direction: where I once had time and energy enough to drag myself to the gym up to three times a week, now I'm impressed with myself if I can make it round the park at the weekend. As a result, while I remain as skinny as ever else-where, what was a relatively flat stomach has become more of a paunch that needs an extra notch on my belt to hold in check and has thus far excluded me from at least one pair of jeans. It's like a built-in life ring implanted just beneath the skin that continues to inflate, to the point that I resemble a stick insect who's swallowed a polo mint. And in a final transformation of indignity, I'm not sure that my breasts aren't growing. As my hard-won pectorals recede, the chub remains, leaving budding man-boobs of the sort that a ten-year-old girl might eye with pride and impatience.

In fact, when coupled with my disappointing lack of fecundity when it comes to a manly thatch of chest hair, I'm starting to grow seriously worried. This sense of androgyny is heightened by Polly's reaction to other men: so much as lean her towards another's manly spread of jet-black lower arm hair, and she begins to bawl in terror, as though she's never encountered a male of the species. It's downright embarrassing; the only thing worse than being a bad male role model is not being recognized as male at all.

Tuesday, 31st July

With Polly down for her morning nap, we're both surprised to feel energetic enough to sneak next door to bed. Despite frequently freezing in fear at every suggestion that our efforts might be waking Polly, the deed is done and we're lying contentedly together when Zoë's face suddenly turns ashen.

'Quick! Get off!'

'Why? What's . . .'

'I forgot to put the diaphragm in! Get *off!*'

'It's too late now . . .' I roll over reluctantly and she rushes off to the bathroom.

I can't believe it. 'Didn't I say you were pretty quick getting ready?'

'Well, pardon me if I was a little distracted by the thought of making love to my husband.'

Good comeback. 'So what now?' I grunt.

'I guess I could have an emergency coil fitted – that would probably be the sensible option, but it costs about £200 and I'd be worried it might damage the uterus lining. Or there's the morning-after pill, though it'll make me feel shit, and leave me wondering where I am in my cycle – assuming I've even started

ovulating again. Because I've not yet had a period and I'm still
– just – breastfeeding, so perhaps there's nothing to worry about.'
 'Another baby ... Oh my God...'
 'I suppose I could take an ovulation test, see if there's any risk.'
 'Do it,' I groan, burying my face in the pillow. 'Do the test.'

Thursday, 2nd August

'Andrew! Can you help me?' comes the familiar cry, launched up
the stairs to where I'm working.
 'What's up?'
 'I'm changing Polly but I need to mix up some formula. Can
you do it? You just need five ladlefuls of powder in a bottle.'
 Without a word, I slouch reluctantly downstairs, take a bottle
from the sterilizer and open the box of formula milk. The ladle
is sitting on top of the powder, and I begin to scoop it into the
bottle.
 'No!' Zoë suddenly screams, throwing herself across the room.
'That ladle isn't level.'
 It's true. Knowing that the second ladleful in my hands is
slightly rounded, I'm intending to compensate with a slightly
emptier third ladleful. But such a casual approach is enough to
push Zoë into meltdown.
 With a glare of exasperation, she speaks like a teacher struggling
to keep her temper with a five-year-old. 'I cannot over-stress how
important it is that you have *precisely* the right amount.'
 'Oh, I think you can,' I reply. Of course.
 Then, as though trying to compensate for her outburst, she
patiently shows me how to level the ladleful against the purpose-
built 'leveller' on the side of the box, thereby ensuring *precisely*
the right amount.
 That I've spent almost 20 years measuring teaspoons of coffee
throughout my days counts for nothing. It has to be exact, it
seems, or else Polly will roll over and die and probably never

forgive me for putting in either too much or too little powder. The question is, will Zoë?

The answer is clear a moment later with her next question: 'Did you put that bottle through the sterilizer?'

'No. It was already in the sterilizer.'

'For God's sake!' she explodes. 'If it's already open, it's not going to be sterile, is it?'

This doesn't bode well.

Friday, 3rd August

Zoë goes out with friends to quote her way through the stage version of *Dirty Dancing*, leaving me holding baby in the corner – a fate I far prefer, having already been forced to sit through the film countless times.

Polly behaves perfectly, though within minutes of Zoë's leaving is firmly crushing the theory that she's 'constipating' beneath a continual stream of sticky, stinking poo that just keeps coming like a third leg. She then feeds far more than usual and settles quickly to sleep.

'Pure cheese,' says Zoë when she gets home and, judging by the smile, that's a compliment. 'It was a bit weird, though.'

'Why?'

'Because for the first time, I didn't identify with Baby.'

'Presumably not just because my pecs are a little wobblier than Patrick Swayze's?'

'Because Polly's almost as close to Baby in age as I am – since she came along, every child I see is an older version of her, not a younger version of me. I found myself watching the story through the eyes of the parents.'

'Well, if you think we're going to be holidaying in the Hamptons, you'd better start working private.'

Saturday, 4th August

In the news today: a man and woman have been charged with manslaughter after the prolonged torture of their 16-month-old child. Amongst other things, they cut the baby in the leg deep enough to reveal tendons, burnt her with cigarettes and broke her arm and ribs. Meanwhile, an eight-year-old has been abducted from the street outside her home.

Where before I would have shrugged off such stories of tortured babies and stolen children with disgust, pity, anger and – ultimately – resignation, now I find myself churning them over in my mind, unable to forget, overwhelmed by such a visceral reaction that I instinctively feel any response against the perpetrators would be justified; any constraint of reason is buried beneath a frenzy for retribution and the wish to annihilate any threat. Because, for the first time, such stories are no longer unimaginable and no longer so far away. My identity has shifted to the point that such thoughts resound; they impact directly.

Sunday, 5th August

If the looming role reversal – Zoë heading out to work while I'm left holding the baby – was threatening to cement a sense of inadequacy, an article in a recent 'dads' mag' offers no relief. It lists the top 17 disasters that can befall a father. Along with a death in the family, an inability to bond, broken spectacles and a puked-on suit, it mentions being 'forced to father from home … while the missus goes out to hunt and gather'. Thus speaks a 'modern' parenting magazine, branding my role in our family a 'disaster'.

Tuesday, 7th August – 24 weeks, 1 day old

A piss-on-a-stick ovulation test indicates we've nothing to worry about from the brief bout of forgetfulness last week. The reprieve allows us to consider dispassionately the practical benefits of having kids almost back to back, but it surely wouldn't be good for Zoë's body, or her work. Or our finances.

And that's one aspect of the transition from breastmilk to formula I hadn't been prepared for: the sheer cost. Zoë's still giving three breastfeeds a day, planning to drop one every Sunday from here on, but already we seem to be romping through the boxes of Aptamil formula.

At 10.20 p.m., having decided to drop the dream feed, I lie in bed staring at the ceiling, with nothing to do but brush my teeth and turn out the light. It's liberating, but given that the late-night feed was the one time of the day set aside for just the two of us to be together – whether Polly knew it or not – the milestone also brings a sense of loss. It makes me wonder what it'll feel like when Polly goes to school, or leaves home. And it certainly gives me more of an insight into Zoë's struggle to give up the breastfeeding.

Friday, 10th August

It's a sunny day so I go for a run round the park, my first exercise in several weeks. My usual route takes me past the play area; I stop in the midst of the slides and swings, surrounded by screaming kids and parked prams, and look around for Zoë and Polly.

In the 1999 remake of *The Thomas Crown Affair*, there's a scene where a beleaguered cop is searching for an art thief in the middle of the gallery. Knowing that the culprit is wearing a black overcoat with matching bowler hat and carrying a briefcase, he spots such a man and grabs him – only to find it's just another faceless businessman dressed in an identical outfit. Then he realizes he's surrounded – every second person is dressed exactly the same way.

That's me in the park, searching for my wife and daughter amongst a crowd of Bugaboos, rows and rows of mothers and children with only the fabric colour of their prams and the design on their Cath Kidston changing bags to distinguish between them.

And because, despite my unconventional career choice, I belong to this demographic more than any other, I can picture their husbands as well, who graduated and probably opted to travel a little before taking up well-paid positions behind desks, who work long hours during the week and still wear collared shirts at weekends, who chat with their friends and wives about club memberships and skiing holidays, and whether or not their Christmas bonus and share options will cover the cost of schooling. Theirs is a world that I almost know, and – had I not stepped off the conveyor belt of expectation after 20-odd years – their world might have been mine.

But here in the park, standing amongst such clear evidence of that well-trodden path I might have followed, I'm reminded only of the mass of benefits such a path can offer: the apportioned security, the comfort of belonging to a group who have tried and tested together, who are fighting the same battle with the same arsenal.

Like jeans beside a tailored suit, the sight only reminds me of the gulf between my days and theirs, and make me think once again that, unless I can make my choices come good, it's my family who will pay the price. So I give up searching for Zoë and Polly, and run back to do more work instead.

Wednesday, 15th August – 25 weeks, 2 days old

Months ago, when Polly was at her most demanding and in need of almost 24-hour attention, Zoë was wishing forlornly for a day off.

'Just one day,' she wailed. 'A day when I don't have to worry about Polly, when I'm not woken by crying or forced to follow the endless routine, when I can eat when I want to eat and be answerable to no one. I just want one day for myself!'

In less than two weeks, Zoë will be turning 30. A while ago, exploiting an uncharacteristic alignment of both organization and memory, I began to plot with the in-laws so that, for 24 hours, we can hand Polly over to her grandparents while Zoë and I head out of London to a place where she can reclaim, for one day only, a life of her own. She doesn't know anything about it yet; I've warned her to keep the weekend free but the rest is to be a surprise. But now the plan's unravelling at the seams.

'God, I'm dreading work and leaving Polly,' she says. I can tell: she's clinging to every minute they've got together. And as she relaxes further into the mothering role and Polly becomes marginally less demanding, I'm not sensing in Zoë the same great desire for a break.

Meanwhile, since it's more a case of weaning Zoë off breastfeeding than weaning our daughter, she's still giving two feeds per day, contrary to her stated timetable at the point of booking, according to which, by the time of our break, Polly would have been fully bottle-fed. Endlessly helpful though the mother-in-law is, I'm not sure even she's prepared to step in on that particular issue.

So I think I'm going to have to tell Zoë now, so she can either refuse to part from Polly and we can plan something else, or she can begin to prepare herself for the separation. Otherwise, at the announcement of my great surprise, Zoë will burst into tears and throw herself at Polly, refusing to let go. In which case, being Scottish, I'll find myself spending a lonely night in the country rather than lose my deposit.

Thursday, 16th August

Zoë and Polly return from their lunch outing, and I begin to outline my plans for our weekend.

'Don't tell me!' she shrieks, cutting me short. 'Because, whatever it is, I'll dread it right up to the point that it happens, and then I'll love it. So if I don't know what it is, I can't dread it.'

I'm impressed. This new level of self-awareness is a form of progress. Her usual manner of dreading any outing and then recanting afterwards frustrates me, because in those dread-full pre-event days, I remind her how we both know she'll actually enjoy whatever it may be, and she'll agree 100% – and then go right on dreading it anyway.

Now, by adopting an approach of ostrich-like ignorance, she's avoiding the knowledge of anything specific onto which to latch her dread. The real problem now is that she knows that she doesn't know where we're going. How dreadful.

Friday, 17th August

When Polly shows no interest in taking anything from the breast, Zoë reluctantly offers a bottle – and Polly downs 3oz.

'It's because I'm only giving her two feeds a day. I'm just not producing enough milk. And my boobs must be shrinking – I keep having to tighten my bra straps.'

But she's determined that her breasts will go down fighting to the end. 'If I can keep expressing and use my milk as a top-up for the next two days, then Polly will have been breastfed for six months!'

The announcement is proclaimed with a grin that mixes triumph with nervous anticipation, like a marathon runner entering the stadium for that last lap. In Zoë's mind, to have achieved the six-month mark will be a validation of the marriage between mother and medic.

The Seventh Month

Tuesday, 21st August – 26 weeks, 1 day old

Walking into the kitchen, I catch Zoë saying, 'Mama ... mama,' over and over to Polly. Aware that she's heading back to work in a few weeks and imagining that, as a result, she'll no longer be the focal figure, she's desperate to stamp her mark while she can.

When I ask her what she's doing, she looks sheepish. 'Babies often manage "Dada" before "Mama",' she says, 'because mums are more likely to talk about the dads than refer to themselves in the third person.'

'Presumably that'll work in the reverse then, when you head back to work and I take over?'

'Maybe,' she agrees, half-heartedly.

But as the day goes on it's clear that Zoë's not going to risk being undermined with even the smallest 'Dada'. Her competitive streak, strengthened by her fear that I'll in some way replace her as the mother, is out in force. Or maybe she's just worried that, left with me, Polly's first words will be 'DVD' or 'Dominos'.

Wednesday, 22nd August

Polly's taking her lunchtime nap and I'm working frantically in the loft when I hear Zoë's urgent whisper.

'Andrew, can you come down here, please?'

I can tell by the tone of her voice that it's serious and by the time I make it to the kitchen, she's already in tears.

'What is it?'

'I'm going back to work soon and I don't want to feel that we've wasted this family time. It's precious.'

I know I should be spending more time with her, learning all about Polly's meals and integrating myself into the routine so that, when the time comes, I can take over with confidence. But, as I try to explain, her return to work – the very reason she's so upset – is the very reason why I'm taking every opportunity to work now.

'But a lot of what you're writing is speculative – there's no guarantee you'll ever be paid for it. And when the next piece of acting or voice work comes along, I'll see even less of you!'

She's right, of course, and at her words I instinctively want to scuttle off upstairs again, to keep plugging away to make a success of it. Or to put through another desperate call to my agent, begging her to find me work. Or to retrain as a plumber. Because only by having a proper job will I negate the need for Zoë to work at all.

'God, I'm dreading leaving her.' As her tears continue to fall, I feel the weight of my guilt like several atmospheres.

Thursday, 23rd August

Zoë's mum comes round for a cup of tea and is so attentive and questioning over every aspect of Polly's care that no sooner has she left the house than Zoë turns to me with a grin.

'Is Mum taking Polly sometime this weekend?'

There doesn't seem to be much choice other than to nod.

'How long for?'

I hesitate. 'Twenty-four hours?'

'Perfect! I wouldn't want to leave her for longer. Even if we just drop Polly off and come straight back here, it would still give me some time off. Just a few hours when I'm not listening out for a baby's cries, one morning with a lie-in.'

I make some soup for our lunch and, while Polly sleeps, sit with Zoë as together we indulge in the luxury of just staring silently out of the window. But while admiring the sight of the countryside and all it offered was a frequent Argyllshire pastime, it doesn't take long for me to lose interest in the backs of huddled houses with their strips of fraying grass, and I'm soon mounting the stairs again to work.

Saturday, 25th August

Knowing that Zoë will notice if our passports have moved, I hide them in the bottom of my sock drawer.

'Is it Paris?' she asks, as we take Polly over to her folks after breakfast.

But when I don't hurry our departure and instead allow her to talk her mum through her meticulous typed schedule covering every minute we're to be away, she rules out the possibility of catching a plane or train.

'Actually,' she admits, 'I wasn't wild about going so far from Polly.'

Finally, we wave goodbye and set off down the A3. Having had a few days to mentally prepare, Zoë surprises even herself at how easy it feels to leave our daughter behind – then ruins it by feeling guilty about how easy it feels.

As we sit in slow-moving traffic, I take her mind off our abandoned daughter by making her guess what activity we could be doing that requires passports, an amusing game for me until it all backfires when her suggestions grow far more exciting than anything I've actually planned.

After a pub lunch in a sunny beer garden, we take a stroll across the foot of the South Downs. In the distance, a couple of horses are running free across the hill, birds are singing from every hedgerow, and Zoë is beaming. 'I'm already feeling totally refreshed!' Her carefree grin lasts precisely three minutes, until the realization that she no longer has mobile reception leads a rapid scurry back to the car.

At the hotel, I proudly reveal that I've booked her in for a massage. 'That's great,' she says, but her enthusiasm is half-hearted.

'What is it?'

'Well . . .' She nods down towards her front, and it takes me a few seconds to realize: her swollen and unhappily neglected breasts are in such a state that an hour lying on her front has no appeal at all. Fortunately a couple of strategically placed, rolled-up towels save the day, and she emerges for a swim soon after with a sleepy smile. Even though her mum has maintained a calming commentary by text since we left, Zoë's still clutching her phone.

As she walks towards me in her swimsuit, her breasts seem dangerously lopsided, as though determined to drag her into the water. The left – the one favoured by Polly – is far bigger, though both are engorged. 'They're really sore,' she admits. 'And I haven't been this off-balance since I fell pregnant.' She laughs, but the implication isn't a joke – the thought of a second is too much for us both right now.

At last, as we're enjoying a pre-dinner drink, Zoë's phone rings. She leaps up to answer it and it's a mix of disappointment and relief to realize it's not her mum but a friend who's recently given birth. Agreeing a time to meet the new arrival, Zoë is relaxed enough to actually forget that any visit has to be arranged around our daughter's schedule – though the mental lapse may be more to do with her first gin and tonic in over a year.

There follows a three-course, early-birthday meal, during which Zoë cradles her phone in her lap and I manage to steer the conversation briefly away from our daughter, and then a blissful collapse, already anticipating our first lie-in for months.

'For the first time in as long as I can remember,' whispers Zoë as she falls asleep, 'I'm happily tired, not exhausted.'

Sunday, 26th August

Her first few alcoholic drinks in over a year wake Zoë with a dull ache in the head and it takes her several dazed minutes before she recognizes it as the return of an old friend.

All the local shops are shut so there's nothing to do after breakfast but sit and read the papers, wallowing in the luxury of every empty minute.

'We must have wasted so much time before Polly came along,' yawns Zoë, stretching lazily on a hotel sofa. But only ten minutes later she's unable to contain herself. 'Do you mind if we head home?'

We're back in London before lunch and become doting parents anew, lavishing attention on Polly who greets our return with grins and squeals. Having slotted so easily back into being a carefree couple, it's a shock to realize afresh that this little person we're collecting is ours and that we're parents, with all the consequent responsibilities.

'That was the perfect incentive to stop breastfeeding,' smiles Zoë as we drive Polly home. 'Something positive, rather than the idea that I'm being forced by work to end it.'

Tuesday, 28th August – 27 weeks, 1 day old

I suppose it was only a matter of time.

We're watching TV and on comes some trite scene involving a parent threatened with the loss of their baby, the sort of anodyne pap I'd never previously have thought twice about, and suddenly I realize I'm welling up, a lump in my throat. Beside me, Zoë is sniffing.

It's such a widespread, primeval emotion, a parent's love for their child, that it's exploited over and over in films and books – and each time I've yawned sceptically at such hollow manipulation.

Only now I feel the real power of that emotion; suddenly it rings true, and I'm torn between hating myself for succumbing to something so obvious, and the confusion of feeling my previous certainty so effectively undermined.

The threat of losing one's own child is the greatest threat I can imagine, and only now can I fully appreciate my granny's experience – and her stoical reaction – as, over the course of so many months, she watched Dad wasting away.

Thursday, 30th August

It's impossible to ignore. Physically, I've peaked. I wake and stretch and crick my neck; I jog round the park and my knees ache for weeks; I sneeze and pull a muscle in my ribs.

Thankfully, though I steadily decline, Polly continues to develop. I've noticed it a couple of times now, her little fist pulsing, the fingers opening and closing like the fronds of an anemone caught in an invisible current, and it's such an autonomous action that, stupidly, I can't help but feel proud. At times that same pulsing makes contact to become a proper scratching – fortunately not the desperate scrape of fingernails suggesting infestation but a casual grazing of her belly, just as we might scratch mindlessly at an elbow or nose.

It's the first sign that she's answering her own needs. Surely, then, it can't be long until she's capable of answering mine, and then my slippers need never go missing again.

Friday, 31st August

Beyond the usual finger sucking, Polly's developed a habit of rubbing her fourth finger along her upper lip, palm turned away from her face. It's a move trademarked by Dad, one that I've caught myself adopting now and again but never, as far as I'm aware, in front of Polly. And it's strange to see, a happy-sad moment to recognize in my daughter such an attributable gesture, coincidental or not.

It's well over three years since Dad died, and we've still not yet found a time we're all available to gather at Ardburdan to mount the plaque on his grave. Regardless, I'm not sure I've yet the stomach to return, and the thought makes me feel guilty, as though we've abandoned him.

Monday, 3rd September – 28 weeks old

Polly seems prone to boogers of such stifling proportions that she wakes in the night gasping for air. It's as though she's got constipation of the nostrils.

Midway through the morning, I walk into our bedroom to find Zoë poised over our sleeping daughter, a pair of tweezers in hand, preparing to delve in and prise the offending snot free.

'It's just too tempting,' she whispers. 'I want to get them while she's asleep.'

Her insistent trawling is rewarded not with a dreamy smile of satisfaction or a sigh of contentment, but a bucking and twisting. Then, just as Polly seems on the verge of waking to scream, Zoë raises a jubilant arm in silent cheer, her face glowing with satisfaction.

Given that – as with all Polly's bodily excretions – the amount is out of all proportion to her size, I find myself staring in wonder at the enormity of what Zoë has plucked out. I'd have thought the sheer relief itself would be enough to prompt Polly to spontaneous speech.

Tuesday, 4th September

At 9.30 a.m., with Polly safely napping, Zoë hands me the monitor and slips out to get her hair done in preparation for her return to work. For a few hours, I'm given a glimpse of the future.

When Polly wakes half an hour later, I pick her up, change her, dress her, and take her for a walk.

The park is relatively empty, but I imagine stares from every direction: either retired men with dogs wondering why I'm not at work, or mothers with kids wondering why I'm not at work.

I talk to Polly as I push her, but peter out self-consciously when others walk past, foolishly embarrassed to be answering her coos.

We arrive in a secluded corner and I sit on a fallen tree. Polly looks cheerfully around with her now standard expression of eternal surprise, her mouth hanging open as though trying to fit the world inside.

I wonder if I should be stimulating her in some way, but she seems happy so I pull out an old newspaper. Within minutes, I'm reading an article that's only feeding my fears, in which a mother, finally sending her youngest off to school and at the end of the road upon which I'm about to embark, lists the mess and the noise and the exhaustion and the boredom of her previous ten years of childcare.

Surprised though she may be to realize that she's actually going to miss it, it's still been messy, noisy, exhausting and boring. And the only thing that's got her through it, she says, is the companionship of all the other mothers she's met along the way.

I look around the park, at the elderly out for their constitutionals, at the nannies with their charges, the mothers with their children, and I wonder – who am *I* going to meet along the way? Suddenly my future seems a pretty isolated place.

Thursday, 6th September

I'm beginning to realize that the question as to whether Polly's first word will be 'Mama' or 'Dada' has far wider implications than mere competitiveness.

It's expected of today's Alpha females that they juggle the demands of a high-paying job with the raising of a family – something I'm confident that Zoë will soon manage. Her concern, though, is that around the ten-month mark – when Polly will apparently develop a fear of abandonment alongside a healthy distrust of strangers – our daughter will, in her mother's frequent absence, automatically turn to her father instead.

219

As a result, she's carrying around a diverse range of emotions: guilt over leaving her daughter behind each day, premature and – to my mind more than a little unnecessary – mourning for the loss of the mother-daughter relationship, and fear of another intruding on her role, all of which is at least sweetened by the excitement of regaining her professional life – though that's probably only an extra cause of guilt in itself.

Meanwhile, by contrast, lurking beneath my swirling mix of excitement and terror, there's an inevitable sense of humiliation at the role reversal. Almost by definition, Alpha males do not stay home to look after the kids. As such, proving myself successful in caring for Polly will not prove me a success.

So the question is this: what would be worse – Polly coming out with 'Dada' first and seeming to confirm all Zoë's fears, or the risk of my insecurities being realized as Polly calls me 'Mama' in public?

Friday, 7th September

'One more week till you take over,' says Zoë during Polly's tea. 'How are you feeling about it?'

She's playing it casual, but I know it's a trick question: too optimistic and I'll be rubbing her face in it; too terrified and she'll not only be resentful but worried for Polly's well-being as well.

'I reckon I'm pretty well prepared,' I tell her, cautiously. 'I'm used to being stuck at home without just turning on the telly. And it's not like I'll have to fight against the habit of nipping into the pub on the way home from the office.'

'So you're looking forward to it?' she asks, still poker-faced.

'Well,' I hesitate, pretending to plumb the depths of her question, 'I'm not underestimating the importance of the role. And obviously it'll be a challenge, like anything else worth doing. But it'll be a privilege as well.' How did this happen? I'm talking to my wife as though this is some sort of job interview.

She stops spooning in Polly's yoghurt and looks directly at me for the first time. 'You're not worried about having to be with Polly every second of the day?' she asks, suspiciously.

'*Having* to be with Polly means *getting* to be with Polly.'

From the way she suddenly swoops to clear the plates, it's clear I've gone too far. 'It'll be exhausting, though,' I say, frantically back-pedalling. 'And it's bound to be restrictive, being stuck at home all day. Especially now it's autumn.'

'You won't just sit inside with her, though, will you?'

'Of course not,' I say, making another immediate about-turn. 'We'll probably be out all the time. Fresh air and all.'

'And what about your work?'

I shrug, as though it's something I've barely considered. 'This won't last for ever, will it? Everyone always says how children grow up so fast, and you don't hear people on their deathbed wishing they'd spent more time working. Besides, with your mum's help and your afternoons off, it's not going to be full time – I'll still be able to work a bit, earn some money.'

'That's good,' she says, walking to the sink, smiling at last. 'So you're not worried?'

'Nope,' I return the smile. 'We'll be fine. Won't we, Polly?'

Zoë's bending down to load the dishwasher, so misses the look of incredulity on our daughter's face. At least I seem to have convinced one of us.

Monday, 10th September – 29 weeks old

'Polly's really showing signs of taste,' Zoë proudly declares.

'You mean she's trying to change the channel when you put on *America's Next Top Model*?'

'Ha ha. I mean that I put a fishfinger on her plate at lunch and after a bit of cautious investigation, she made it quite clear she was far from impressed.'

I notice similar touches of discernment at dinner. Refusing to finish her chicken stock and vegetable slush, she then gets a taste of puréed pear and suddenly I just can't shovel it in fast enough.

'Imagine what it must be like,' says Zoë, watching from the safety of the other side of the table. 'She's gone from the monotony of breastmilk to the full spectrum of Annabel Karmel's dishes in just a few weeks. Doesn't it make you appreciate the mass of different tastes we take for granted every day?'

Still Polly's knocking back the pear, the spoon barely touching her lips before its contents disappear down her gullet.

'It feels like she's reached a new level,' says Zoë. 'Having a preference for one type of food over another shows that she's her own person and learning to make her own choices.'

Instead of an automaton baby to be changed and winded and fed in a never-ending circle without question, she's becoming a real individual, exhibiting characteristics and preferences for which we now have to make allowance.

As final confirmation of this development, Polly forces down a last mouthful of pear and then, seconds later, sicks it all up over my shoes.

There's something endearingly vivacious and strangely life affirming in her not knowing when she's had too much of a good thing.

Tuesday, 11th September

All day, Zoë is close to losing her temper. We eat dinner in silence and, by 8.30 p.m. she's donned earplugs and disappeared to the loft. Forty-five minutes later she's back, doubled over with nausea and searching for paracetamol while she mumbles about going to the hospital. And I find it impossible to know whether that's the professional recommendation of a medic or the moan of one who's exhausted and physically sick at the thought of leaving her daughter while she goes back to work.

Polly has been waking so often these last few nights that Zoë's terrified it'll become a pattern, especially as the emerging tooth we've been blaming it on has, so far, failed to appear, and an examination of the other side of her gum shows that the ridging we'd thought to presage its arrival is on both sides anyway. Even the constant dribbling like a broken tap and the chewing of anything she can get her hands on, from newspapers to tables, could be attributed to normal baby behaviour. Which means that, with no apparent cause for this degeneration in our nights, we've no way of gauging how long it'll last.

'It's just a phase,' I tell Zoë. 'It'll pass.'

'When?' she snaps, and stuffs in the earplugs again.

Wednesday, 12th September

Zoë takes Polly over to her mum's for the day, to introduce her to the schedule so she's ready to take over the childcare for one day a week. Since Polly seems to have experimented freely and finally settled on almost the exact timings that 'Gina says', Zoë carefully photocopies the relevant page from her now well-thumbed book.

'This is a silly routine,' says her mum, a veteran of three children, when presented with the schedule. 'These timings can't be right.'

'It's what Polly seems comfortable with. So, please, just humour me.'

With Polly taking her morning nap, she nips out to the shops, and gets back to find Polly still asleep, the printed timetable ignored.

That evening, Zoë's ranting before she's even through the door. 'I specifically asked her to wake Polly after half an hour! Now look at her!'

She points to the car seat where our daughter is fast asleep. 'Because she had such a long morning sleep, she didn't sleep at all this afternoon. God knows what tonight's going to be like.'

We struggle to wake Polly for her bath and then, dreading what might follow, put her down to sleep at the usual time. And by the time Zoë and I get to bed, she's slept more peacefully than she has in weeks.

'The worst thing,' whispers Zoë as she rolls over to sleep, 'is that it's going to look like Mum was right.'

Friday, 14th September

One of those alignments of happenings you couldn't dream up.

Zoë and I are pushing the pram towards the park to meet up with her dad and, given that this is her last day of maternity leave, the conversation is on the now typical topic – can we afford for Zoë to go part time?

'The main problem,' she tells me, 'is that although it would give you more time to work, you can't guarantee enough income to replace what we'd be losing.'

'I could work evenings and weekends to compensate.'

'But you still can't guarantee you'd be able to sell what you write! And then I'd be paying the price twice over – we'd still have less money, and I'd see even less of you!'

'True. But unless I get a proper job and put Polly into childcare full time, I've got to make the most of the few means of earning I've got.'

Then, within minutes of us arriving in the park, my agent calls.

'We've got you an audition,' she says. 'It's for *River City* again, and this time it's perfect for you.' She reads the character description: a Scot with a mild accent, my age, my build, athletic from an outdoorsy life but likes his books as well.

As she reads out the details, I grow more and more excited. It's as though the writers have based every aspect of this character on my life – except the alcoholic lesbian mother, perhaps.

I'm grinning in anticipation, because this feels like an eleventh-hour reprieve, the opportunity not just to escape the househusbandry but to claim the career I've spent the last six years fighting for. 'So when is it?' I ask. 'When's the audition?'

'Monday.'

Shit – Zoë's first day back at work, and my first full day of childcare. I hang up with muted thanks and break the news to my wife.

'You'll have to call Mum,' she says, lips pursed. 'See if she can take Polly.'

Two minutes later I know that she can't.

'Where's the meeting?' asks Zoë's dad.

'Just by Oxford Circus.'

'That's just round the corner from my office,' he says. 'You could leave her with me.'

It's embarrassing, to be begging for back-up already, on my first day of looking after Polly. But I've no alternative, and jump at the offer.

Beside me, Zoë's sitting in heavy silence, and I know what she's thinking. Although this opportunity could lead to a future the like of which we were dreaming of just minutes ago, she's far from happy. Because, as ever, this audition offers no guarantees. And meanwhile, as ever, it's everyone else – from Polly to the in-laws – paying the price for my hopes.

Sunday, 16th September

Zoë remains surprisingly calm about tomorrow's return to work – until she interrupts my script-learning to take me through Polly's schedule, like a general addressing his nervous troops. Except these troops are apparently so incapable that, by the end of the half-hour pep talk, the general's ready to give up the fight herself.

Polly doesn't help the situation, waking around 10 p.m. having tugged out her dummy. Unfortunately, although she's sufficiently coordinated to remove it, she's not yet up to stuffing it back in, so by midnight I've already staggered through to the nursery four times, each time deliberately not turning on the light and avoiding all eye contact that might get her excited, fumbling in the darkness of the cot for the dummy and then, finally, trying to force it into her ear.

'She can't settle herself now without it,' groans Zoë from somewhere beneath her pillow. And I can't avoid a feeling of guilt because, after all, it's me who's been championing that little plastic teat while Zoë's only ever used it reluctantly, suspiciously, as though it was a threat to her nipples from the start.

Monday, 17th September – 30 weeks old

Zoë's first day back at work. Being a Monday, she's also the doctor on call, giving her all the emergency patients on top of the routine. She drives off around 7.30 a.m. already close to despair, with no choice but to leave me to sink or swim in the deepest of deep ends I could ever be thrown into – a potentially career-launching audition of the sort I can't afford to screw up, all while holding the baby alone for the first time.

No battening down the hatches and taking things easy, no mastering the home routine before venturing further afield – by early afternoon I'm part-pushing, part-carrying Polly and her pram towards the heart of Oxford Circus.

Deciding to ignore plans for a sleep on the tube, she opts instead to stare at our fellow travellers – not smiling, just gawping with a mildly scornful look of incredulity as though every single person has stepped out wearing horribly clashing clothes or mismatched shoes. So by the time we arrive at Zoë's dad's office, Polly's too fractious to take her two o'clock milk, and both she and the secretary seem equally unmoved by my best rendition of 'The Ugly Duckling'. I jiggle her desperately, realizing I couldn't have engineered a more tired or hungry baby to dump on my father-in-law.

As I head across the street to the casting studio, frantically trying to focus on my reason for being there, Zoë's dad sets off to push Polly around Portland Square. My stomach is churning with nerves while my head's spinning with guilt: already, on my first day of childcare, my daughter is paying the price of my lifestyle. I walk into the studio determined to prove myself, to make the disruption worthwhile by bagging the job.

Naturally, the auditions are running late. For half an hour I squirm on a bench, waiting, all the time expecting to hear Polly's cries reverberate around the West End. And then, all of five minutes later, I'm running back across the street to heat her milk before it gets any closer to her teatime.

'How did it go?' asks Zoë's dad.

'I think it went well. I think. At least, I didn't make any mistakes. But it's impossible to tell. Either they like the look of me, or they don't. And how's Polly been?'

'Great! She fell asleep the moment you left and has only just woken up.'

'I don't believe it!' I peer down into the pram where Polly's smiling sleepily. 'She was so moody when I handed her over.'

'Were you nervous before the audition?'

'Absolutely.'

'So maybe Polly picked up on your nerves. They do say babies can tune in to their parents' feelings.'

'That doesn't seem very fair.'

'Why not?'

'Because babies already have a sufficient arsenal of techniques to make parents' lives difficult without having the ability to read minds as well.'

Polly's home and in the bath when Zoë staggers through the door, exhausted.

'How was it?' I ask.

She smiles, as though uncertain. 'Good and bad. I sat for a whole hour at lunch just gossiping and reading a magazine, but it was really frustrating wasting time like that when I could've been with Polly. And it was great seeing all my regular patients again. A few of them – including one 92-year-old – have refused to see any other doctors for the last seven months. Which meant they'd been saving up all their problems for me to deal with.'

On her insistence, we turn our lights out around 9.15. Half an hour later, I give up and use my phone as a reading light, my mind whirling with the possibility of a future we've already agreed there's no point in considering. But I can't help it, and the questions circulate unbidden. What would happen if I got this part? What effect would it have on Polly? On my marriage? Would it pay enough for Zoë to stop working and join me in Scotland? Or would she be forced to remain in London, to all intents and purposes a single working mum?

This feels like my last chance to be something other than a househusband. Two possible futures rear before me – top-level acting, or bottom-level wiping – and all I can do is wait to see which will be mine.

Tuesday, 18th September

Zoë leaves at a quarter to eight, by which time I'm already too busy with Polly to know if she's crying as she walks out the door. She lasts less than half an hour before calling.

'How is she?'

'She's fine. How are you?'

'Annoyed. One of my patients hasn't turned up so I could've had a few more minutes with Polly this morning.'

'You should make the most of it, reclaim some time for yourself.'

'I know, but I can't help feeling guilty.'

Zoë and I seem to be hoarding so much guilt, it would be nice to think that somewhere in the world they're having to ration it as a consequence.

The Eighth Month

Wednesday, 19th September

Cowering behind a sheep-shaped musical 'learning centre', I tentatively offer Polly spoonfuls of puréed breakfast. Since she's taken to blowing raspberries through every meal, it's the only way to escape the worst of the splattering.

It's her first day with Grandma so, having made sure the front airbag is safely off, I load up the car and drive round to Putney.

By 9.30 I'm back at my desk, tapping away on the laptop. And even though I know it's too early, I'm waiting as ever with fluttering hope for the phone to ring. It seems as though any minute could release an avalanche that will sweep through our lives and change everything. Then again, it may be that nothing will happen, nothing but more of the same.

Friday, 21st September

By mid-afternoon, I buckle and call my agent, desperate for news.

'Nothing yet, Andrew. I spoke to them yesterday and they liked your reading a lot, but they've a couple more days of auditioning here in London and then they're doing more in Glasgow. And the shoot doesn't start for a few months anyway.'

My future, and perhaps my sanity, is beyond my control. Meanwhile a week of caring for Polly through the days and settling her through the nights and then running off to work whenever she takes a nap has left me bone tired. So I'm more than happy to comply when Zoë returns around one o'clock, grabbing Polly out of my hands and declaring, 'I want to do everything over the weekend.'

Saturday, 22nd September

It's not yet noon, and already Zoë's grumbling because I'm not helping enough. 'I'd forgotten how exhausting it can be,' she says.

Sunday, 23rd September

I can tell something's up by the way Zoë's barely said a word all evening, and I dread having to ask what's wrong only to be told the obvious, to be reminded once more that it's my lack of secure income that's forcing her apart from her daughter. But her answer surprises me, and in some terrible way comforts me.

'I'm just feeling really guilty,' she says, undressing for bed.

'Why?'

'Because I'm really looking forward to going back to work tomorrow – it's so much easier than looking after Polly.'

'How?'

'Because in the surgery I'm in charge of every minute – it's predictable. But you lose that element of control when you're looking after a baby. And there's also the time off: the lunch hour or the commute, the minutes between patients.'

In comparison, I think of the day awaiting me: an ancient bag of mozzarella fell out of the fridge this evening and exploded across the floor so there's mopping to be done and – thanks to Zoë cooking a roast dinner last night – there's a chicken carcass to be stripped and stock to be made, there's a big pile of nappies to be washed and, of course, all while taking care of an eight-month-old baby.

Fifty minutes after turning out the light, I still haven't shrugged myself free of the usual thoughts, from my dread of the week ahead to the loss of Dad and Ardburdan – and that's when Polly begins to cry. For the first time.

By midnight, Zoë has gone to sleep upstairs and I've just settled Polly for the third time. Crawling back to bed, the realization strikes me: *this is it.* Unless I get that *River City* job, this is my life for the foreseeable future: minutes carved from the weekends and evenings to write, and for the rest of the time I'll be changing nappies and reading the same stories and singing the same songs again and again.

For the first time since the misery of boarding school, I turn into the depths of my bed for a comfort I already know I'll never find.

Tuesday, 25th September – 31 weeks, 1 day old

It's 5.45 a.m. We wake to the sound of Polly's cries and share what's now the usual glance across the pillow in recognition of the continuing irony – that Zoë, who would love to be spending more time with Polly, is forced to go to work, while I, who would love to be spending more time working, am forced to look after Polly, all the time carrying out my duties with one eye on the phone, waiting for the call that will absolve me from the responsibility and rescue me from the routine. Worst of all, I wonder what effect such a dynamic must be having on Polly, who deserves so much better.

After all – even were I fully committed to childcare as a lifelong ambition – surely there's *some* difference between the way a man and a woman care for a child? And what of the indirect effects, as exhibited through the attitudes of those around her? Will the mothers of Polly's friends really be as willing to invite her back to play in their homes if it means a man has to come along as well, or will I have to offer to shift garden furniture or put up shelves at the same time?

Allowing the dad to raise the child while the mum goes out to work seems dangerously like testing a new drug, or using one of those latest-generation, ultra-powerful mobile phones, or beaming wi-fi around the home. Have househusbands really been around long enough for us to know what impact such a parental role reversal can have?

The more time Polly has to spend with me, the more chance there is that I'll get something wrong. And as one used to indulging a desire for frequent bouts of solitude, I'm not sure *I'd* want to be forced into my company every waking hour.

The one consolation is that, at this age, she should be too young to remember the sight of me on the toilet.

Friday, 28th September

It's 6 a.m. when Polly begins to cry.

'I'll get her,' offers Zoë, leaping from bed with the enthusiasm of one desperate for every minute with her daughter. And even at that time of the morning it doesn't take much – the approaching weekend, a warm bed to hide in while someone else soothes Polly's wails – for me to appreciate that, in tears or without, our daughter is an amazing addition to our lives. After over seven months, it's still a constant source of bafflement how something so perfect could have come from the two of us.

Today Zoë is holding her first minor surgery clinic in months. As I pull the bed covers tight, I wonder if the queue of patients lining up before her scalpel would be quite so willing if they knew how little sleep their doctor actually gets, or how keen she always is to finish her work and get home as quickly as possible.

Monday, 1st October – 32 weeks old

This is only my third week of caring for Polly, and already I'm forced to seriously consider that sweeping generalization according to which women create while men control: in the most authentic sense of the word, women are the creative sex – they nurture the world they have made – while men step out the front door each day to subordinate the world unto themselves.

Although time may yet ease our adjustment, our set-up not only seems to confirm the rectitude of such historical roles but, worse, it lends credence to the theory that women are taking over. Because, having created life, Zoë steps out each day to perpetuate it, dominating both the domestic and professional spheres. Meanwhile, my relative lack of professional success has forced a retreat into the domestic sphere, and I'm struggling there as well.

Every wipe of the muslin feels like the waving of a white flag.

Tuesday, 2nd October

After another broken night as Polly repeatedly spits out her dummy then cries for its return, we're all as tired as ever – but at least the baby's allowed to show her tears. Zoë's out the door by 7.30, and I know immediately that I lack the energy to manage.

I take Polly for a walk, but get no further than the end of the street before her cries make me turn around and head for home. In the afternoon, after trying for half an hour to rock her to sleep without success, I try again, slipping her under the pram's rainproof cover and heading out the door.

I thought it was an acknowledged and acceptable means of settling a baby, to walk her quiet, but the glares of the few mothers also out braving the rain make me very aware that, just as they might have to work twice as hard in business to be considered equal to men, in the world of childcare, I'm guilty until proven innocent.

Merely being with their children, it seems, qualifies a woman as a good mother; men, however, have to prove themselves capable. And because I continue to walk along the street, trying to ignore the crying pram before me, I'm clearly under suspicion.

Friday, 5th October

I live in fear of being asked what I do for a living. Where before the answer 'actor and writer' stimulated a reasonable amount of interest, now my principal job description is met with an awkward politeness, that same pitiful nod I've seen ending all discussion on receiving the answer 'housewife' – a role that, however worthy, is still viewed as essentially a job by default. But at least housewives have the consoling and accepting expectation of centuries.

Three weeks after the audition and my agent's still heard nothing more about it. The silence in itself isn't conclusive, but it's a long way short of a job offer. With each passing day, my hope shrivels further while my desperation increases.

Sunday, 7th October

Dad regularly used to muddle up the names of his three sons to the point that he'd frequently run through all three before getting it right: 'Nathan ... Andrew ... I mean Rob...'

I used to wonder how he could get something like that wrong. But now, bogged down in the intellectual wasteland of the nursery, I get it wrong all the time – and that's with only *two* names to choose from in Zoë and Polly. By contrast, Dad was a genius.

History was his pet subject and, while he never remembered our telephone numbers, he could instantly recall every detail of the most obscure event from centuries ago. Mention of a minor skirmish or inconsequential treaty would prompt a flourish of dates as he reeled off the ages of everyone involved. I, meanwhile, find myself unable to remember my *own* age, and have to work it out by counting up from the year in which I was born.

My brain is frazzled and, less than eight months down the line, I fear the damage could be irrevocable. Yet despite mourning the agility of those few brain cells I used to muster, a small part of me recognizes the evident deterioration with a shrug – I've lost something that these days I just don't need: my exhaustion and Zoë's at the end of each day precludes any chat more meaningful than the TV schedule. And though the radio offers some mental stimulation, it is – perhaps fortunately – unable to mount much of a riposte to my contributions.

Day by day, I'm de-skilling; I live in dread of the moment Polly comes in from school to ask for help with her homework.

Monday, 8th October – 33 weeks old

Soon after midnight, when Polly refuses to settle for the third time, it dawns on us that the steady trickle of snot is not just from her crying. She has a cold. The moment I lay her down and she closes her mouth, she wakes in a fog of confusion, bawling at the inexplicable sense of suffocation.

'I *knew* that kid looked ill!' spits Zoë, furious. 'His parents should never have brought him along.' She's talking about the birthday party on Saturday and the small boy, a roving bundle of phlegm and germs, who sneezed in Polly's face.

'Typical!' she fumes. 'Just as she was getting more settled.'

Polly's two short, mid-afternoon naps have been merging into one lengthy, deeper sleep and, though she's still waking with the loss of the dummy, she has seemed better rested, and more cheerful through even her normally grisly evening period.

After breakfast I pull something from Polly's nose so abundant and stringy that I'm forced to wrap it round my finger three times before it breaks free. I take her to the chemist at the end of the street and am sold a small bottle of nasal drops.

'How am I meant to give her this?' I ask. 'Do I hold her by the feet and just pour it in?' Either the pharmacist fails to hear the frustration in my voice, or he simply ignores it.

'No,' he laughs, and when no further advice is forthcoming, I head for home.

Ten minutes later, Polly's face is so liberally sprayed it looks like she's been crying for months, and still not a single drop has gone up her nose. She stares at my suggestive miming as though I've gone mad.

Around lunchtime, Zoë calls for her customary update.

'Yeah, I'd have given you nose drops in that situation as well, but it's just saline.'

'So I've just spent £1.99 on a bottle of salty water?'

'Exactly. It's next to useless. Have you taken her temperature?

Zoë waits while I press the little monitor against Polly's forehead.

'It's 37.4°.'

'That's fine – anything up to 37.5° is normal.'

But by the time she gets home, Zoë's obviously decided that one thermometer isn't enough; a second, more expensive model is soon stuffed into Polly's ear – and then all hell breaks loose.

'It's gone up,' shrieks Zoë. '38.3°!'

'What does that mean?'

'It could be anything,' she answers, mind spinning. 'Tonsillitis, an ear infection, maybe even pneumonia!'

I look at Polly sitting in her cot, still determinedly licking the snot from her top lip and playing quite cheerfully with the packaging for her mummy's new toy. 'She doesn't seem any worse.'

'Her first temperature!' Zoë frets. 'Oh God, Andrew!'

'It's not that high.'

'But it might still be climbing!'

Just then Polly turns the box upside down and a small bag falls out, full of what look like small transparent attachments. 'Zoë?' I point.

Two minutes later, this time with the proper plastic 'hygiene cap' fitted over the end of the thermometer, Zoë shoves it once more into Polly's ear. One beep later, her temperature reads 37.3°.

'Oh,' says Zoë, deflated. 'Maybe it's just a cold.'

Delving into her bag, she pulls out another new purchase: a plug-in vaporizer, and soon Polly's asleep in a room that's leaking menthol throughout the entire house.

Tuesday, 9th October

Polly continues to suck on her top lip with such relish that, were it not coming from her in the first place, I'd worry about her salt intake. Although beyond her snot-blocked nose there's nothing wrong with her – as the near-drained batteries in the thermometer will attest – the consequences of a single ailment are wide reaching.

I give her a spoonful of food and she spits it out within seconds, fighting for breath. I lay her down to sleep and, despite the Vicks rubbed plentifully into her chest and the pervasive stink of the menthol vaporizer, you can almost hear the fluid gurgling to form an air-tight seal deep inside the nostrils. Which, naturally, makes her cry. Which, naturally, makes the snot problem worse.

When she does finally settle, I have to tiptoe gently back from the cot – a move I've done so often in the last few days that my calf muscles ache. And thanks to the squealing of the floorboards that I thought I'd secured months ago with a multitude of screws and nails, getting out of the nursery is like a choreographed dance.

One positive consequence of her cold is that, unable to close her mouth for any length of time, Polly begins to reject her dummy. One negative consequence is that she continues to wake regularly and fight off any attempt to be settled, so she cries until the hair from her temples to the back of her head is soaked with her tears. And there are few things more disturbing than staggering through to your daughter's cot in the middle of the night, doped with fatigue, to see her beautiful face contort with each exhalation as two large, skin-like bubbles inflate beneath each nostril like the swelling of a toad's throat.

Wednesday, 10th October

I've seen more sunrises in the last eight months than in the whole of the rest of my life put together, and there are moments when I'm surprised to find that London can be silent, properly silent, so quiet that my ears ring with the settled air. No trains click-clacking down from Clapham, no planes roaring overhead, no sirens, no birds trumpeting the early hour or cars hurling themselves down our street, no children shouting and stomping or babies crying next door. And no sound from Polly. The trouble is, it's those moments when the world is finally quiet that I'd rather be asleep.

As for Polly, we seem to be weaning her off the dummy and onto the wave machine – a plug-in box offering typical New Age noises like waterfalls, crashing waves and rainforests. It's a gift which months ago I thought a terrible waste of generosity but now have come to appreciate, particularly as soon our daughter won't be able to rest unless we're living by the coast, far from the sound of London traffic. If only it emitted the smell of Irn Bru, haggis and deep-fried Mars Bars at the same time, I'd never turn it off.

Thursday, 11th October

Polly can now shake her head. Since she can't yet nod, communication remains somewhat stilted, but it's great to have even the illusion that we're exchanging thoughts. As the day progresses, a few lengthy discussions establish a number of fundamentals: I'm not Polly, she's not a cow and, reassuringly, I'm not Mummy. Choose the question carefully and she's liable to reveal a firmly held opinion on everything from the wisdom of withdrawing from Afghanistan to whether or not it's safe to place a tenner on the Springboks.

Sally calls in the afternoon, kindly asking if I'd like to join her and baby Stephen for a walk in the park. I wait for them by the gates, Polly calm in the pram beside me.

A little boy walks past, gesturing towards me. 'Mummy,' he says, 'what's that man doing?'

By the swings, a little girl points and turns to the woman beside her. 'Look, Mummy! There's a man.'

The apparent novelty of a male adult in the playground midweek makes me feel like a celebrity. Unfortunately, though, more Gary Glitter than Tom Cruise.

Friday, 12th October

Ignoring that little voice that says I shouldn't have to go in search of friends, I set off for the local dads' group with Polly in a sling and a changing bag over my shoulder.

By the time I'm opening the door of the church hall to be met by a barrage of screams and chatter, it feels like my first day at school. Only this time I do at least have a best friend strapped to my chest.

Beyond an initial welcome from the guys in charge, I pretty soon find myself anchored to a mat in the middle of the room: Polly's the youngest there and, as the other kids run around and, in some cases, run *over* one another in little plastic buggies, she needs constant attention. At best she stretches to allow her curiosity local rein amongst the plastic toys that look like they've been in at least a hundred teething mouths already.

I look around. The majority of dads, freed from direct childcare by the relative self-sufficiency of their children in a room full of toys, huddle around the coffee machine and biscuit tin, discussing the previous night's football results with lively good humour.

By contrast, on the low benches surrounding the mat, three dads stare at their babies, silent and morose, as though waiting for a bell to ring and free them from their duty. The obvious cheer elsewhere in the hall only highlights their gloom.

For 45 minutes, I struggle to rouse them in conversation between self-conscious efforts to engage Polly with toy trains, books and puzzles. She stares occasionally at the other babies but is too young to interact, and we fathers seem to feel too old. When I mutter my goodbyes, saying I have to get Polly back for her lunch, it's a convenient excuse, and I walk home wondering what either of us has really gained from the outing.

'Well?' asks Zoë when she gets home after lunch.

'I think it's one of those things where you get out of it what you put in,' I tell her, mindful that it's not necessarily for my benefit anyway. 'I'll give it another go.'

Sunday, 14th October

I'm sitting with Polly on the sofa reading her a story when, in a move so understated and natural that it makes my heart swell, her little hand seeks out mine and grasps it tight.

'I held my father's hand on the day that he died,' Dad used to tell us. 'I held his hand and I told him that I loved him.'

Such an intimacy, related so proudly and with such sincerity, always made an impact. So as I sit holding hands with my daughter, I'm unavoidably reminded of the day that he died, as he sat on the edge of his bed fighting back the choking coughs. Sitting beside him, I looked at his hand, the callused palm pale, the nicotine-stained fingers curled and inert, and I wanted to take his hand in mine. I wanted to tell him that I loved him, and to thank him for everything he'd ever done for me. I wanted in some small way to offer a sense of closure, an expression of a cycle that was now complete.

But to do so would have been too much like a goodbye, a gesture too recognizable as a parting. And so, although he was never anything but overtly practical about what lay ahead, I couldn't bring myself to acknowledge it so brazenly.

The moment passed. Instead of taking his hand, I sat with him as he struggled for air and slipped in and out of sleep.

'Do you want to go to the hospital?' I asked at last, the agreed plan for when the tumour began to restrict his breathing.

'Not yet...' he managed, raising one hand to wave the idea away. 'Not yet...'

Although never explicitly mentioned, we were all – doctors included – quietly hoping that his body would give up before it became necessary to open an airway through his throat. So I helped him back into bed and made him as comfortable as I could without seeming to fuss, and we woke the next morning to find him gone.

After seeing him fight through so many false alarms to linger for so long, I shied away from acknowledging what could be our last moment together. And although I know that he loved me and I'm sure he knew that I loved him, I still regret not having taken what I realized at the time was an opportunity.

The thought makes me gather Polly into my arms and, in the face of her tolerant bemusement, squeeze her tight as though to draw out the memory.

Monday, 15th October – 34 weeks old

Even though Polly's now entirely off the dummy, she's never really taken to sucking her thumb. Yet she's quite willing to hold it out for others to suck, an admirable display of economy of effort akin to Blackadder's demand that Baldrick run into his fist.

Zoë returns from work with a CD intended to lull Polly to sleep with the sort of banal muzak you'd hear dribbling from the speakers in shopping centres. And it works, which means that when we tiptoe out of the room, sneak downstairs and turn on the monitor, we find ourselves eating dinner to a chorus of pan-piping whales.

Hopefully, trusting to Pavlov, years from now Polly will find future shopping trips just too lethargic to do any damage to my credit card.

The Ninth Month

Saturday, 20th October

'You can't send that!'

Zoë's mum has come round to babysit and caught sight of a thank-you card waiting to be posted, one of those ones that allow you to make a postcard of your own photo. Unsurprisingly, Zoë has inserted a snap of Polly.

'Why not?' asks Zoë. 'I thought that was a nice shot of her.'

'It's not that. If you send that as it is, people will know that Polly lives here.'

Refraining from asking why that might matter, Zoë points out that there's nothing on the card to link the baby on the front to either our name or address.

'But they'll know that baby lives around here!' insists her mum.

'Fine. We're going out to New Malden. I'll post it there.'

'Oh, no, Zoë! Don't post it like that. Please!'

Listening in to the discussion, I can't but agree with Zoë's firmly independent approach. 'She's *my* daughter. And there's nothing to worry about anyway.'

Her mum manages five seconds of silence before she tries again. 'Why don't you put it in an envelope?'

I can't work out if I should be more amazed at Zoë's forbearance or her mother's nervousness.

'Let me take it, then,' says her mum. 'I'll post it for you.' Not the most secretive of plans, the obviousness of what she intends being all too clear. But Zoë's gratitude at her babysitting melts her refusal into an offer to provide an envelope and, by the time we leave, the photocard of Polly is tucked away and out of sight.

As we drive away, I try to work out what the danger is – presumably that someone will spy the photo of Polly (while either emptying the letterbox or sorting the mail) and become so besotted with her that they stake out the entire neighbourhood awaiting an opportunity to grab her.

It's nothing less than priceless having a besotted grandmother on our side, but there are enough things to worry about without grasping at more tenuous scares.

'She's far, far more nervous with Polly than she ever was with me,' says Zoë, in a bid to explain.

'So has she just grown more nervous over time, or is she admitting at last that London's not such a great place to raise a child?'

A loyal silence, but the opportunity's too great to miss.

'Perhaps Polly would be safer in Scotland?'

'Just drive the car.'

Friday, 26th October – 35 weeks, 4 days old

We're making decisions all the time in answer to questions we've not yet guessed. Only now do I see how that one simple act all those months ago was ruling out possibilities and turning me away from paths I didn't even know existed. Now they may never exist.

I accepted long ago that having a baby means we're unable to head out together for an impromptu pub night, or drop everything and disappear for a weekend on the continent. Thanks to my loyalty to an unadventurous life of relative domesticity, I can easily live with such a loss.

What I hadn't appreciated is the loss of another freedom: the power to change profession – that aspect of ourselves that, rightly or wrongly, defines and demands so much of us. Before Polly came along, I naively imagined I could be anything I chose, because that sometimes bewildering array of career options is also reassuringly fluid. I could have been an architect or lawyer. I could have devoted my life to saving the dolphins, become a Vegas drag queen or founded my own cult.

But now that Zoë and I are agreed that we want to bring up our child ourselves rather than handing over her formative years to a relative stranger, my life is no longer so malleable; this role of househusband is a Herculean hold. It's what I now am, and there's no room to change. Staying at home to raise kids doesn't bear comparison with any other career one may choose to follow – exactly because, with a career, there is a choice.

Unless I can somehow earn enough to allow Zoë to step back from work (assuming she'd even want to), then my new role is a permanent one. As such, acceptance of the job seems to equate to an acknowledgement akin to saying, 'Very well – at least until this child is of school-going age, I renounce my own potential in favour of fostering theirs.'

Of course, women have been giving up their options in order to raise children for generations, and perhaps it's about time that a few men did the same. But when you're suffering from claustrophobia, it's no consolation to think about all the others who've felt restricted in the same way.

'The hand that rocks the cradle is the hand that rules the world,' runs the poem. Try telling that to Alexander the Great – I don't remember hearing about his post-feed burping technique, or Napoleon's grumbling because Junior cried right through the night. Although I've no immediate plans to take over the planet, it might be a little restrictive if I've got to stop to change nappies every few minutes.

So although I may be shaping my own child's future while rocking the cradle, it's hard to see how I'm helping to shape my own. As such, I can't help feeling I'm standing down from any thought of standing out.

Monday, 29th October – 36 weeks old

Polly begins wheezing with each intake of breath. Alarmed, I call Zoë.

'That sounds like stridor,' she says, obviously frightened. 'Has she got anything stuck in her throat?'

'Nothing I can see.'

'Is she red in the face?'

'No.'

'It might be an infection. Take her temperature – I'll wait.'

When Polly's temperature is confirmed as normal, Zoë relaxes only marginally. 'Keep a close eye on her. If she gets any worse, you need to take her straight to Casualty.'

In fact, aside from the strange breathing, Polly seems totally normal, so I've just begun to prepare her lunch when the doorbell rings – it's Zoë's mum. At the sight of her, Polly's wheezing immediately grows heavier, but rather than the expected concern, her grandma's face breaks into an enormous grin.

'That's right, Polly!' she coos. 'A cow!'

'A cow?' I ask, stupefied.

'Yes! I've been teaching her animal noises,' she says proudly. 'And that's a cow.' She inhales, matching Polly's strained gasp. 'Clever girl, Polly!'

Promising myself that one day soon I'll get Polly into the countryside to introduce her to the real thing, I pick up the phone to tell Zoë that our daughter is not, in fact, fatally ill. Behind me, a gleeful though severely asthmatic herd is rampaging around the front room.

Tuesday, 30th October

I'm used to seeing Zoë's long blonde hairs everywhere, from the pillow to the kitchen table. But it's a shock to glance down at the sofa and spot a small curl of fair hair too short to be hers and too light to be mine.

Although our home's now covered in endless baby paraphernalia, from playmats and board books to walkers and coats, somehow a single baby hair highlights the existence of another family member more than anything else.

Friday, 2nd November

'Maybe we should have got the train,' says Zoë, looking nervously through the window of the plane as she tightens Polly's safety belt across her lap. 'That would feel safer somehow.'

'Are we never going to fly anywhere again now we've got Polly?'

'I guess not. It's just a risk, isn't it?'

Of course, everything's a risk – but having Polly to worry about increases our exposure. And it doesn't help to read stories in the press about babies being abused or snatched from prams, or to console ourselves with the thought that while it might be headline news if one child is abducted, in the same day perhaps 50 lost children have been independently reunited with their parents by helpful strangers. Because even if most of our fears are shadows, that one occurrence just proves that abduction happens.

The desire to ensure our daughter's safety and happiness is so strong that I feel an impossible urge to bundle up all safeguards, to lock in a steel chest all the qualities that could make her life better – love, health, understanding, kindness, wealth, friendship – and bury them at the bottom of the garden so we can sit back, confident that they'll all be there for her when needed. But it doesn't work like that. Instead, for years to come, it'll be a daily task, balancing our worries for her security against her living her own life.

As much as anything else, parenthood seems to be about managing risk, and so far my attitude has been similar to the one I find myself adopting now on the plane. Innumerable things could go wrong, the worst of which could, ultimately, end in death. And yet, after a certain point, there's just nothing I can do. From the possibility of her choking or catching chickenpox to the ever-present terror of cot death, parents cannot ward off every evil. An element of fatalism seems essential every time I kiss Polly goodnight.

Soon we're airborne en route to Edinburgh, and Polly is behaving better than her parents, reading a book and taking her food with such attentive urgency that Zoë and I find ourselves almost crying with laughter. I shovel it down her gob as fast as my giggles will allow, until a disastrous clash of heavily laden spoon and turning page.

The day before his wedding, I meet most of Nathan's family-in-law for the first time with a crotch seemingly encrusted with moulding cottage cheese.

Saturday, 3rd November

In a sumptuously decorated hotel castle in the heart of Edinburgh, Nathan and Rowena are married. Between the celebrations, Polly gets to meet more of her family. There's a bushy red beard from the west, and a neatly clipped moustache from Germany. There's an American accent over from Boston, a few bilingual tongues from Paris and, given that Rowena's family are Irish, more than a few lilts and brogues. All of which I hope will distract Polly from the shock of seeing her dad in a tartan skirt.

Sunday, 4th November

The weekend has only reminded me how much I love Edinburgh: the accessibility of its compact centre and the countryside around it; the greater proportion of smiles as opposed to scowls and, above all, my family and friends.

'It's people like him who'd persuade me to move to Scotland,' says Zoë of our cheerfully chatty cab driver as he drops us at the airport, and instantly I'm regretting not having tipped more generously.

Monday, 5th November – 37 weeks

It's late morning and Polly's screaming. It started without provocation in the park and continued all the way home, unchecked even by the sight of her toy panda dancing along the top of the garden walls lining the street.

Thinking she must be hungry, I take her straight through to the kitchen to start on her lunch – mashed potato and melted cheese with beans. But she won't let me put her down and, hurrying to get it ready with a shrieking baby on my arm, I grate a slice of knuckle into the dish as well.

Soon my throbbing hand's wrapped in reddening kitchen towel, Polly's in her chair with a few choice books laid out before her, and the food's approaching her mouth. At the last moment she twitches away, arms flailing deliberately to knock the spoon out of my hand. It falls to the floor having unloaded its contents all over me.

And for just a second, as I struggle with the instinctive urge to retaliate even with just a shout, I see how some – the impatient, the intemperate, the unsupported, the frustrated or the just plain exhausted – could lose their temper and do something worse.

There's something about that first mouthful of every meal, as though Polly's making a point of resisting but then, won over, realizing it's not so bad after all – like an asceticism proudly guarded that, once lost, is willingly and repeatedly annulled.

But today, even with the typical distraction of a book, Polly refuses to take that first spoonful. I try singing to her. I try swooping the food in like an aeroplane. I try feeding some to Panda, then to myself. In desperation, I'm about to call Zoë for help when my mobile rings. Although I'm reluctant to get distracted, I can see it's my agent calling.

'Andrew?'

'Hi.' I have to shout over the cries.

'Is this a good time?'

'I'm just feeding Polly.'

'I'll be quick. I just got a call from *River City*.'

With just those few words, I'm raised instantly to a watershed – to one side, a move to Scotland that offers professional vindication, financial reward, profile and promise; to the other, months and months of identical days, all of them pre-allocated to boredom, exhaustion and routine. Even my heart stops what it's doing to hear the verdict.

'It's not going to work, I'm afraid. They loved meeting you, they said, and they really want to use you at some point, but they...'

She's still talking, but I've stopped listening. Polly's cries have reached a new crescendo, her lunch is now cold and, after months of desperate hope, it's finally been confirmed: this is my life.

Thursday, 8th November

For the last few days, with Polly's waning appetite, her meals have become not so much nutritional as attritional. Although she's got plenty of weight in reserve, and although she's perfectly entitled just like anyone else to have a few days of eating less, I can't stop myself equating every spoonful to another 15 minutes of sleep for us all. So despite the risk of turning every lunch and tea into an hour-long trauma as she loses all faith in the power of a shaken head, still I cajole and tease, desperate to shovel Zoë's carefully prepared casserole down her gullet.

The kitchen's already a battleground littered with the debris of our every skirmish. Each broccoli-smeared chair tells its tale, each toast-crumbed tile, each soup-stained toy or fruit-smudged book. As forensic scientists retrace the sequence of a crime from the liberal blood spatters across the walls and floor, visitors to our kitchen could read the course of the struggles in the flicked banana and sticky patches of drying juice.

From the radio to the TV, every distraction has been tried and failed. The fingerprints on the glass door from where I tried to divert her to look into the garden; the spat yoghurt that's cascaded from her chin like rain from an overflowing gutter, trailing a path from table to sofa; the tumbled pots of fromage frais; the soggy bibs and my own crusted clothes – they all bear witness to our mutual grief and Polly's uncanny ability to shake her head so as to maximize the spray of food around the house, like a great furry dog emerging from the sea.

At what point is it all meant to get easier? Already I'm daydreaming of the moment Polly's old enough to start school or leave home, and I hate myself for it.

Before Zoë went back to work, I never understood that urge that prompts people to collapse at the end of the day with the moan, 'I need a drink.' But now, although it's barely noon, as I replace in the fridge the rejected remains of Polly's lunch, I find myself eyeing up that open bottle of wine.

Friday, 9th November

Every day is identical to the last – not difficult, just insufferably boring.

When Polly wakes from her morning nap, we go for the same walk to the same park – even the same swing. Some mums talk into phones while pushing their prams, and I long for someone to divert me with a call. Back home, when someone does ring – from India as part of a survey about electricity suppliers – I linger willingly through a 15-minute conversation about unit prices and green tariffs.

The arrival of the postman, with his latent potential to offer variety, constitutes one of the highlights of the day – potential that dwindles with each brown envelope thrust through the letterbox.

All the chores that can be done while Polly's around, from hanging up washing to returning phone calls, are done before her lunchtime, so that when the time comes for another meal, another change and another nap, I can put her down and race upstairs to the computer, desperate to achieve something for myself, to wring maximum value from these jealously hoarded minutes before the schedule drags me back down.

Despite a good afternoon nap, Polly wakes grouchy and difficult to calm. Zoë calls to say she's been held up at work and I hang up, head aching with exhaustion and nearly falling asleep despite the crying baby in my arms, and for the first time wonder whether I'll cope.

The thought of this future stretching out ahead, indefinitely, leaves me miserable. I'd rather cut back on all expenses, eat beans on toast for the years to come, if it means that Zoë can relieve me and let me return to a world I know.

I sit down to play with Polly on her mat and find myself falling asleep, splayed across the floor, head resting on an outstretched arm, as she rolls around my tumbled body. I'm daydreaming of the sound of Zoë's key in the lock, counting the minutes like a schoolboy waiting for the bell to announce the start of the summer holiday.

Dad would have been 65 today. Brooding on the date while Polly amuses herself, I retreat into memory, and am standing again outside the church, minutes after his funeral. We've carried his body down the aisle and squeezed awkwardly through the narrow door and are now standing beside the hearse at the bottom of the steps. The church is perched on the ridge of the hill and the wind is blowing up off the water, freezing, piercing – because Rob doesn't have a suitable dark-coloured coat, a sense of solidarity has left us all three without, and so we stand beside Mum and hop from foot to foot against the cold, shaking hands, thanking people for coming.

I'm surprised at how easily I can pretend to be OK, at how readily a smile comes to my face with each passing nod, until Zoë's dad steps forward from the line and, before I can do anything, smothers me in a squeezing embrace. And I have to fight the urge to collapse, resist the breaking of the dam that would have me sinking in tears.

Monday, 12th November – 38 weeks old

The dads' group again. I'm busy propping up a daughter insistent on awkwardly straddling a plastic garage when I hear a voice above the usual hubbub of the hall.

'Hi! We haven't met. I'm Ian.'

I look up from the playmat to see a thickly bearded man settle himself down onto the benches alongside.

'I'm Andrew.' I nod, with both hands full. 'And this is Polly.'

'Hello, Polly,' says Ian, leaning forward to knee level, but his effort earns him only a fierce eyeballing. 'How old is she then?'

'Coming up for ten months. How old is yours?'

'I've got two. Five and three. That's one of mine: Gemma.' He points to where a curly-haired blonde girl is marching around inside a plastic fire truck, holding it up as if it's meant to be worn tight around the hips. 'Harriet's at school.'

'So you live nearby?'

'No, I have to drive in from Twickenham.'

'There aren't any groups like this nearer?'

'There are the usual mothers' groups, but the last time I tried one of them with Harriet, they all went quiet when we walked in.'

'Because you're not a woman?'

'Because it was a swimming class and I forgot my trunks. I had boxer shorts on, but I think they were a bit clingy after the shower.'

I'm still wondering how to reply when he offers me a drink. 'I'll get it for you,' he says. 'You look like you'll be stuck to that mat for a while.'

Within minutes I'm struggling to balance a boiling hot coffee in one hand and a baby daughter in the other. 'Do you look after your girls full time?'

'Absolutely.'

'So how did you get into it?'

'The usual question,' he chuckles. 'And I'm afraid it's the usual answer: money. My wife earns far more than I'd ever manage, and I didn't really enjoy my job anyway. Plus we didn't want to hand our children over to be raised by someone else. We're just incredibly lucky – we can get by on one income, and I get to see my daughters grow up.'

His cheer is so obviously genuine, it's hard to refute. So I wonder what I'm missing; it's like we're both staring at the same painting but I, like a philistine, am seeing only a mess of squiggly colours while he's gaining some deeper message that offers meaning and inner fulfilment.

'It does get easier, you know,' he grins, as though well aware what I'm thinking. 'When they're as young as Polly here, they dictate every second, and I found that really tough. But wait till she starts to understand what you're saying and talking herself, then you'll start getting something back. If you're anything like I was, you'll find the first few months the hardest.'

As Polly and I head back for lunch, I wonder if I am anything like Ian. Not only because I've never dared take Polly swimming alone but because, if I discovered I'd left my trunks behind, I'd more than likely give up and go home. That in itself seems to say something about our differing approaches to the job.

Thursday, 15th November

Zoë has left for work and Polly's playing on her mat on the kitchen floor as I clear away her breakfast. Noticing that everything has gone ominously quiet, I peer round to see her using the front cross-struts of a chair to pull herself up onto her knees. As I watch, she twice forgets to hang on, leaving her wobbling unsteadily. Both times, just as she begins to fall forward, she manages to catch at the chair to break her fall.

I watch her – and the looming inevitable – in a quandary. 'Isn't this what parenting's about?' I wonder. 'Isn't this what they say about letting them learn from their mistakes?'

Pretty soon, as expected, Polly loses her balance and topples forward. Only this time it's her head that stops her fall where her hands failed, and soon she's face down on the mat, bawling.

Immediately, I pick her up and within 30 seconds have distracted her with a toy. No harm done, I think, as she giggles and grabs. Then a bruise begins to grow beside her right eye. Where the skin is slightly broken, a deepening reddish blotch screams 'neglect'. In a wave of guilt, I wonder if she's not a little young to be presented to a world where every move has to have a moral. I begin to dread our afternoon trip to the supermarket, as I push a bruised and battered advert to my parenting skills around the aisles.

When the time comes for her first nap of the day, I take Polly upstairs, change her nappy and put her in a clean vest. It's a few minutes later, as I lean over to kiss her before turning out the light, that I realize which top Zoë has dressed her in today: a long-sleeved t-shirt with 'Daddy's Girl' spelt out in diamanté. But while the word 'Girl' is still perfectly formed, the glittering specks forming the word 'Daddy's' have come off in the wash. Or have they, I wonder, been picked off in resentment by little fingernails?

The Tenth Month

Monday, 19th November – 39 weeks old

It's early evening. Polly's playing on the floor, babbling endlessly, while I read yesterday's paper. I'm waiting for the usual routine that inevitably follows Zoë's return home: the slam of the front door, the urgent shout of 'Where are you?' as bags are thrown to the floor, then the insistent stomp as she tracks us down, determined not to lose another second with her daughter, followed by the squeals of delight as the two girls are reunited.

And as I sit there anticipating the scene, working my way distractedly through the endless supplements, a word leaps out of the jumbled mess of noise coming from Polly, a single word so unexpected and powerful that it casts the autumn clouds aside and throws rainbows across the sky. 'Dada.' I couldn't be more surprised or delighted if a line of dancing girls had burst through the door to a cannonade of champagne corks.

In truth, it's more like, 'Brrr-gzzzz-wawawa-dada-dadadada-brrrrr,' and clearly the noise Polly's found herself making has no connection whatsoever with the man now kneeling before her with a big grin on his face, nodding encouragement as he laughs and repeats the noise over and over again. But it's a start.

How could I have known that hearing that noise would have such an effect? Not for much longer will I be able to console my immature self with the idea that I'm really just looking after this baby for someone else. When she actually starts calling me 'Daddy', the fact that I'm a father will be pretty hard to deny. And harder still to live up to. Hearing it from the lips of my daughter, that single word – or even Polly's approximation of it – becomes so much more than a mere name. It's so laden with association and heavy with suggestion that it almost feels like a challenge.

Perhaps over-sensitive to Zoë's fear of missing out while at work, I don't mention it when she finally storms into the house and crushes our baby in an ecstatic bear hug. Instead, I wait for Polly to repeat it later and for Zoë to notice it herself. I can only hope I'll be there when she hears Polly managing 'Mama' for the first time – if only to shield my daughter from the inevitable onslaught of delight.

Tuesday, 20th November

I'm working upstairs, a whole free afternoon ahead. When Polly wakes from her lunchtime nap with a cry, I hear Zoë bounding up the stairs to grab her. Moments later, there's a loud and ominous crack, a brief silence, and then a tentative call, 'Andrew?'

I go down to find Zoë and Polly lying side by side in the cot. 'What are you doing in there?'

'She looked so cute! I couldn't resist getting in beside her.'

'So you've broken the cot?'

'I'm not sure. I did hear a bit of a crack.'

'A bit of a crack? It sounded like a giant redwood falling to earth.'

While Zoë dresses Polly, I inspect the damage: one of the main support bars has split in two and will need to be splinted or replaced entirely. In an instant, my precious free hours have disappeared.

My annoyance is offset by amusement as I catch sight of Polly, now fully dressed head-to-toe in pink velour. 'What *have* you put her in?'

'It's got to be pink. Only the more expensive shops offer anything other than pink or blue.'

'But why has she got turn-ups?'

'Because of the washable nappies – they're so bulky I've had to put her in 12-to–18-month clothes so they fit round her bum. Which means they're too long in the leg.'

With her wispy hair, baggy backside and toothless gums, our daughter looks like one of those elderly women who've retired to Florida to play bridge.

That evening we're in the front room watching Polly doing her usual trick: reaching out to grab everything she can and – as likely as not – shoving it straight in her mouth. Having not yet mastered the principles of perspective, it usually results in an outstretched little arm grasping at something at least six feet away, like Luke Skywalker working on his Jedi mind tricks. Except I don't remember Luke ever sticking his tongue out of one side of his mouth.

Suddenly Polly freezes, fixes Zoë in a red-faced stare, and begins to grunt.

Zoë and I share a weary look but neither of us moves.

'She's looking at you,' I say.

'That's irrelevant – I've been looking after her all afternoon.'

'That's because I've been fixing a broken cot.'

It's a trump card. With a sigh of acceptance, Zoë hauls herself off the sofa. 'All right, Polly. Let's go and change you.'

Thursday, 22nd November

'Have you seen Panda?'

Zoë's urgent shout interrupts my work, prompting an automatic reply. 'No!'

'Did you have him earlier?'

I think back to our standard trip to the park. 'Polly was holding him on the swings but...' As the implication dawns, my next few words feel like the greatest admission of failure. '... I haven't seen him since.'

'You'll have to go and look for him, then. She'll not settle otherwise. And quick! Before the park closes.'

Grumbling, I retrace our steps through the strengthening streetlight towards the park, one eye on the pavement and another on the walls and railings alongside – the common resting place for stray items of clothing found gusted into corners, or stuffed animals curled in gutters, to the point that walking the streets can be like a tour of a toyshop, interspersed with odd socks, shoes and gloves.

I'm imagining what will happen if I can't find Panda: how long it'll be before Polly falls asleep without her best friend, and how hard it'll be to calm her wailings at 3 a.m. when she wakes all alone.

Most neighbourhoods have, on trees, walls and lampposts, scores of desperate flyposters offering rewards for help in tracking down runaway cats and dogs. Around here, where you're more likely to step on a discarded dummy than a dog turd, there are just as many flyposters offering enormous sums for the return of favourite dolls and other cuddly toys. The railway underpass at the park entrance often looks like a rogue's gallery of ursine mugshots, and already I'm composing in my head the words of Panda's 'Missing' poster, and imagining his face staring out from local milk cartons.

Within minutes, I've arrived at the park – too late. It's way past dusk and the gates are already locked. Peering desperately through the fence, I picture the park officials stumbling across Polly's little bear, picking him up and flinging him carelessly into a crate of forgotten toys that's then forklifted into a vast council warehouse somewhere, like that hangar at the end of *Raiders of the Lost Ark.*

At the thought of what Zoë will say to me, I begin to eye up the barbed wire around the top of the fence, wondering if I can scramble over to check out the playground.

That's when I spot him, hanging limp on a nearby railing, like an impaled criminal on the spikes of old London Bridge. Brushing off the worst of the dirt clinging to his ragged, black-and-once-white fur, I can see that he's none the worse for his ordeal and I check no one's around before quickly giving him a brief hug in the darkness.

When I get in, the house is full of Polly's cries. I step into her room holding Panda before me like a gold medal, undaunted by Zoë's critical shake of the head. At the sight of him, Polly's face turns instantly from misery to joy, her cries morphing in the way only hers can do into gleeful chuckles. She grabs Panda out of my hand, wrestles lovingly with him for a few seconds and then, having landed him a full body drop that would have snapped his back in an instant, she rolls over to sleep.

For the first time in months I feel like a successful father. Nothing – not the boredom, nor the exhaustion, nor the endless repetition of my days – can negate her smile of gratitude.

Admittedly, it was my fault that Panda got lost in the first place, but even the ability to right a wrong is a start.

Friday, 23rd November

Zoë gets back from work and rushes round the house before finding us in the nursery.

'The house is a tip,' she says with weary resignation as I hand Polly over, and instantly I'm defensive.

'What do you mean?'

'Polly's toys are all over the floor downstairs. Her lunch is spread around the kitchen. And your computer stuff is all over the sofa.'

'Because I've been trying to fix the broadband! Polly's toys are all over the floor because that's where she plays with them. And her lunch is spread around the kitchen because it's a nightmare trying to feed her at the moment!'

I appreciate that the mess is a stain on her otherwise happy homecoming, but to me it's a regrettable inevitability, the debris of another day's work, like the medical notes or overdue phone calls to a patient she has to complete over dinner. And although I know I'm being over-sensitive to what's intended as nothing more than a passing observation, it feels as if she's rubbing her own meticulousness in my face. Tired and prickly, I'm seeking justification for my self-pity.

Slouching downstairs to tidy up, I realize I've become the stereotypical little housewife – I may as well shout at her for treading mud into the carpet, or not hanging up her coat. Once again I'm counting down the days until March, when Polly begins at nursery.

Weighed down by exhaustion, guilt and our own brands of self-imposed pressure, we're both feeling the strain and both looking to nursery for some sort of relief: for me, it'll be two extra mornings a week to reclaim my life; for Zoë, it'll mean I no longer dominate the childcare so overwhelmingly. After all, it's as much about competitive parenting as our family's well-being, and the knowledge that I'm no longer spending *that* much more time with our daughter should go some way towards assuaging her guilt.

Until then, we're struggling to hold it together, and neither is giving the other of our best.

Sunday, 25th November

Given that attitudes, mannerisms and phobias can be inherited or inculcated, the thought of what we could be heedlessly passing on to Polly every second is terrifying.

Will she be a hoarder or a thrower-out? Unable to shower in less than 15 minutes, or incapable of solitude? Will she want the bathroom door emphatically locked, or happily hold audience while sitting on the toilet?

Will she learn to spend far too much money on books, or boots? Will she leave notepads scattered around the house, or nail clippings? Be fanatical about films, or insistent on pausing them every few minutes to have the plot explained? Repeat the same tired stories over and over, or never quite pin down which is left and which is right?

Will she insist on having the radio volume only on even numbers? Or unpacking her suitcase the minute she's back from holiday – even if it's four in the morning? Will she be a sucker for Waitrose clotted cream ice cream, or McDonalds cheeseburgers?

Above all, when it comes to issues of stress, will Polly inherit her mother's propensity to ignite or her father's tendency – born of necessity – to firefight?

Supposedly, children are especially prone to the influence of the parent of the same sex, and Polly's already proving herself truly her mother's daughter, wailing at the first suggestion that she's being left to sit alone. Yet, as her principal carer, surely a few of my characteristics will inevitably rub off on her as well?

Thankfully Zoë and I are well suited to each other – but we also differ in many ways. So I pity Polly the internal conflict the years ahead may bring. Perhaps we should prepare ourselves now for a daughter who, in her inherited turmoil, locks her friends in the toilet to discuss films, interrupting herself every few minutes to explain why she hoards nail clippings and can only eat cheeseburgers in even numbers.

Tuesday, 27th November – 40 weeks, 1 day old

I'm coming back from some voice work in town and am crammed into the tube, alone amongst hundreds of others, when a group of aggressive, logo-ed guys who can't be much more than 20 years old lever themselves into the crowd. Before the doors are even closing, they're shouting abuse at each other, while the rest of us do what we can to ignore them and their noise by burying ourselves in our books or staring at the floor or the adverts or the passing views of back yards and warehouses.

At last, from somewhere in the tight huddle of bodies, a man's quiet voice breaks through their torrent of obscenities. 'Why don't you just shut up?'

Instantly, the nearest guy, tall and scrawny in a white baseball cap, stands on tiptoe to search the crowd. 'Who f***in' said that?

You wanna say that again? Come out at the next stop, ya f***, and say that to my face! Come on, who said that?'

There's no answer.

'I wish it had been me,' I'm dying to say. After all, there are perhaps 50 people in this carriage alone – were these few guys going to take us all on?

But, of course, because we've all read reports of teenagers with knives, and how passers-by have witnessed assaults and kept on passing by, I say nothing. Like everyone else, from white-collar executives to paint-smeared tradesmen, I remain motionless, staring out of my own little world.

Eventually the group gets off, swaggering at our silence and throwing further abuse over their shoulders. A few stops later I walk home, enraged as much at myself as them.

'I hate people like that,' I tell Zoë back home. 'I hate them for intruding so brazenly on everyone's day, and for so casually making the lives of so many that little bit worse. I wish I'd said something as well.'

'I'm glad you didn't,' says Zoë. 'I'd rather you were a cowardly father than a dead hero.'

As I consider my reaction to that white baseball cap surfing his wave of fear, I can't help thinking of Dad: 15 years ago and down in London for a party, he was waiting for an early morning train at King's Cross when a guy with a knife demanded his wallet. Having been a university boxer, Dad punched the guy to the floor. When he mentioned it casually a few weeks later, I almost burst with admiration.

So I'm wondering now, would Polly be more admiring of a father who cowers amongst the meek masses, or who stands up for the right to head home unmolested? The answer seems obvious – until I remember the rest of what Dad told me.

'Did you knock him out?' I asked at the time, hungry for detail to pass on to friends.

'No, it was a punch to the stomach. I just winded him.'

'So what did he do then?'

'I don't know – I didn't stick around to find out.'

And that's the real lesson: react if it's unavoidable, but don't go looking for trouble.

The first rule of self-defence, they say, is to remove the target, to minimize exposure to risk. The thought only makes me want to get my family out of London all the more.

Wednesday, 28th November

I've so much to be grateful for.

My opportunities for acting work may be restricted, but I'm still able to write and therefore earn money, however little, which means I retain a little self-respect and at least a tenuous connection with a world outside our home. Nor have we stretched ourselves into a mortgage or lifestyle that forces us to hand our daughter over to another while I sit through my days in an office. Instead, I get to share my life with my daughter, and to watch her grow.

Because I can appreciate how lucky I am, because I love Polly and love being with her, it's hard to know what it is I'm finding so difficult to deal with: the life I'm living, or the life I'm not?

Is it the boredom of childcare day after day, where every moment mercilessly dictates its own function, where identical minutes stretch into identical hours, unrolling at a snail's pace until the moment Zoë walks back through the door to take over?

Or is it the frustration of never having the time to grasp what few professional opportunities I do have, and suffering the consequent desperate desire to make something more of myself? Because while Zoë and my friends – male and female, working parents or not – have proved themselves in their chosen spheres, I remain largely untested, my brain ossifying, restricted to a job that requires no special qualification and with no guarantee that I'm any good at it. And every day I seem to hear another door close, another possible future lost.

It's hard not to resent that.

Friday, 30th November

Rob's got a free day so, grateful for variety, I strap Polly in the car and set off for Hammersmith. The radio's on, and it's not long before I recognize Take That – the same song that welcomed her into this world and haunted her first summer. Sacrificing my own self-respect, I start singing along, hoping it will ease her journey.

Given the trauma of her birth, perhaps Polly's reaction is not surprising: she stares across from the seat beside me with such an expression of contempt, with such incredulous disappointment, that it's hard not to feel a little proud.

Naturally I take great delight in pointing out our daughter's disgust when Zoë returns from work.

'But that's her favourite song!' she says. 'Polly must have been making a face at your singing, not the song.'

That seems to be one of the risks (and, perversely, the delights) of having a baby of Polly's age – we can ascribe to her every expression an accompanying thought or attitude. Denying her the freedom to simply experiment, we force a meaning on every gesture, funny face or strange noise, imposing on each a logical motivation. The problem is that so often the motivation Zoë and I choose to inflict differs so much.

So until Polly can sign an affidavit, Zoë and I are fated to argue. While I translate her expression as a sign of success in my efforts to instil taste, Zoë reads in it simple straightforward contempt for my crooning. The books say that, around the nine-month mark, Polly will start trying to assert her independence. She doesn't stand a chance.

Tuesday, 4th December – 41 weeks, 1 day old

In the car to the shops, Polly's sick all over herself and the seat. By lunchtime, it's more than just the familiar streaming, bubbling nose and diminished hunger of a cold; now there's a hacking cough, poos that are either mucus-strung or sticky avalanches, occasional bouts of growled breathing like a cornered dog, and a nappy rash that's so blistered it's painful just to look at. I resort to using olive oil rather than water on cotton wool to wipe her, anything to avoid getting the skin wet or adding more chemicals to the mix from wetwipes.

Throughout the day, Zoë's brought high or low with reports that her baby daughter has slept well or eaten little, smiled or had another painful poo. But already by the evening, the nappy rash has improved: from a screaming red, blistered blotch, it's shrunk to two narrow strips of raw flesh, though still quite tender enough to start Polly crying as soon as I lie her down to be changed.

She wakes around 11 p.m., crying inconsolably just as we're trying to get to sleep ourselves. Zoë squirms in bed, miserable at the sound of Polly's pain, and eventually she cracks, applying the thermometer to Polly's forehead for perhaps the thirtieth time today. This time, it shows a slight rise.

Since administering medicine seems to have become my job while Zoë hovers ready to provide the comfort immediately afterwards (not the fairest division of labour, that she gets to make the heroic rescue while I'm cast as the sadistic baddie), I look out a syringe and the bottle of Medised.

No sooner have I squirted 5 ml of the stuff into Polly's mouth than Zoë is wrenching our screaming, kicking daughter out of my hands, all the while making appropriate clucking noises. And not a second too soon, because the moment she's in her mother's arms, Polly vomits what seems like half her body weight in an explosive outburst of torrential, milky mush.

My guilt at the thought that perhaps my infliction of the medicine has prompted the eruption is soon forgotten at the sight of Zoë, stunned and sticky, as though a passing clown has ducked her face in a plate of cottage cream. I, however – aside from the usual caked snot on my shoulder where Polly has lunged in for a nose-wiping cuddle – have escaped unsplattered. That's the kind of pantomime I like: when the hero gets the custard pie and the villain leaves laughing.

Friday, 7th December

'Andrew! Can you watch Polly for five minutes? I'm going to put on a wash.'

'Andrew! Can you give me a hand distracting her during tea?'

'Andrew! The TV isn't working.'

'Andrew! Do you think this nappy rash is getting any better?'

Whatever the issue of the moment, a shout upstairs seems to be Zoë's solution. Even on her afternoons off, when I'm officially working and Zoë's caring for Polly, because I'm still in the house I face a continual bombardment of requests, all for things I'm forced to handle every day without dragging Zoë away from *her* work.

Then this morning she phones from the surgery.

'I'm really sorry, but I'm going to be back late. We've got a lunchtime meeting and then I've got a whole load of home visits to make.'

Instantly, what should have been a half-day of Polly-care has become a full day, and I don't know who resents it more: Zoë because she loses her few precious hours with Polly, or me because I lose another afternoon's work.

With the writing always taking second place to everything else, from a trip to the dentist to an inspection of Polly's backside, the result is increased pressure on the short amount of time I *do* have to work, and increased pressure on our time together as a family when I'm always dragging with me the need to catch up. I have to guard against resenting all obligations of normal life, from weekend lunches to drinks with friends.

Life has become a tightrope of guilt and frustration, and nursery the Holy Grail, the one possibility on the horizon of retaining my sanity. It's more than just the isolation and repetition – it's because, rightly or wrongly, my self-esteem demands more of myself. At the moment, I just don't feel I'm giving all I can, or being all I can be.

Tuesday, 11th December – 42 weeks, 1 day old

A perfect day: incredibly cold but sunshine sparkling brightly off the frosted lawn. A single cloud perches above Clapham like a question mark, while the frozen damp retreats up the rooftops to crouch, paling, behind walls and chimney pots.

It's so crisp and beautiful that I can't help remembering what it *could* be, were we surrounded, not by mile after mile of flat concrete, tarmac, brick and slate, but by curving, open land, by water and mountains, by countryside and space.

My mood's not helped by the bags under my eyes. Although Polly's nose is still running, her cough has dried up, the blisters on her backside have subsided, and she's back to distributing her meals a little more equally between her mouth and the floor.

Fortunately for her, she can make up for lost sleep during the day, extending her morning nap to an hour or fitting in a quick snooze before tea. Unfortunately for her parents, we can't. Perhaps that's why she's now all smiles and I've come down with whatever she had – though with marginally less nappy rash. Maybe I'm teething?

Whatever the reason, I'm waking through the night and now feel I'm carrying everywhere an exhaustion as heavy as a sodden blanket jammed in a broken washing machine still full of water after the spin cycle. And thanks to our low-budget choice of kitchen appliances, I know exactly how heavy that is.

Thursday, 13th December

Just as we've put our heads to the pillow already lamenting how little is left of the night, Polly begins to scream – not cry, not moan, but scream, as though milk's just been uninvented and Panda's announced he's emigrating to Australia.

In an instant, Zoë has picked her up, but for the next five minutes, Polly ignores all comfort and continues to yell, her little eyes screwed shut.

Only when she finally falls quiet, opens them to look around and immediately begins to smile do we realize she's been asleep throughout.

'Do you think she's teething?' asks Zoë, but I'm wary of that old favourite attribution of every symptom for the last few months, especially given the persistent non-arrival of teeth.

'Shall we try some medicine?' I ask, already squirming at the thought of another coating of yack.

'She doesn't have a temperature. Maybe it's night terrors?'

As she jostles a now cheerful Polly around the room, I turn to the manual. 'It says here that night terrors don't usually start until around the first birthday. But Polly's under nine months!' I can't help feeling a flash of pride at the prospect of such remarkable precociousness.

'So maybe she's just cold?' wonders Zoë.

'It's no colder than any other night.'

'I'm going to buy her a heater with a thermostat tomorrow,' she declares, regardless, and I'm too tired to argue.

Finally, having changed Polly, rocked and cuddled her, only for the bawling to continue the moment she's put down, Zoë and I give up. We lie next door, desperate for sleep, and listen to our daughter's screams. For the best part of an hour, Polly howls, Zoë squirms as though pierced with needles, and I try to crawl under the pillow. At last the three of us drift off to sleep, at an hour perhaps known only to our neighbours.

Friday, 14th December

If Polly wants something enough, she's perfectly capable of stretching an impressive distance. Her preferred method, though, is to get down on her front then push herself back until she eventually ends up in a sitting position again; though it often leaves her facing the wrong direction, it does tend to deliver her nearer her target.

Her crawl, when it comes, is usually backwards, bum first, and that's exactly what she does as I look on, watching her end up wedged and bent double beneath the cross-struts of a chair.

I can see the thought process as she looks around, calmly evaluates the situation and then, with nothing else for it, bursts into tears.

Monday, 17th December – 43 weeks old

Presumably it was man's larger frame, greater muscles and lack of breasts that dictated his role as the hunter-gatherer while his wife stayed at home. Now, though, in a world where muscle is seldom a prerequisite for bringing home the bacon and where formula can replace breastmilk, I'm wondering whether a man's physicality doesn't actually leave him better suited to a life at home?

I'm talking gross generalizations, of course, but who's better equipped, physically, to lug six bags of shopping, one folded pram, a bumper pack of loo roll, two bags of nappies and a baby from the car to the front door? Who's better built for the household chores like mowing the lawn, or shunting the sofa to hoover underneath? Or better able to cope with a car that won't start or bags full of dirty clothes that need to be carried to the laundrette because a faulty washing machine still hasn't been fixed?

Admittedly, none of these physical attributes take into account the principal reason for staying at home: raising the children. And I do live in fear of discovering – when it'll be too late to make amends – that my role as childcarer has impacted in any negative way on Polly.

But perhaps, with the ever-increasing numbers of househusbands around the world, evolution is telling us something. Perhaps the time has come to recognize an impending seismic shift in the typical distribution of work and childcare.

I like that idea, and the thought that I may find my place in history after all; perhaps, millennia from now, my remains will be dug up and put on display, my brittle bones exhibiting an early example of what that world will have come to consider normal, as they mark the early development of a major societal transition – the birth of *homo nappiens.*

The Eleventh Month

Wednesday, 19th December

Every time I pick Polly up after a day with her grandma, I'm reminded of that joke about a new sheriff arriving in town to see bullseyes painted on every wall, bullet holes perfectly placed through each one's centre.

Keen to meet the local sharpshooter, he's introduced to the local idiot. Amazed, he asks the guy to demonstrate his skills, so the idiot pulls out a gun, shoots the nearest wall, then paints a bullseye around the hole.

That's what Zoë's mum does with Polly, painting in hindsight around every gesture and noise a deeper meaning as a demonstration of genius and then, when I arrive to take my daughter home, proudly reciting a list of supposed 'firsts', each one outdoing the last.

As Polly sees me step through the door, she greets me with what's now a typical swooping squeak that Zoë and I have generously interpreted as 'Hi!'

'See!' says Zoë's mum. 'She's started singing!'

Then, reaching for a toy, Polly does her typical fruitless roll on her arse. At which there's another immediate shriek of delight from the mother-in-law. 'Look! She's crawling!'

If I hadn't witnessed the reality of these imagined breakthroughs for myself, I'd be growing seriously concerned that my presence is somehow hindering Polly's development throughout the rest of the week, forcing her to compensate in a burst of brilliance every Wednesday.

Friday, 21st December

About ten years ago I read a book in which a character is feted for his night-time ability to tell the make and model of a car simply by the shape of its headlights in his rear mirror. Whether really possible or not, I accepted it at the time as one of those casually worn skills that mark out real men, like the ability to recite statistics from the European Cup quarter-final of 1967, or to tell the time from the sun.

My own interest in cars has never really grown beyond the functional, I'm no great football fan and, when it comes to telling the time, I've been lucky enough to have a watch. So as though to compensate for such benchmarks of virility, my eyes have started fixing instantly on prams in the street, homing in on their appearance in an effort to discern the make and model.

Why should that be? Apart from the fact that I don't really care, as manly skills go, the ability to identify a pram at 50 paces isn't quite the same, is it?

Monday, 24th December – 44 weeks old

Leaving Zoë and Polly to an afternoon of mince pies and girly chatter before roaring log fires, I drive out of Edinburgh and join up with a group of friends for a walk across the Pentland Hills.

We're barely three miles from the centre of Scotland's capital, yet we're surrounded by countryside the likes of which we'd have had to drive for hours to find around London.

Dad used to judge cities according to how easy they are to escape and, as I stop to appreciate the views across the city and the Firth of Forth, fighting off the winter winds with sips from a variety of well-stocked flasks, it's impossible to disagree.

Tuesday, 25th December – Christmas Day

Polly's first Christmas, and she loves every minute – not because she wakes with excitement at the thought of a chunky stocking at the foot of her cot, nor because she's overjoyed to be dressed as 'Santa's little helper' (complete with white-trimmed cap) by an uncle who should know better. Polly's loving her first Christmas because she has the unbroken attention not only of both her parents, but all her Scottish family as well.

No less than four generations gather to tear open presents and tuck into turkey, so there are dozens of willing hands reaching out to pick her up and play, or scrutinize her every move through a camera. So while her dad celebrates his return north with Irn Bru, the occasional cocktail and a bucket of mulled wine, Polly is drunk on the attention.

Thursday, 27th December

Back home again, Polly's hangover is hitting hard. She's moping because so much stimulation has diminished – with Zoë's return to work – to a mere Daddy, himself suffering from the return to London and solo childcare. Exhibiting all the symptoms of her withdrawal, she groans reluctantly when I try to put her down and grumpily refuses to amuse herself.

'How's she getting on?' asks Zoë, calling for yet another update.

I consider my response carefully. I could placate her with a lie, but it seems cruel to suggest that Polly's barely noticed her absence. So I opt for honesty instead.

'She didn't eat much lunch,' I admit. 'And she's been pretty clingy all day. I think she's missing her mummy a bit.'

Cue immediate wails of self-reproach. 'It's ten times harder now than it ever was before.'

The glimpse of another life has only shown us all what we're missing in ours. And it's pleasing no one.

273

Friday, 28th December

Polly's grouchiness isn't helped by the arrival – at last – of her first tooth. It had cried wolf so many times that we'd given up hope and resigned ourselves to her gummy chomping for months to come.

But now that a little slice of white has appeared at the front of her lower jaw, it's prompting endless fascination as she taps her toys against it, and lengthy tears as she's put to bed screaming at the darkness with nothing to distract her from the pain.

At least, that's what we assume she's crying about – it could just be a recurring nightmare about the day she brings home a boyfriend she's desperate to impress, only to be presented with a photo of herself dressed as a North Pole pixie.

Saturday, 29th December

Polly lies on our bed, peaceful and innocent, one little index finger running through the hair of her teddy like a chimp searching for nits, unaware of her daddy less than two feet away, stalking her with a hypodermic needle.

Having found a blister on the outside of her little toe, just around the nail, the plan is to pierce and drain it. Or, rather, Zoë's plan is for *me* to pierce and drain it while she shrieks and runs out the room.

Sunday, 30th December

Having dried up as planned, Polly's blistered flap of skin solidifies and falls off. Unfortunately – and this bit *wasn't* planned – her little toenail is still attached and comes off as well. Although it looks to us frighteningly like her entire tiny toe has separated itself from her foot, Polly seems oblivious. Zoë and I inspect it, fascinated, unsure whether to frame this tiny chunk of daughter, bin it, or bury it.

Monday, 31st December – 45 weeks old

For the first time in perhaps 20 years, I fall asleep before the New Year.

Then, thanks to the mass of fireworks and the party across the street, I'm awake again before midnight, and greet the year ahead like a grumpy old man, with a string of expletives thrown out from my pillow. At times the crackers are so loud they wake Polly, who briefly roars her annoyance then settles again to sleep.

Tuesday, 1st January – New Year's Day

'I've made a New Year's resolution,' I mumble when we're woken at 6.30 by cries from the nursery. 'I'm going to take Polly across the street and leave her on the doorstep of that party house.'

Fortunately, like most New Year's resolutions, the urge lasts only a matter of minutes, by which time Polly is tucked up alongside her mum, warm and cosy, sucking happily from her milk bottle while Zoë sips her tea. And as I slurp my coffee, I contemplate the aptness of last night's disruption.

At times, I used to think that life was passing me by, that there was always a party going on somewhere else, where everyone was more attractive and more intelligent, where life was more interesting and more meaningful, more fun. Then I met Zoë and, if we ever talked of that party, we were actually quite content to find ourselves sitting together on the sofa instead.

But for this last year, ever since Polly landed amongst us with all the disruptive force of a meteorite, the party has been here, in our own home. Of course, I use the word 'party' deliberately: it's been noisy, messy, utterly exhausting, and the music isn't always to my taste. The responsible people who should be in control seem to have disappeared for the night, we've experienced frequent cravings for alcohol, we're forever clearing up or wiping stains off the sofa, and our neighbours probably hate us.

However, just like that party nine years ago when, for the first time, I was grateful to be indecently assaulted by a judgementally impaired Zoë, it's been a party I wouldn't have missed for the world.

Friday, 4th January

Zoë comes home from work desperate for a cuddle with Polly, and bursts into tears.

'I'm finding it so hard,' she cries. 'I hate being away from her and miss her like crazy. The worst of it is, I know Polly's doing fine. So if I go part time it would be for my benefit, not for hers.'

Deliberately not calculating the loss of income, I swallow and try to sound supportive. 'That's no reason not to investigate the possibility – you've as much right to be happy with your life as Polly does.'

We spend the evening doing the maths. Could we get by if Zoë cuts back? And would her partners even allow it?

'It's the same old problem,' I tell her. 'Until I've got more time to work, I can't even try to make up the lost income. And until you go part time, I won't have more time.'

'You need to get a regular acting job, like a series,' she says, as though it's simply a matter of choice. 'Then I could cut back. At the moment I just feel torn in so many directions, I'm going mad.'

'It's a risky strategy, to base your future sanity on my job prospects.'

'I want it like we had it over Christmas, with nothing to care about but ourselves, spending time as a family, the three of us together. At the moment, one of us is always working. It's relentless. I feel like my head's only just above water.'

Wednesday, 9th January – 46 weeks, 2 days old

Zoë arrives home just as her mum's dropping Polly off, so the two of them catch up over a cup of tea while Polly staggers between the two of them.

Her mum's only just left the house when out rolls Zoë's bottom lip. 'I knew it would happen. Polly spends so much time with Mum – and all of it pure, quality time – that she thinks *she's* her mum!' she cries. 'Now she loves her more than she loves me!'

'How do you work that out?'

'I was holding her, and she kept reaching for Mum.'

'But she always does that! She always reaches for whoever's not holding her. If she's in my arms, she reaches for you. And if you're holding her, she'll reach for your mum.'

Zoë turns to the stairs, Polly in hand, heading for the bathroom. And halfway up, as though to prove my point, Polly lunges – just as she did for her grandma – for a painting of a morose-looking cow, staring out of the frame as though searching for pastures new.

'You see!' I say, following behind. 'It's totally indiscriminate. She just wants whoever she's not with, even if it's a cow.' I'm about to crack a weak joke about the grass always being greener when Zoë's sad face stops me.

'I'm finding it really difficult,' she says. 'Polly's acting and reacting more and more; I'm finding it harder than ever to leave her each morning.'

Monday, 14th January – 47 weeks old

Kate invites us to join her at her 'mothers and babies' group. Since it's in the hall alongside the nursery where Polly's due to start in six weeks, I think it'll do her good to get familiar with the area and have a little company her own age, so, swallowing my apprehension, I step through the door, and am pleasantly surprised to see another man mingling amongst the mums.

'He's a full timer,' whispers Kate.

Throughout the morning, I feel strangely duty bound to chat to him, as though we're united in some comradely struggle. Yet to do so seems to risk suggesting there's something remarkable about a man caring for his kids, so I don't. And anyway, I'm too busy marvelling at how relaxed I feel despite being a minority amongst all these women, some of them still breastfeeding, some of them chasing their kids around the hall, all of them chatting cheerfully, gossiping as though they're in their own kitchens.

I can't help comparing it to the dads' group, and it takes a while to work out why this atmosphere seems so much more relaxed.

Very generally – and this may well be more about me than an accurate reflection of the groups – the women seem less self-conscious, more natural; they'd be doing what they're doing whether the kids were there or not. Most of them have worked and so know what they're missing and, having got into the swing of caring for kids, are happy to have the time now simply to sit and chat with friends over a cup of tea. They're fulfilling a role they probably always expected to have – and in some cases may have yearned for. As a result, they're happy, which makes their gatherings a happy place to be.

Those dads new to the stay-at-home role and forced to sit around the playmat, meanwhile, gave me the impression of being there – like me – for the benefit of their children. Most likely having never considered a time when their wives would be earning more, they've taken on the role of childcarer by default, for financial reasons, and the result is a gathering with a classroom feeling, as though it's something of a chore, a dutiful self-sacrifice of time that could be usefully spent elsewhere.

So it's a relief – if not a little disconcerting – to feel so much at home amongst the girls. I even look around during the songs to see who's singing with such a low voice.

The Twelfth Month

Thursday, 17th January

Zoë collapses on the sofa beside me with a sigh. 'You know those people at the circus who spin plates on wobbly sticks?'

'You mean wobbly stick plate-spinners?'

'Yeah. *That's* what I feel like. I feel like every day I'm running from stick to stick, only able to give each plate just enough attention to keep it spinning intact. And the only reason none of our plates has so far come crashing down to earth is because we're forced to leave so many other plates untouched, piling up at the side.'

'If this is about the dishwasher...'

'Andrew! I'm being serious. I feel like we're so busy dealing with all the mundane necessities that we're missing out on the good stuff.'

'Like what?'

'Like the chance to just waste a weekend's afternoon together, or take a drive into the country. Or go for a walk as a family without hurrying back so one of us can work. Between looking after Polly, paying the bills, washing the clothes and shopping, cooking and cleaning, answering letters, dealing with this and dealing with that...'

Her voice is quiet, close to tears. 'I don't want to live like this any more,' she says.

Friday, 18th January

Polly refuses to say anything other than 'Mama'. Despite her earlier seeming glee at the sound, there's now not a 'Dada' to be heard. Even the barrages of screams or gurgles have diminished in favour of an endlessly looping 'mamamamamama'.

In the privacy of our front room, it feels fair to correct her, counteracting her chant with a reply of 'dadadadadada' in the hope that she'll relent. But in front of others, in the supermarket or on the swings, it's just embarrassing, as though my effort to put her right lends credence to what could otherwise be shrugged off as mindless noise, as though in her repetition Polly really is expressing her thoughts on my identity.

There is an advantage, though. Just as we're falling asleep, Polly wakes and starts babbling, allowing me to turn to Zoë with a smile. 'Listen! It's you she wants – close the door quietly on your way out.'

Monday, 21st January – 48 weeks old

It's 7.30 p.m. Long after Zoë's typical exuberance over her daily reunion with Polly has faded, a contented smile remains.

'A patient came in last week with a cold,' she says, 'and I spotted a mole on her neck I wasn't happy with, so I sent her to get it checked out. Turns out it was cancerous, but we got it in time.'

As so often, I'm in awe of the difference that Zoë makes to people's lives, whether it's in saving them from the worst, supporting them through it, or just offering up a sympathetic ear.

But while I'm proud that her attentiveness and professionalism have potentially saved a life, I'm also a little terrified – I can't help wondering, as it nears the end of each day and she begins to think about hurrying home to see her daughter, what has she missed?

That in turn makes me wonder: what were all those doctors really thinking about when they met a 60-year-old man from Argyll complaining of a sore throat?

Tuesday, 22nd January

Like so many others hoping to better themselves in the New Year, it's as though Polly has got herself a personal trainer. How else can we explain the rapid developments? Where before she'd watch a ball rolling past with thinly disguised scorn, mocking my efforts for being just so obvious in my scheming to get her moving, now she's sufficiently motivated to chase after it with a big grin, mauling it like an angry bull pawing the ground, until it rolls back to me and the game can continue.

Up until now, she's sat lazily and watched the world go by, content as an old man on his front porch. At best, she might have risked a calculated stretch for the nearest toy before returning to the safety of her backside. But now she just won't sit still, and is moving so quickly we daren't take our eyes off her.

And there are other signs of her progress: she's clapping (both to order and for her own amusement), the top of a second tooth has appeared alongside the first, and she's even walking – albeit shakily – with the support of a couple of fingers, raising each foot so high with each step it's as though she's trying to overstride a fallen tree. With much grunting, she pulls herself up on everything she can find. I'm sitting on the sofa when her face appears suddenly alongside my knee, grinning a grin of utter triumph before greeting me with a glass-shattering 'Hi!'

But progress also brings problems. She attacks stairs with admirable determination, only to lose impetus halfway up where she'll wobble until rescued. Unfortunately, she's no longer so easily fooled by her own battery-less TV remote, and insistently searches out the real thing at the most dramatic moment of whatever we're watching. To stop her clambering out of her cot, we've had to lower the mattress level – worse still for my back, particularly as she's not getting any lighter. And with all the increased chasing around the carpet, I'm forced to throw out what I'm sure will be the first of many trousers worn through at the knees. Most disconcertingly, she's taken to copying my attempts to make her laugh by going cross-eyed, her eyeballs swinging in their sockets like the loose hands of a broken clock.

Wednesday, 23rd January

The second Polly's head touches her cot, she starts screaming and reaching out to be picked up again. Rather than leave her to cry down as I've done so often before, I lift her back out of the cot and give her a cuddle, her arms immediately snapping round my neck as her head rests on my shoulder.

We stay like that, swaying slightly, and I feel as though I'm gaining every bit as much as her from the hug.

After a minute or so, I risk bringing it to an end. 'OK, Polly,' I whisper. 'Time to sleep.'

At my words she pulls back, gives me a deliberate grin, then leans towards her cot.

As I walk out of the nursery, we're both smiling quietly. And I'm feeling a strange sense of achievement, as though in picking her up I exhibited an unconscious skill, the result of a new level of understanding. All Polly wanted was a last cuddle before sleep and, in defiance of the usual routine, I instinctively agreed – for the benefit of us both.

Could it be that I'm finally getting the hang of this?

Saturday, 26th January

Hamish and Felicity are round for dinner and tentatively talking about thinking about starting to wonder about trying for a baby.

'I'm really glad we decided to have a baby when we did,' I say, meaning to be encouraging.

'Why's that?'

'Because I hadn't yet learnt from other new parents how much it can change your life.'

Zoë shoots me a warning glance as Hamish shifts uncomfortably. 'What do you mean?' he asks.

'Just that the easiest way of describing how a baby changes your life is by talking about all those practicalities that, on the face of it, don't sound all that appealing: the restricted freedom and shortened nights, the nappies that grow steadily heavier and the wallet that grows rapidly lighter.'

'It's not all that bad,' says Zoë, mindful of Felicity's nervous nodding.

'That's exactly my point – but when I hear myself trying to tell people what it's like, I realize I'm focusing on all the bad things.'

'Why?'

'Because if they don't have kids themselves, then I imagine that's the only stuff they'll be able to relate to. Everyone knows what it's like to be delayed getting out the door, or stuck in a supermarket queue, so it's easy to talk about the 15 minutes it takes to prepare for a trip to the park, or to share the difficulties of getting round the shops in time to get Polly home for lunch. And everyone can imagine the delights of dealing with a brimming nappy.'

I can hear myself leaning towards that patronizing phrase, 'If you haven't kids yourself, you wouldn't understand,' and though I loathe myself for it, I can't help feeling it's true: without Polly, *I* wouldn't understand the depth of the red rage that rises from nowhere when an adult without even a kid's car seat – let alone a kid – parks in the last bay for Parents and Children. Or the impact it makes to read the detail that Jewish mothers stripping before their Auschwitz showers tried to hide their babies amongst their discarded clothes.

'So have a go,' Hamish says. 'Tell me something good about it.'

'That's just the thing,' I say. 'It's impossible to explain all the good stuff without resorting to cliché...'

'Try!' he says, almost pleading.

'Well ... if I'd heard you talking in my pre-Polly days about the look in your daughter's eyes when she catches yours and grins, or the way she says "Dada" and reaches out when you walk in through the door, or the moment when she quietly leans into your shoulder for a hug...' Unbelievably, I'm actually talking myself close to tears. 'It's precisely those instances that render the dry and tedious practicalities insignificant, and precisely those instances that would have meant nothing to me before.'

In the silence that follows, I see Hamish's awkward smile and can't work out whether he's convinced, or if I've just proved my point.

Monday, 28th January – 49 weeks old

It's mid-morning and raining outside, so Polly and I are playing in the front room when my mobile rings.

'Is that Andrew?'

'Yes.'

'I got your number from a colleague of mine, Anna Bowen – I hope you don't mind. I was wondering if you've got a few minutes to talk?'

I look across to where Polly's hunched happily by her Fisher Price kitchen, her tongue extended in concentration as she tries to stuff Panda into the oven. 'A few minutes should be fine,' I say. 'Who am I talking to?'

I listen. A few seconds later I sit down, still listening. Then I hang up. And then, within seconds, I'm dialling Zoë's number, whooping and prancing around the front room while Polly looks on in cautious amusement.

'Zoë? Zoë! Guess what!'

'What?'

'I just got a call from a friend of Anna's at her parenting magazine. Remember I sent in some material from my diary ages ago?'

'Yeah.'

'They've offered me a column!'

'*What?*'

'A column! And I can base it on my diary, so it'll only need minor rewrites. They want me to go in and meet with them to chat it through.'

'Oh my God! That's *amazing!*'

'I know! It means I might actually get *paid* for all I've been doing over the last six months!'

Around 6.30, when Zoë runs through the door, she actually throws down her bag and steps *past* Polly to wrap her arms around me first.

'I'm so proud of you!' she says, and I'm glad we're still hugging so she can't see my eyes welling up. 'Didn't I always tell you you're a brilliant writer? That's *such* good news! I can't wait to tell everyone.'

At last, she pulls away and looks down at our daughter. 'Your Daddy's so clever, isn't he, Polly?'

Polly looks up from where she's on her knees systematically emptying the contents of Zoë's bag across the floor, and she smiles. 'Uh!' she grunts. And until she can tell me otherwise, I'm taking that as affirmative.

Thursday, 31st January

It's 6.15 a.m. 'Oh my God!' laughs Zoë, walking into the nursery. 'Look, Andrew, Polly's managed to lower the side of the cot!'

Polly is one small clamber away from freedom. Caught in the act of escape, she pauses, considers the situation, and then beams an angelic smile as though butter wouldn't melt.

In the afternoon, it's another trip to the supermarket, one of those frantic snatch-and-grab trips carefully timed between meals and naps. And while in the past she's been content to stare from the child seat as items fly past her face (economy beans for us, organic butternut squash for her), this time we're barely at the dairy aisle before she's restlessly kicking and screeching. I hand her one of the two cheese wedges I've tossed into the trolley, and she nibbles in vain on the packaging as I whisk her around the rest of the store before rushing to the shortest queue at the checkouts. There Polly lets loose that same gummy grin, fluttering her eyelids at the woman on the till who, enchanted, matches Polly's every coo with one of her own.

Only when we're outside and I'm wheeling her towards the car does she reach deep within the folds of her jacket before flourishing her small clump of Dutch cheese to the skies, whooping and chuckling over her loot like a criminal mastermind whose evil plan has come to fruition.

Much is made of the role of parents in our crime-riddled society, so I feel a little ashamed that, instead of buying extra parking time, relocking the car and returning to Customer Services with an apology and £1.07, instead I quickly smuggle both baby and booty into the car and head straight for the state line. Besides, with her new-found ability to escape from behind bars, what good would it do to shop her in?

It does make me suspicious, though, as this evening I proudly watch her pulling herself up on my trousers, wobbling unsteadily on her little legs as she smiles and reaches up. Is she trying to give her daddy a hug, or making a play for my wallet?

Monday, 4th February – 50 weeks old

I'm beginning to suspect that nursery will become the only 'normal' time for Polly. Thus far, she's only ever really spent much time with her daddy, a grandma who drowns her in attention once a week, and a mummy spurred to manic energy by her guilt at not being around. The consistency of nursery, where she'll be treated like any other, should only do her good.

Yet so far the nursery's only able to offer us two mornings a week

– one of which is Monday. And since we have to pay in advance regardless of bank holidays, when they're closed, that'll be the equivalent of a whole month's nursery fees wasted every year.

The only answer is for other kids to drop out, so we're reliant on a high turnover of foreign workers being relocated. Not such a forlorn hope, perhaps; you can tell that this corner of London is a real multinational neighbourhood because, faced with imminent head-to-head collisions while pushing Polly's pram to the park, so many mothers instinctively veer straight into my path.

The situation isn't helped by the tracking on our pram, which insists on pulling to the left. We're on our way home from the lake, Polly having fed herself on the stale bread she was meant to be offering the ducks, when I spot a little dachshund up ahead and, between steering and making the necessary 'Woof! Woof!' noises, I nearly run over the damn thing.

Saturday, 9th February

Helen comes round to see Zoë and I take the opportunity to sneak upstairs for the evening to get on with work. Returning downstairs a few hours later, I find Helen has succeeded where I long ago failed.

'I've decided,' declares Zoë, with full knowledge of the enormity of her announcement, 'that I'd like to move to Scotland.'

'What?'

'Well, you know I don't want to be in London for ever. Even Mum and Dad agree it's not what it was when I was growing up. And when I told Helen that we were thinking about somewhere neutral like Oxfordshire, she thought I was mad. She pointed out how lucky we are, with a ready social network and family support in Edinburgh. And, ultimately, as she said, I don't need to look at it as the last move we ever make. It could be just another chapter in our lives, not necessarily the final one. Thinking of it like that, it's quite exciting.'

I sit down to digest the news. 'What would your mum say?'

Zoë smiles sadly. 'I think she's been preparing herself for us moving to Scotland ever since we got married. Anyway, she wouldn't want to feel she's stopping us doing what's best. So what do you think?'

I consider my principal reason for being in London, Zoë aside – to be near the opportunities for acting work – and I shrug.

'There's lots of acting work in Scotland. And I'd still be accessible to London for auditions. Although, to be honest, the idea of abandoning you and Polly while I disappear to some regional theatre for two months to live in some stranger's spare room doesn't really appeal so much any more.'

'You could write equally well anywhere, couldn't you?'

'Sure.'

'And now that you've got that column, you'll be earning more, too – especially when your fiction book's published. That'll compensate for me dropping a session or two, won't it?'

'You're not just saying all this because you want to move out of London? Because life would still follow us to Scotland, you know. We'd still have to earn money, we'd still have to pay the bills and empty the bins.'

'I know. But I don't want to be here any more. And I definitely don't want Polly to grow up in London – it's too busy, too frenetic. I'd worry myself to death every time she walked out the door. And it's not just about getting out of London – it's more about getting all the things that I want: a bit of space, a calmer life, with more time as a family. There'll be plenty of chances to work when Polly's grown up and left us. This is the time we should all be together. If we can still pay the bills, wouldn't that be worth it?'

I think of playing with Polly on the beaches around Edinburgh, and consider living again within sight of the sea. I think of my friends and my family, and of introducing Polly to so much that I've loved. And I think that, if it's the sides of a mountain that sustain life, perhaps we should all be doing what we can to enjoy the climb a little more. Because who knows if we'll ever reach the top?

'Andrew? It would be worth earning a little less to get all that, wouldn't it?'

'I think it would. Yes.'

Monday, 11th February – 51 weeks old

'You know those policies I'm planning for when I'm dictator-for-life?'

'What policies?' Already, Zoë has adopted her humouring tone, the one that offers least resistance in the hope that the conversation will end that little bit quicker.

'Those ones I'm always talking about, like drinking fountains on every street corner, four-day working weeks and obligatory siestas.'

'Uh-huh.' She still hasn't looked up from her magazine.

'I've got a new one.'

'Oh yes?' she says, utterly uninterested.

'Yeah. These last 12 months have convinced me that the path to parenthood is just too easy.'

'Tell that to all my patients worrying about their fertility.'

'In general, I mean. The implications of almost every other commitment we might be tempted to make in life are assiduously detailed in advance, for good or for bad: if you want to hire a car for the day or sign up for a mobile phone – let alone borrow hundreds of thousands to buy a house – you're forced to wade through pages of small print packed with warnings of hidden charges, long-standing obligations and the risks associated with being unable to finish what you've started.'

'So?'

'So, make the decision to take on the life-changing role of parent and you need only find a similar-minded partner and half an hour.'

'Half an hour?'

'All right, 20 minutes.'

She lets out a derisive snort and turns a page.

'The point is, getting someone pregnant shouldn't be a mere matter of having the right equipment and finding someone willing to let you use it – though I admit I have actually found that quite difficult at times. Anyway, what I'm saying is – we need parenting small print.'

'*What?*'

'Yes! Where are the dire warnings of the insidious costs that'll be charged to your credit card? Who's there to advise that without considerable additional expense you'll no longer be free to roam? That your level of contentment may go down as well as up, or that your home may be possessed by dropped raisins and plastic toys if you do not keep up the tidying?'

'So *that's* your new policy? *More* small print?'

'No. Until there's a regulatory authority committed to protecting consumers from such ruthless exploitation by our loins, until the European courts are prepared to insist on a greater transparency between those few pleasure-packed minutes–'

'That's more like it.'

'–and a lifetime of parenthood, this is my proposal.'

I pause for effect, which only gives Zoë time to raise one sceptical eyebrow.

'*Parenting Krypton Factor!*'

'Oh, for God's–'

'Wait! Hear me out! In my world, the effort required to get pregnant would be brought into line with the effort required to care for the result. OK? All aspiring breeders would be forced to attend a week-long boot camp. Starved of sleep and robbed of money, they'd be stretched to their physical, mental and emotional limits, challenged on everything from common sense and multi-tasking to an ability to resist marketing and peer pressure, and all the while forced to listen to a persistent, high-pitched screech above the loud ticking of a clock.'

'I see what you're getting at,' nods Zoë. 'But I think eugenics went out of fashion sometime around the 1930s.'

'No, this isn't a suitability test. All participants would remain free to choose their next step – whether that's to return home to get it on, or to spend the money on a holiday instead. The point is that, should they still decide to embark on parenthood, they'd be making a marginally more informed decision rather than simply rushing to fulfil a fantasy or obey their more feral urges.'

'OK. Good idea. Although it may, of course, lead to the extinction of our species.'

'How?'

'Because your boot camp misses out all the good stuff about parenthood to balance the bad. How will you demonstrate that?'

'That's for my advisors to sort out. We dictators don't claim to have all the answers.'

Wednesday, 13th February

Showing off in front of her grandma, I ask Polly where her head is – a safe bet as, whether inquiring after her nose, tummy or toes, she invariably points to her head. In reply, her gesture is so joyful and vigorous that she jabs herself in the eye and immediately bursts into tears.

When she reaches out to be comforted, I begin to empathize with those parents who prod their babies to cry just so they can offer them a cuddle; there's something strangely empowering about being one of a very few who can give her the comfort and security she wants.

Thursday, 14th February

Polly's leaning against the full-length glass back door, staring, silent and motionless, as though hypnotized, at a blank stretch of sky.

'Polly?'

In response, she points upwards. I squint into the distance, but see nothing.

'There's nothing there, Polly.'

She briefly turns her slightly ominous, hamster-cheeked stare towards me, and her excessively rounded look of scorn – not to mention the bracelets of chub on either arm – remind me of Brando in *The Godfather*, as though she's about to pronounce my future swimming with the fishes.

Then, just to prove her point, an aeroplane floats into view, exactly where she's been staring. She's like a mini-radar. Who'd have thought there'd be anything positive about owning a home beneath the Heathrow flight path? But just the sound of a plane overhead is enough to make Polly scuttle towards the window in the hope of catching a glimpse.

Finally, with no planes in sight, she loses interest and crab-walks across the kitchen with such ease that I expect her to stand up and walk at any minute. As so often, she makes for the oven, where the horizontal door handle acts as the perfect support to allow her to pull herself up and admire her reflection in the glass. She won't quite be strolling around by the weekend, when family and friends are gathering to celebrate her first birthday, but she won't be far off. Given her particular fondness for pulling herself up on every pair of legs she can find, I'd better warn guests in trousers to wear a belt.

Saturday, 16th February

Polly wakes at 6 a.m., refusing to settle herself, and I lie in bed asking myself the standard Saturday morning question: is she likely to sleep later tomorrow? Because if she *is*, then I should pretend to be asleep now so Zoë takes her downstairs, and when it's my turn tomorrow it'll be a later start. Beside me, I know Zoë's doing the same calculation, but eventually the tugging on her heartstrings becomes too much – however exhausted, she hauls herself from the bed, leaving me to lie in.

Once again, I dream I'm back at Ardburdan, in the kitchen. But this time Polly is with me, and it's first thing in the morning and, as on so many mornings, Dad steps through the door in worn jeans and riddled green cardigan, mug of coffee in hand, strolling in as though it's just another day.

The enormity of my mistake in thinking that he'd died only flashes across my mind, overwhelmed as it is by the realization of what's now possible. But instead of immediately introducing him to his granddaughter, I deliberately decide at last to do what I've so many times regretted not doing.

With far less emotion and self-consciousness than I expect, I look him full in the face and, without any preamble, say, 'Dad, I want to tell you how much I love you, and how much I appreciate all you've done for me over the years.'

He turns away slightly to put down his mug on the kitchen counter, an action obviously intended to shield his embarrassment at such naked emotion. But, driven by a new confidence as I hold Polly in my arms, I lean forward and kiss him, and then lunge in for a hug, and I can smell his smell and feel the bristles of his beard on my cheek, the rough wool of that worn cardigan. And as I proudly hold Polly up for his inspection, I wake, not emotional, but just glad to have seen him again so vividly, and to have seen in his eyes the acknowledgement of my words.

It's 8 a.m. Downstairs, Polly is squawking and chuckling as Zoë berates Panda for falling off the sofa.

Monday, 18th February

'Life is just too busy,' sighs Zoë, collapsing into bed.

'Especially Mondays.'

'If Polly settles into nursery next week, Mondays will be easy for you.'

'I'll still be working, you know.' But inwardly I'm smiling in anticipation of two whole mornings every week, not just to work but finally to feel on top of all those tedious, unavoidable, mundane intricacies that are done and done again just to get from one day to the next. In my mind, nursery promises the chance to re-engage with the wider world beyond our shrunken horizons, and offers a little breathing space around the work for all those little acts I previously took for granted that help the world revolve, from catching up with friends to a quiet moment with a good book.

'I think we're trying to juggle too much,' says Zoë. 'Nursery should make life easier for you, but it doesn't change anything for me. And I need to know that things are going to change. So I've got a plan.'

'What's that?' Knowing what I know about Zoë and her plans, I'm instinctively on guard.

'With Polly at nursery, you'll be working more, won't you?'

'That's the idea.' Tentative agreement.

'So if you're earning more, then I should be able to cut back.'

'Ideally, yes.' Even more tentative.

'But I don't want to give up work entirely.'

'OK.' Relief. Begin to nod.

'I'm thinking three days a week rather than four.'

'Right.' Seems fair enough. More nodding.

'And we don't want to be in London for ever, do we?'

'No.' Firm agreement. Emphatic shake of the head.

'So the obvious place to go is Scotland. Near your mum, so she can help with Polly.'

'Sounds good.' Sounds great. Nodding again.

'So I need to get a job somewhere near.'

'I guess so.' Nothing wrong here. Keep nodding.

'And any jobs around there are going to be pretty popular.'

'True.' Exchange nodding for a look of serious thought.

'So I might have to locum for a while.'

'Possibly.' Problem solved. Continue nodding.

'But I won't get a maternity package if I'm a locum.'

'No.' Good point. Nod, but retain look of serious thought.

'And even if I find something for three days a week, it'll pay a lot less than I got last time.'

'True.' Another good point. Still nodding, but cautiously, sensing ambush.

'So unless we want Polly to be an only child, it makes financial sense to take maternity leave from my current position, full time.'

'. . . Right.' Abort. Stop nodding. Immediately.

'So we should have another baby soon. Then I can take full maternity pay and spend the time looking for a job in Scotland. Helen's getting married in May and I've got to fit into the bridesmaid dress, so I think we should start trying after that.'

There's an admirable practicality to Zoë's motivation, but I can't help feeling it's the sort of logic that would have us shelter from a storm under a tree. 'So you want to make life easier by having another baby?'

'Exactly. What do you think?'

I consider her grand plan for an instant, then have to ask. 'What does Gina say?'

Zoë laughs. 'Gina says if you can get me pregnant, then you can move back to Scotland.'

Never underestimate a wife's ability to exploit the weakest point in your defence. Somehow, with just a few words, sex has become my patriotic duty.

Tuesday, 19th February – Polly's first birthday

Despite a string of interrupted nights as a result of a fifth tooth tearing its way through Polly's gums, Zoë throws herself into preparations for a party with characteristic gusto. Fuelled by that typical working mother's sense of guilt, she insists on baking rather than buying a cake, and by the time our guests arrive has whipped up a much-admired chocolate hedgehog using a forest of flakes as spines.

With four godparents in attendance, in a home brimming with friends and family, Polly is blessed by the same person who blessed our marriage almost three years ago. And, by the end of the day, the debris testifies to the event's success: surfaces are littered with empty glasses, the floor is flaked in flakes, and the previously buoyant hedgehog looks more like deflated roadkill.

Of course, as well as enjoying the milestone, it gives us opportunity to reflect, and to quietly congratulate each other on our daughter's survival to date as I assess the damage to us all.

My body and mind clearly chart the effect of 12 months of parenthood: I now have permanent bruises beneath my eyes, I'm as unfit as I've ever been, there are white tufts in my hair, and my hearing seems to be stuck on a baby setting – wherever I am, I hear snuffles and murmurings from phantom monitors, snippets of song from cot-side CD players that aren't turned on.

I wake around 6 a.m. even when Polly's still asleep, and catch myself humming lullabies as I walk down the street. Many of the things I once thought I'd achieve have been postponed – perhaps indefinitely – and I'm a sentimental wreck.

I'd feared a woeful decrease in my knowledge of the world as all doors beyond the kitchen and nursery slammed shut, but in fact, thanks to the radio and a new interest in the world often roused on Polly's behalf, the doors have been flung wide open. That's not to say that I could hold my own in Prime Minister's Questions, but it's something more than I'd expected. And there are other positives too: my extra little ring of belly has proven itself very useful as a portable shelf on which to rest an increasingly heavy daughter.

Meanwhile this house we so carefully prepared has also suffered the impact of our daughter's arrival, from walker-scraped skirting boards to an infestation of mice more than happy to nibble up what Polly's discarded. And of course it rings with the sound of both her and her belongings, the worst being her jigsaw puzzles fitted with light sensors – every night I turn out the kitchen lights ready for bed and am chased up the stairs by an eruption of foghorns and duck whistles, racing engines, nursery rhymes and animal noises.

One whole year further on it's easy to see that, for all her fears and the pain of almost daily separation, Zoë has juggled motherhood and a demanding full-time job with enormous success. I do still wonder who, in the future, will decide if our child is ill – the resident doctor, determined not to appear over-anxious perhaps at the risk of downplaying something serious, or the nervous mother, with her natural predilection for the dramatic? But we've come this far, and I suppose if you've got to live with a split personality it's better if they at least balance each other out.

In a way, I think we approached parenthood at an advantage, having previously been tested. Over our years together, we'd already faced trials – from straightforward geographical distance to the death of my father, from the loss of the life I loved in Argyll to the reunion of Take That – all of which we overcame to feel stronger and more confident of our place alongside each other.

But there's nothing else as potentially binding as becoming parents together, nothing else that requires the same teamwork, responsibility and support, and the same need to feel your way through the mass of conflicting advice. There's nothing else that provides the same opportunity for shared love and shared enjoyment. And there's nothing else that offers the same chance to get so familiar with your wife's most intimate, physical, visceral, excreting, anatomical bodily bits – and only love her all the more.

From the ultrasound that showed our daughter as a matchstick-sized bundle of cells, to the sight of Zoë's insides as the doctors tore our baby free, from the breast leakages to her superhuman ability to function without sleep – the entire process has been a revelation inspiring nothing but respect for all that she's capable of.

Meanwhile the process has produced something that remains, even after 12 months, a consistently overwhelming mystery. Future siblings aside, nothing else Zoë or I could ever do will come close in terms of the wonder that Polly generates in us, and the love and the pride. Nothing else we ever do will be so worthwhile, so ... if not perfect, then so close to perfection. One year after she was wrenched awkwardly into the world, I'm still in awe of what we've created, still feel thoroughly undeserving, and uncomprehending of how anything I've done could have resulted in this beautiful baby girl.

And as Polly has gone from strength to strength, as she increasingly rewards those around her with an ever-growing variety of responses, there have been other developments as well. I used to long for that magic moment in the day when I'd hear Zoë's key in the lock, watch with genuine pleasure as Polly flapped in a circle of utter delight at the recognition of her voice, and then I'd hand our daughter over and disappear upstairs to get on with what I thought was truly important.

Now, though, I'm glad to realize I've begun to look at things differently: I've grown from reluctantly spending time with her, to appreciating the importance of spending time with her, to actually *wanting* to spend time with her. Rather than restricting me, fatherhood has given me a greater realization: Polly has become the keel that provides greater awareness and control of my direction. And with the ballast of my new role comes a new stability and strength to weather the storms.

I'm mindful of the clichés; mindful, too, of the triteness of the remark, but though it may not seem so at 4 a.m. after an hour of inconsolable screaming or when faced with yet another aromatic, overflowing nappy, it really does seem to be the hardest challenges that are the most rewarding, and I wouldn't have wanted Polly to join us even one day later than she did. However alien to my heritage of deep emotion lurking beneath a stiff upper lip, I hope my own lips will never stop voicing that same depth of love.

Months ago I realized we're making decisions all the time in answer to questions we've not yet guessed, and I still think that's true. But what I hadn't appreciated then is what I understand now – that sometimes, without even knowing it, we're answering those questions *correctly*. I realize now that, in asking myself if I was ready to become a father, I was asking myself something that was, to that person then, essentially meaningless, being so far beyond my comprehension. How could I have ever known that this would be the life I'd always wanted?

Epilogue

At last, more than four years after we buried him, Mum, Nathan, Rob and I gather in Edinburgh for the drive west to Ardburdan, to lay the plaque on Dad's grave.

After lengthy discussion, Zoë and I have agreed that she'll stay behind with Polly – six hours strapped to a car seat to look at a patch of grass that, to her, would be just like any other doesn't seem fair. And fitting though it would have been to return for the first time with a wife and daughter, it seems equally fitting that, as a father, I've learnt to relegate my own priorities beneath those of my family.

A month ago, Zoë and I began trying for another baby, the trigger planned to instigate our lifestyle transformation from hectic Londoners torn in every direction to a relaxed, rural family, each of us with the perfect balance of work and children. And though we're not there yet, I can see on Zoë's face that the idea of a whole day with Polly to imagine herself already living that life appeals.

So, having kissed them goodbye, the rest of us set off for the other side of the country. I'm hoping for a typical Argyllshire day, a day of mist and dampness to hurry us along and remind us of its worst. Instead, the sky is rolled out to the horizon in rich blues, the sort of weather that used to tempt Dad to leave his work for another day and take us out in the boat, pushing off into the calm waters of the loch to look back on a land shining with summer, the warm air shimmering above the white pebbles of the beach.

It's a largely silent journey along the familiar roads, my dread slowly smothered beneath a rising excitement that seems somehow inappropriate. Yet you don't stop loving something just because you've lost it.

The colours of the roadside flash by as the land rises and falls to peaks and lochs: the wisps of cotton hanging above the heather,

300

the fields of glowing rapeseed and the golden flowering gorse, the foxgloves and scattered buttercups, all succumbing to the bright purple splashes of smothering rhododendron.

When we step out of the car by the front gate, the air is fresh like spring water. The windows of the house are diplomatically inscrutable as we walk past and on, down towards the graveyard. In the strip of woodland running alongside us to the beach, trees are rotting where they've fallen. By the gate halfway down we see the beech beneath which Dad once reluctantly posed for a photo. The ancient tree has lost a limb – it's split and fallen across the burn below – and I'm relieved that he's not around to witness what work there is to be done.

With the plague of encroaching rhododendron cut well back, the graveyard has become a charming, sun-dappled glade, and now I'm grateful that it's a beautiful summer's day rather than the grim one I'd been hoping for, because this seems the perfect place to lie.

Slowly, the four of us walk forward into the clearing, the pebbled path giving way to grass as we approach the millstone in the graveyard's centre. And there, on the side of the lichen- and moss-covered stone, beside the plaques commemorating his parents, glinting brass letters spell out Dad's name. Beneath are the lines we chose from the song he'd often sing, the high notes ringing through the house:

> And I shall hear though soft you tread above me
> And in my grave will richer, sweeter be
> And you'll bend down and tell me that you love me
> And I will rest in peace until you come to me.

We've come prepared, and Nathan, Rob and I each break open a cold Strongbow in commemoration, raising the cans above the green turf, so established and firm. And as I stand there in the peace of the sunlight, I can appreciate how lucky I am to be able to balance against all I've lost, all that I've since gained.

It was one year after Dad died that Zoë and I were married, and two years after that Polly was born. However much I may have longed to have him back ever since, however many times I've wished for his advice and support as I try to be the father to Polly that he was to me, her arrival has at least brought a consoling perspective that makes his passing easier to bear.

Dad moved to Ardburdan to live the life he loved with the wife he loved, and it was their daily efforts together that gave me the memories of my childhood. Now that he's gone and Mum has moved on, it suddenly becomes clear in a way that it couldn't had I not returned, that nothing remains for me here but the past. And sad though that realization may be, how much happier it is to think of what's waiting for me elsewhere, in my present and my future.

Taking one last swig from the cider can, I pour the remains around the base of Dad's gravestone like a libation. Then, grateful for so many memories, I turn away, determined to create them afresh for a family of my own.